OLD WORLD ECHOES

COMPILATION AND INTRODUCTION BY
Jennifer Courtney

MULTIMEDIA

Old World Echoes (Copper Lodge Library)
© 2019 Classical Conversations® MultiMedia. All rights reserved.

Published by Classical Conversations, Inc.
255 Air Tool Drive
Southern Pines, NC 28387

CLASSICALCONVERSATIONS.COM
CLASSICALCONVERSATIONSBOOKS.COM

Cover design by Classical Conversations.

The cover artwork and illustrations were collected from a variety of illustrators.

Printed in the United States of America

ISBN: 978-1-7329640-1-3

ACKNOWLEDGMENTS

Since childhood, I have loved stories—stories from around the world that my family read to me, and stories from our own family that they told to me. I'm grateful to my parents and grandparents for these precious memories.

Thanks to. . .

Leigh Bortins for being excited about this project with me while we were swimming in the lake.

Heather Shirley for loving beautiful stories and supporting this book.

Jen Greenholt for discussing these stories with me and giving me so much freedom to explore.

Jasmine Flood and Kathi James for making the book beautiful and persevering with me through all the changes!

Emily Shirley for finding so many stories and poems for me—a researcher par excellence.

Lisa Bailey for reading alongside me and getting equally excited. Cyndi Widman for thoughtfully editing so that my words are clear and meaningful.

My children (Ben, Abby, Susannah, and Mia) who have been my read-aloud companions for many years and especially to my daughters to whom I have read many of the stories in this little volume.

My husband, Tim, for listening patiently as I imagined this project and wrestled with ideas. Thanks for always supporting me!

Lastly, thanks to families everywhere who take time each day to curl up with their children and share a great story. You are building a beautiful life.

TABLE OF CONTENTS

INTRODUCTION

My children were enchanted by echoes. There is something magical about standing on one side of a canyon and shouting across, waiting to hear your own voice boomerang back to you, slowly fading into silence until you shout again. I was once in a public restroom with my three-year-old son. He immediately noticed the acoustics of the space and loudly shouted "echo" over and over again to hear his voice come back to him. (I hope our restroom neighbors were also delighted, or at least amused.) The discovery and delight of an echo are as amazing as the discovery of one's own shadow.

Our children learn to speak by echoing back the words, phrases, and sentences that we say to them. They become part of our family culture as they echo back the stories that we tell: stories about our ancestors, last summer's vacation, and the baby's latest achievement. These echoes bind our families together. Shared stories that echo through the ages bind whole civilizations together.

Just as children thrill to sound echoes, they can thrill to literary echoes. Part of the amazing magic of C. S. Lewis's novel *The Lion, The Witch and the Wardrobe* is the thrill of recognizing echoes. Children read the story of Aslan's death at the Stone Table and hear the echo from Scripture of Christ's crucifixion and resurrection. When the tiny mice come to tend to Aslan, children thrill again as they hear two echoes: they hear the echo from Scripture of the women coming to Jesus' tomb and the echo of Aesop's fable about the mouse and the lion. Just as it is exciting to hear the echoes, it is sad to miss them if you do not know the original stories. As we read aloud the stories that have formed our culture, we hear more and more echoes. And, the more echoes we hear, the richer literature becomes.

If you think about it, you will realize that this happens in your own family. You hand down family stories by telling them again and again at family gatherings. So, too, civilizations have handed down their stories. In this volume, I have included stories from oral tradition such as Norse mythology, Arthurian legends, Robin Hood stories, and even Grimm's fairy tales. Eventually, these oral tales have been compiled in written records. Other stories in this collection first existed in writing but borrowed heavily from other sources (Shakespeare) or followed the conventions of folk and fairy tales (Andersen and Kipling). Shakespeare retold stories from historical and literary writers before him. J. R. R. Tolkien and C. S. Lewis echoed the mythology that they grew up reading. In recent years, movies and musicals have borrowed the characters and plots from fairy tales. The echoes repeat on and on.

Fairy tales, myths, and legends are not just bedtime stories for children. Indeed, the whole family can relish the tales of heroism and self-sacrifice, of loyalty and lifelong friendships, of providential rescues by supernatural helpers, of cunning escapes, and of growing into one's adult responsibilities. Because these stories are not just children's stories, they often speak of dark or difficult situations, but that is the power of fairy tales. They give concrete form to emotions and abstractions. For example, "Little Red Riding Hood" contains dark and tense moments. In our contemporary culture, we might ask ourselves, "Why is she sent out into the woods alone?" or "Why does a fairy tale include people being eaten by wolves?" These stories take abstract concepts like evil and make them concrete by having them take on the form of a lurking wolf or a wicked witch. By the same token, the magical elements of fantasy allow us to see the very real conflicts in our lives in a new light. The woodcutter in Little Red Riding Hood echoes the savior who sees our distress and rescues us from danger. Our children need to read about these conflicts and resolutions in order to form a moral imagination that will allow them to make good choices and to trust in a savior. As C. S. Lewis writes:

"I think it is possible that by confining your child to blameless stories of child life in which nothing at all alarming ever happens, you would fail to banish the terrors and would succeed in banishing all that can ennoble them or make them endurable. For in the fairy tales, side by side with the terrible figures, we find the immemorial comforters and protectors, the radiant ones. . . It would be nice if no little boy in bed, hearing or thinking he hears a sound, were ever at all frightened. But if he is going to be frightened, I think it better that he should think of giants and dragons than merely of burglars. And I think St. George, or any bright champion in armour, is a better comfort than the idea of the police" (*Three Ways of Writing for Children*, 40).

The truth is that we do have an enemy and we do have a Savior. We should train ourselves to step forth bravely, willing to sacrifice ourselves for others, and we always should be on the lookout for our Savior and Friend.

As we have begun to see, the echoes from the past are powerful. The stories have the power to change us by showing us human nature in a new light and by showing us characters who made heroic choices even in the face of great personal cost. We see characters who were forced to accept their adult responsibilities and correct their flaws. This same power of story appears in Scripture when Nathan the prophet confronts King David with his sins. Rather than confronting the king directly, the prophet tells David a story of a rich man who took away a poor man's beloved pet lamb. The story moves David to anger and eventually to repentance. The Israelites were commanded to remember God's faithfulness to them and to tell the stories to generations of their children. As Jesus taught, He told parables to teach important truths. God is weaving each of us into a unique story of our own and into the fabric of His story. These Scriptural examples tell us that "story" is an essential part of our human flourishing. Stories of the Prodigal Son, the Lost Sheep, and the Widow's Mite have all been echoed in stories and poems. The echoes repeat on and on.

Just like Nathan's story of the pet lamb, the stories in this volume help us to see human nature in a fresh way. For example, all of us have known a childless couple who longed for children. This wish is played out again and again in fairy tales. Often, the longed-for child comes only to be taken away on an adventure. Hans Christian Andersen's "Thumbelina" contains echoes of these wishes and of the biblical tale of Hannah and Samuel. The child who reads the story has his moral imagination strengthened by the sacrifices Thumbelina makes on behalf of her friends. The mother who reads the story has her resolve strengthened to let her beloved child go out into the world.

The stories in this volume echo our deepest longings and our challenging temptations. The parents' deep-seated longing for a child in Thumbelina is a good wish. As Mitchell Kalpakgian reflects: "Human beings are created for happiness, and this happiness depends on having true, natural wishes that distinguish human beings—the desire for children, for marriage, for truth, for goodness, for beauty—and seeking the fulfillment of these wishes in legitimate, moral ways that do not oppose the will of God" (*The Mysteries of Life in Children's Literature*, 23–24). It does not seem too much of a stretch to suggest that wishes made to fairy godmothers teach us about praying fervently and waiting on God's will.

Of course, just as there are good wishes and fairy godmothers, there are also bad wishes and bad witches who tempt us to do the wrong thing. Some fairy tales, like "The Fisherman and His Wife," provide warnings about greed. Fairy tales are full of temptations to grasp those things that are harmful. The stories display both the good rewards for good choices and the dire consequences of wrong ones. Every time we enjoy one of these stories with our families, we are strengthening their moral imagination. If education is about giving children the wisdom to know right from wrong, it is also about strengthening their virtue—their resolve to reject the bad and act on the good. Repeated examples from stories give them the courage to do just that. These tales do not form the moral imagination in the form of a lecture, but put before us a compelling vision of the true, the good, and the beautiful. Vigen Guroian writes: "Mere instruction in morality is not sufficient to nurture the virtues. It might even backfire, especially when the presentation is heavily exhortative and the pupil's will is coerced. Instead, a compelling vision of the goodness of goodness itself needs to be presented in a way that is attractive and stirs the imagination" (*Tending the Heart of Virtue*, 20). We should be irresistibly drawn to Thumbelina's kindness to the wounded bird. The beauty of her action stirs in us a longing and ability to be compassionate.

The echoes of fairy tales are perhaps more needed in our day than ever before. Our children are being raised in a culture that tells them that every individual should decide what is best for themselves. Fairy tales argue that virtue lies in the common good and often makes us subdue our whims and passions in order to love our neighbors well. Because there was a break in the tradition, sometimes our culture echoes the past without knowing what it means. Let us reject this world in which everything is echo without substance. Rather, let us embrace the old tradition of fairy tales, which argued that the world is a mysterious place. The ability to accept the mystery nurtures faith, hope, and love. Like little children, we must believe that miracles happen and that the unseen is palpably real. As my friend Jen argues, "Postmodernism says we only ever see in a glass darkly. Scripture tells us that we only see in a glass darkly temporarily."

Remember, too, that the echo is not an end, it is a beginning. We can keep it running through the ages, but it will fade unless we take up the chant again. It is my prayer that this book will start the echo for a new generation; for, although the times and people change, the echoes of truth, goodness, and beauty will continue to reverberate through the ages.

—Jennifer Courtney

HOW TO SAVOR THIS BOOK

This book is designed to give you one or two classic stories and a read-aloud poem to relish with your whole family each week (yes, even the high schoolers and adults). This book is NOT designed to burden an already full homeschool day, but to provide a beautiful space to gather as a family for about thirty minutes to read and discuss together. My family likes to gather first thing in the morning with a delicious breakfast and beautiful stories. In the warm weather, we read outside. In the winter, we cozy up around the fire. Other families may like to read around the dinner table or in mom and dad's bed. If you only get to one story this week, that is terrific.

Do not be easily discouraged. Even if you only have time to read the stories and poems, you are relishing beauty together. For the glorious days when you have time to dig deeper, the following guide will help you discuss the stories with your family and recite and delight in the poetry. Let's walk through the 5 Core Habits of Grammar and the 5 Common Topics with the first story in the book, "Magic Apples."

5 CORE HABITS OF GRAMMAR

NAMING

Young children like to learn the names of things: the characters, magical creatures, and enchanted weapons. After listening closely, they can tell you the names of people and places they remember. Older children can attend to the meaning attached to these names.

Example: Who was in this story? Odin, Loki, Hoenir, Thiasse, Idun, and Thor.

ATTENDING

Young children will often attend to the surface details of the stories better than older children and adults. This is excellent because those surface details will contribute to the deep meaning of each story. Help younger children attend to patterns like the number of days or repeated phrases. Encourage them to engage all five main senses.

Setting: When and where does this story take place?

Draw out the details using their five senses. How big do you think the giant eagle was? What do you think it sounded like when he flapped his mighty wings? What do you think it felt like for Loki to be carried away by the eagle? What do you think it sounded like when the giant eagle screeched? What do you think the magic apples tasted like? How did the bonfire of Odin, Loki, and Hoenir smell? What do you think it felt like to wear Freia's falcon dress?

Character(s): Who are the people in this story? (see Naming)

Plot: Can you tell me the main things that happen in the story? Does this remind you of other stories or movies?

This is an exercise called "narration." Have the child tell the story back to you. Other children in the family can add missed details, or you can ask questions to help them fill in some gaps.

Conflict: What is the main struggle the character faces or problem he must solve? How does the character solve the problem?

Example: Loki must get Idun back from the giants so that the Aesir (the Norse gods) can have the magic apples back. The gods' problem is that, without the apples, they will grow old and die. Loki borrows the falcon dress, flies to the giants, turns Idun into a nut, and carries her home in the falcon claws.

Theme: Did the characters in the story learn a lesson? Did you? Was Loki right to save his life by betraying Idun and the Norse gods? Did he make things right by getting Idun back? Did the Aesir forgive him?

MEMORIZING

Young children first build their language skills through memorizing. This is how they learned to speak their mother tongue. They will likely memorize and retell many of these stories. Their memorization of poetry will be aided by rhythm, rhyme, and repetition. Be sure to read the poem aloud several times each week. Have them make up a tune or pat out a rhythm on their lap to help them remember.

EXPRESSING

Young children have very active bodies that are intimately connected to their minds. There are several ways for them to express what they have learned from your reading:

Recitation: Have a formal recitation at the end of the year in which they deliver memorized poems to the grandparents or use the poems as presentations in your Classical Conversations Foundations community.

Narration: Give the children a few minutes to tell back the story or poem they have just heard. Putting it into their own words makes it theirs.

Acting: Allow the children to act out the story throughout the week. They will almost always find simple costumes and props around the house to add to the fun.

Drawing: Children often attend better to read-alouds if their hands are busy. They can illustrate the stories and poems while you read.

Copywork: Have the children copy the poetry in their best handwriting and then illustrate them. It will be a keepsake to treasure.

STORYTELLING

Children love to tell stories. They can re-tell the stories and poems you are reading to them. Allow them to be creative, changing the setting or plot or characters. Many will likely be inspired to write their own fairy tales, myths, legends, and poems.

5 COMMON TOPICS

There is a relatively simple set of questions that you can practice as a family to help them contemplate meaning. (For more information on the five common topics, read *The Question: Teaching Your Child the Essentials of Classical Education* by Leigh Bortins.)

DEFINITION

What is a thing and what are its parts? Who is a character? What groups of people does he belong to? What distinguishes him from other members in the group?

Example: Take one of the characters and list every trait they have in order to get a unique and precise definition. You could define Loki as one of the Norse gods of Asgard, son of Odin, brother of Thor, and mischievous trickster.

Have fun with this exercise by including as many characteristics as your children can find.

COMPARISON

How are two characters or situations the same? How are they different?

Example: Compare Loki to the giant. What characteristics do they have that are the same? Different? (Who are they?) How do they behave the same? Differently? (What do they do?)

CIRCUMSTANCES

What else is going on in the world? Closely examining the circumstances in which a character has been placed helps us to understand the decisions they make and to empathize with them.

Example: The giants and the Norse gods are enemies. The gods are very tired and hungry when the giant steals their food and then kidnaps Loki. The giant is growing old and wants the magic apples to preserve his life. Loki wants his freedom.

Unpacking the circumstances helps us to empathize with others and to attempt to make the wisest decisions we can. Encourage your children to think about how both the Norse gods and the giant felt throughout the story and to imagine what choices they would make if faced with these circumstances.

RELATIONSHIP

What happened before? After? What are the causes/effects?

Example: What happened before the giant showed up? The gods had traveled a long way and were tired and hungry. They built a bonfire and attempted to roast some meat, but due to an enchantment, the meat would not cook. Then, the giant stole their food. What happened after? Loki attempted to hit the giant (who was disguised as an eagle) with a stick and the giant kidnapped him. What happened after that? The giant demanded Idun's magic apples in exchange for Loki's freedom. And then? The gods began to age. Loki managed to bring Idun home. What do you think will happen after the story? Do you think there will be more peace or less peace between the gods and the giants? Do you think the gods will trust Loki?

Peering into the causes and effects of other characters' decisions allows us to practice for the big choices we will face. We can learn to weigh the consequences (effects) through story long before we face weighty choices in our own lives.

TESTIMONY

Who has something to say about this? Are they trustworthy?

Example: Odin should have been the ultimate authority, but he repeatedly fails to punish Loki. Throughout the story, the gods are guided by the advice of Loki. Should they have listened to him?

From the evening news to the Internet, our children will be bombarded with people who claim to be authorities in their lives. Through story, we can teach them to evaluate whether these authorities and witnesses are reliable and trustworthy so that they can decide whether to accept or reject them.

Sometimes your family will want to ask lots of questions about a story. Other times, you may only have time to just pick up the book and read. That is valuable, too. Delight in the sounds of the words and lose yourselves in the story. Like my son who delighted in the echoes he could create, I hope you will fill your home with echoes this year.

"Iduna [*sic*] giving the magic apples." Illustration by Louis Huard for E. and A. Keary in *The Heroes of Asgard; Tales of Scandinavian Mythology* (London, New York: Macmillan, 1909).

Week One:
MAGIC APPLES
Norse Mythology

It is not very amusing to be a king. Father Odin often grew tired of sitting all day long upon his golden throne in Valhalla above the heavens. He wearied of welcoming the new heroes whom the Valkyries brought him from wars upon the earth, and of watching the old heroes fight their daily deathless battles. He wearied of his wise ravens, and the constant gossip which they brought him from the four corners of the world; and he longed to escape from every one who knew him to some place where he could pass for a mere stranger, instead of the great king of the Aesir, the mightiest being in the whole universe, of whom every one was afraid.

Sometimes he longed so much that he could not bear it. Then—he would run away. He disguised himself as a tall old man, with white hair and a long gray beard. Around his shoulders he threw a huge blue cloak, that covered him from top to toe, and over his face he pulled a big slouch hat, to hide his eyes. For his eyes Odin could not change—no magician has ever learned how to do that. One was empty; he had given the eye to the giant Mimer in exchange for wisdom.

Usually Odin loved to go upon these wanderings alone; for an adventure is a double adventure when one meets it single-handed. It was a fine game for Odin to see how near he could come to danger without feeling the grip of its teeth. But sometimes, when he wanted company, he would whisper to his two brothers, Hoenir and red Loki.

They three would creep out of the palace by the back way; and, with a finger on the lip to Heimdal, the watchman, would silently steal over the rainbow bridge which led from Asgard into the places of men and dwarfs and giants.

Wonderful adventures they had, these three, with Loki to help make things happen. Loki was a sly, mischievous fellow, full of his pranks and his capers, not always kindly ones. But he was clever, as well as malicious; and when he had pushed folk into trouble, he could often help them out again, as safe as ever. He could be the jolliest of companions when he chose, and Odin liked his merriment and his witty talk.

One day Loki did something which was no mere jest nor easily forgiven, for it brought all Asgard into danger. And after that Father Odin and his children thought twice before inviting Loki to join them in any journey or undertaking. This which I am about to tell was the first really wicked deed of which Loki was found guilty, though I am sure his red beard had dabbled in secret wrongs before.

One night the three high gods, Odin, Hoenir, and Loki, stole away from Asgard in search of adventure. Over mountains and deserts, great rivers and stony places, they wandered until they grew very hungry. But there was no food to be found—not even a berry or a nut.

"Magic Apples." Illlustration by E. Boyd Smith for Abbie Farwell Brown, *In The Days of Giants: A Book of Norse Tales* (Boston and New York: Houghton Mifflin Company, 1902). Project Gutenberg EBook.

Oh, how footsore and tired they were! And oh, how faint! The worst of it ever is that—as you must often have noticed—the heavier one's feet grow, the lighter and more hollow becomes one's stomach; which seems a strange thing, when you think of it. If only one's feet became as light as the rest of one feels, folk could fairly fly with hunger. Alas! this is not so.

The three Aesir drooped and drooped, and seemed on the point of starving, when they came to the edge of a valley. Here, looking down, they saw a herd of oxen feeding on the grass.

"Hola!" shouted Loki. "Behold our supper!" Going down into the valley, they caught and killed one of the oxen, and, building a great bonfire, hung up the meat to roast. Then the three sat around the fire and smacked their lips, waiting for the meat to cook. They waited for a long time.

"Surely, it is done now," said Loki, at last; and he took the meat from the fire. Strange to say, however, it was raw as ere the fire was lighted. What could it mean? Never before had meat required so long a time to roast. They made the fire brighter and re-hung the beef for a thorough basting, cooking it even longer than they had done at first. When again they came to carve the meat, they found it still uneatable. Then, indeed, they looked at one another in surprise.

"What can this mean?" cried Loki, with round eyes.

"There is some trick!" whispered Hoenir, looking around as if he expected to see a fairy or a witch meddling with the food.

"We must find out what this mystery betokens," said Odin thoughtfully. Just then there was a strange sound in the oak-tree under which they had built their fire.

"What is that?" Loki shouted, springing to his feet. They looked up into the tree, and far above in the branches, near the top, they spied an enormous eagle, who was staring down at them, and making a queer sound, as if he were laughing.

"Ho-ho!" croaked the eagle. "I know why your meat will not cook. It is all my doing, masters."

The three Aesir stared in surprise. Then Odin said sternly: "Who are you, Master Eagle? And what do you mean by those rude words?"

"Give me my share of the ox, and you shall see," rasped the eagle, in his harsh voice. "Give me my share, and you will find that your meat will cook as fast as you please."

Now the three on the ground were nearly famished. So, although it seemed very strange to be arguing with an eagle, they cried, as if in one voice: "Come down, then, and take your share." They thought that, being a mere bird, he would want but a small piece.

The eagle flapped down from the top of the tree. Dear me! What a mighty bird he was! Eight feet across the wings was the smallest measure, and his claws were as long and strong as ice-hooks. He fanned the air like a whirlwind as he flew down to perch beside the bonfire. Then in his beak and claws he seized a leg and both shoulders of the ox, and started to fly away.

"Hold, thief!" roared Loki angrily, when he saw how much the eagle was taking. "That is not your share; you are no lion, but you are taking the lion's share of our feast. Begone, Scarecrow, and leave the meat as you found it!" Thereat, seizing a pole, he struck at the eagle with all his might.

Then a strange thing happened. As the great bird flapped upward with his prey, giving a scream of malicious laughter, the pole which Loki still held stuck fast to the eagle's back, and Loki was unable to let go of the other end.

"Help, help!" he shouted to Odin and to Hoenir, as he felt himself lifted off his feet. But they could not help him. "Help, help!" he screamed, as the eagle flew with him, now high, now low, through brush and bog and briar, over treetops and the peaks of mountains. On and on they went, until Loki thought his arm would be pulled out, like a weed torn up by the roots. The eagle would not listen to his cries nor pause in his flight, until Loki was almost dead with pain and fatigue.

"Hark you, Loki," screamed the eagle, going a little more slowly; "no one can help you except me. You are bewitched, and you cannot pull away from this pole, nor loose the pole from me, until I choose. But if you will promise what I ask, you shall go free."

Then Loki groaned: "O eagle, only let me go, and tell me who you really are, and I will promise whatever you wish."

The eagle answered: "I am the giant Thiasse, the enemy of the Aesir. But you ought to love me, Loki, for you yourself married a giantess."

Loki moaned: "Oh, yes! I dearly love all my wife's family, great Thiasse. Tell me what you want of me?"

"I want this," quoth Thiasse gruffly. "I am growing old, and I want the apples which Idun keeps in her golden casket, to make me young again. You must get them for me."

Now these apples were the fruit of a magic tree, and were more beautiful to look at and more delicious to taste than any fruit that ever grew. The best thing about them was that whoever tasted one, be he ever so old, grew young and strong again. The apples belonged to a beautiful lady named Idun, who kept them in a golden casket. Every morning the Aesir came to her to be refreshed and made over by a bite of her precious fruit. That is why in Asgard no one ever waxed old or ugly. Even Father Odin, Hoenir, and Loki, the three travelers who had seen the very beginning of everything, when the world was made, were still sturdy and young. And so long as Idun kept her apples safe, the faces of the family who sat about the table of Valhalla would be rosy and fair like the faces of children.

"O friend giant!" cried Loki. "You know not what you ask! The apples are the most precious treasure of Asgard, and Idun keeps watch over them as if they were dearer to her than life itself. I never could steal them from her, Thiasse; for at her call all Asgard would rush to the rescue, and trouble would buzz about my ears like a hive of bees let loose."

"Then you must steal Idun herself, apples and all. For the apples I must have, and you have promised, Loki, to do my bidding."

Loki sniffed and thought, thought and sniffed again. Already his mischievous heart was planning how he might steal Idun away. He could hardly help laughing to think how angry the Aesir would be when they found their beauty-medicine gone forever. But he hoped that, when he had done this trick for Thiasse, now and then the giant would let him have a nibble of the magic apples; so that Loki himself would remain young long after the other Aesir were grown old and feeble. This thought suited Loki's malicious nature well.

"I think I can manage it for you, Thiasse," he said craftily. "In a week I promise to bring Idun and her apples to you. But you must not forget the great risk which I am running, nor that I am your relative by marriage. I may have a favor to ask in return, Thiasse."

Then the eagle gently dropped Loki from his claws. Falling on a soft bed of moss, Loki jumped up and ran back to his traveling companions, who were glad and surprised to see him again. They had feared that the eagle was carrying him away to feed his young eaglets in some far-off nest. Ah, you may be sure that Loki did not tell them who the eagle really was, nor confess the wicked promise which he had made about Idun and her apples.

After that the three went back to Asgard, for they had had adventure enough for one day.

The days flew by, and the time came when Loki must fulfill his promise to Thiasse. So one morning he strolled out into the meadow where Idun loved to roam among the flowers. There he found her, sitting by a tiny spring, and holding her precious casket of apples on her lap. She was combing her long golden hair, which fell from under a wreath of spring flowers, and she was very beautiful. Her green robe was embroidered with buds and blossoms of silk in many colors, and she wore a golden girdle about her waist. She smiled as Loki came, and tossed him a posy, saying: "Good-morrow, red Loki. Have you come for a bite of my apples? I see a wrinkle over each of your eyes which I can smooth away."

"Nay, fair lady," answered Loki politely, "I have just nibbled of another apple, which I found this morning. Verily, I think it is sweeter and more magical than yours."

Idun was hurt and surprised.

"That cannot be, Loki," she cried. "There are no apples anywhere like mine. Where found you this fine fruit?" and she wrinkled up her little nose scornfully.

"Oho! I will not tell any one the place," chuckled Loki, "except that it is not far, in a little wood. There is a gnarled old apple-tree, and on its branches grow the most beautiful red-cheeked apples you ever saw. But you could never find it."

"I should like to see these apples, Loki, if only to prove how far less good they are than mine. Will you bring me some?"

"That I will not," said Loki teasingly. "Oh, no! I have my own magic apples now, and folk will be coming to me for help instead of to you."

Idun began to coax him, as he had guessed that she would: "Please, please, Loki, show me the place!"

At first he would not, for he was a sly fellow, and knew how to lead her on. At last, he pretended to yield.

"Well, then, because I love you, Idun, better than all the rest, I will show you the place, if you will come with me. But it must be a secret— no one must ever know."

All girls like secrets.

"Yes—yes!" cried Idun eagerly. "Let us steal away now, while no one is looking."

This was just what Loki hoped for.

"Bring your own apples," he said, "that we may compare them with mine. But I know mine are better."

"I know mine are the best in all the world," returned Idun, pouting. "I will bring them, to show you the difference."

Off they started together, she with the golden casket under her arm; and Loki chuckled wickedly as they went. He led her for some distance, further than she had ever strayed before, and at last she grew frightened.

"Where are you taking me, Loki?" she cried. "You said it was not far. I see no little wood, no old apple-tree."

"It is just beyond, just a little step beyond," he answered. So on they went. But that little step took them beyond the boundary of

Asgard—just a little step beyond, into the space where the giants lurked and waited for mischief.

Then there was a rustling of wings, and whirr-rr-rr! Down came Thiasse in his eagle dress. Before Idun suspected what was happening, he fastened his claws into her girdle and flapped away with her, magic apples and all, to his palace in Jotunheim, the Land of Giants.

Loki stole back to Asgard, thinking that he was quite safe, and that no one would discover his villainy. At first Idun was not missed. But after a little the gods began to feel signs of age, and went for their usual bite of her apples. Then they found that she had disappeared, and a great terror fell upon them. Where had she gone? Suppose she should not come back!

The hours and days went by, and still she did not return. Their fright became almost a panic. Their hair began to turn gray, and their limbs grew stiff and gouty so that they hobbled down Asgard streets. Even Freia, the loveliest, was afraid to look in her mirror, and Balder the beautiful grew pale and haggard. The happy land of Asgard was like a garden over which a burning wind had blown,—all the flower-faces were faded and withered, and springtime was turned into yellow fall.

If Idun and her apples were not quickly found, the gods seemed likely to shrivel and blow away like autumn leaves. They held a council to inquire into the matter, endeavoring to learn who had seen Idun last, and whither she had gone. It turned out that one morning Heimdal had seen her strolling out of Asgard with Loki, and no one had seen her since. Then the gods understood; Loki was the last person who had been with her—this must be one of Loki's tricks. They were filled with anger. They seized and bound Loki and brought him before the council. They threatened him with torture and with death unless he should tell the truth. And Loki was so frightened that finally he confessed what he had done.

Then indeed there was horror in Asgard. Idun stolen away by a wicked giant! Idun and her apples lost, and Asgard growing older every minute! What was to be done? Big Thor seized Loki and threw him up in the air again and again, so that his heels touched first the moon and then the sea; you can still see the marks upon the moon's white face. "If you do not bring Idun back from the land of your wicked wife, you shall have worse than this!" he roared. "Go and bring her now."

"How can I do that?" asked Loki, trembling.

"That is for you to find," growled Thor. "Bring her you must. Go!"

Loki thought for a moment. Then he said:—

"I will bring her back if Freia will loan me her falcon dress. The giant dresses as an eagle. I, too, must guise me as a bird, or we cannot outwit him."

Then Freia hemmed and hawed. She did not wish to loan her feather dress, for it was very precious. But all the Aesir begged; and finally she consented.

It was a beautiful great dress of brown feathers and gray, and in it Freia loved to skim like a falcon among the clouds and stars. Loki put it on, and when he had done so he looked exactly like a great brown hawk. Only his bright black eyes remained the same, glancing here and there, so that they lost sight of nothing.

With a whirr of his wings Loki flew off to the north, across mountains and valleys and the great river Ifing, which lay between Asgard and Giant Land. And at last he came to the palace of Thiasse the giant.

It happened, fortunately, that Thiasse had gone fishing in the sea, and Idun was left alone, weeping and broken-hearted. Presently she heard a little tap on her window, and, looking up, she saw a great brown bird perching on the ledge. He was so big that Idun was frightened and gave a scream. But the bird nodded pleasantly and croaked: "Don't be afraid, Idun. I am a friend. I am Loki, come to set you free."

"Loki! Loki is no friend of mine. He brought me here," she sobbed. "I don't believe you came to save me."

"That is indeed why I am here," he replied, "and a dangerous business it is, if Thiasse should come back before we start for home."

"How will you get me out?" asked Idun doubtfully. "The door is locked, and the window is barred."

"I will change you into a nut," said he, "and carry you in my claws."

"What of the casket of apples?" queried Idun. "Can you carry that also?"

Then Loki laughed long and loudly.

"What welcome to Asgard do you think I should receive without the apples?" he cried. "Yes, we must take them, indeed."

Idun came to the window, and Loki, who was a skillful magician, turned her into a nut and took her in one claw, while in the other he seized the casket of apples. Then off he whirred out of the palace grounds and away toward Asgard's safety.

In a little while Thiasse returned home, and when he found Idun and her apples gone, there was a hubbub, you may be sure! However, he lost little time by smashing mountains and breaking trees in his giant rage; that fit was soon over. He put on his eagle plumage and started in pursuit of the falcon.

Now an eagle is bigger and stronger than any other bird, and usually in a long race he can beat even the swift hawk who has an hour's start. Presently Loki heard behind him the shrill scream of a giant eagle, and his heart turned sick. But he had crossed the great river, and already was in sight of Asgard. The aged Aesir were gathered on the rainbow bridge watching eagerly for Loki's return; and when they spied the falcon with the nut and the casket in his talons, they knew who it was. A great cheer went up, but it was hushed in a moment, for they saw the eagle close after the falcon; and they guessed that this must be the giant Thiasse, the stealer of Idun.

Then there was a great shouting of commands, and a rushing to and fro. All the gods, even Father Odin and his two wise ravens, were busy gathering chips into great heaps on the walls of Asgard. As soon as Loki, with his precious burden, had fluttered weakly over the wall, dropping to the ground beyond, the gods lighted the heaps of chips which they had piled, and soon there was a wall of fire, over which the eagle must fly. He was going too fast to stop. The flames roared and crackled, but Thiasse flew straight into them, with a scream of fear and rage. His feathers caught fire and burned, so that he could no longer fly, but fell headlong to the ground inside the walls. Then Thor, the thunder-lord, and Tyr, the mighty war-king, fell upon him and slew him, so that he could never trouble the Aesir any more.

There was great rejoicing in Asgard that night, for Loki changed Idun again to a fair lady; whereupon she gave each of the eager gods a bite of her life-giving fruit, so that they grew young and happy once more, as if all these horrors had never happened.

Not one of them, however, forgot the evil part which Loki had played in these doings. They hid the memory, like a buried seed, deep in their hearts. Thenceforward the word of Loki and the honor of his name were poor coin in Asgard; which is no wonder.

"Meadow Lark." Illustration by John James Audubon, *The Birds of America*, Plate 136
(Philadelphia: J. B. Chevalier, 1839).

Week One:
"FOR SATURDAY"

Now's the time for mirth and play,
Saturday's an holyday;
Praise to heav'n unceasing yield,
I've found a lark's nest in the field.

A lark's nest, then your play-mate begs
You'd spare herself and speckled eggs;
Soon she shall ascend and sing
Your praises to th' eternal King.

CHRISTOPHER SMART
(1722–1771)

"Thor." Illustration by A. Grobe for Annie Klingensmith, *Old Norse Wonder Tales* (Chicago: A. Flanagan Company, 1923).

Week Two:
The Dwarf's Gifts
Norse Mythology

Red Loki had been up to mischief again! Loki, who made quarrels and brought trouble wherever he went. He had a wicked heart, and he loved no one. He envied Father Odin his wisdom and his throne above the world. He envied Balder his beauty, and Tyr his courage, and Thor his strength. He envied all the good Aesir who were happy; but he would not take the trouble to be good himself. So he was always unhappy, spiteful, and sour. And if anything went wrong in Asgard, the kingdom of the gods, one was almost sure to find Loki at the bottom of the trouble.

Now Thor, the strongest of all the gods, was very proud of his wife's beautiful hair, which fell in golden waves to her feet, and covered her like a veil. He loved it better than anything, except Sif herself. One day, while Thor was away from home, Loki stole into Thrudheim, the realm of clouds, and cut off all Sif's golden hair, till her head was as round and fuzzy as a yellow dandelion. Fancy how angry Thor was when he came rattling home that night in his thunder-chariot and found Sif so ugly to look at! He stamped up and down till the five hundred and forty floors of his cloud palace shook like an earthquake, and lightning flashed from his blue eyes. The people down in the world below cried: "Dear, dear! What a terrible thunderstorm! Thor must be very angry about something. Loki has been up to mischief, it is likely." You see, they also knew Loki and his tricks.

At last Thor calmed himself a little. "Sif, my love," he said, "you shall be beautiful again. Red Loki shall make you so, since his was the unmaking. The villain! He shall pay for this!"

Then, without more ado, off set Thor to find red Loki. He went in his thunder-chariot, drawn by two goats, and the clouds rumbled and the lightning flashed wherever he went; for Thor was the mighty god of thunder. At last he came upon the sly rascal, who was trying to hide.

Big Thor seized him by the throat.

"You scoundrel!" he cried, "I will break every bone in your body if you do not put back Sif's beautiful hair upon her head."

"Ow—ow! You hurt me!" howled Loki. "Take off your big hand, Thor. What is done, is done. I cannot put back Sif's hair. You know that very well."

"Then you must get her another head of hair," growled Thor. "That you can do. You must find for her hair of real gold, and it must grow upon her head as if it were her own. Do this, or you shall die."

"Where shall I get this famous hair?" whined Loki, though he knew well enough.

"The third gift—an enormous hammer." Illustration by E. Boyd Smith for Abbie Farwell Brown, *In The Days of Giants: A Book of Norse Tales* (Boston and New York: Houghton Mifflin Company, 1902).

"Get it of the black elves," said Thor; "they are cunning jewelers, and they are your friends. Go, Loki, and go quickly, for I long to see Sif as beautiful as ever."

Then Loki of the burning beard slunk away to the hills where, far under ground, the dwarfs have their furnaces and their workshops. Among great heaps of gold and silver and shining jewels, which they have dug up out of the earth, the little crooked men in brown blink and chatter and scold one another; for they are ugly fellows—the dwarfs. Tink-tank! tink-tank! go their little hammers all day long and all night long, while they make wonderful things such as no man has ever seen, though you shall hear about them.

They had no trouble to make a head of hair for Sif. It was for them a simple matter, indeed. The dwarfs work fast for such a customer as Loki, and in a little while the golden wires were beaten out, and drawn out, made smooth and soft and curly, and braided into a thick golden braid. But when Loki came away, he carried with him also two other treasures which the clever dwarfs had made. One was a golden spear, and the other was a ship.

Now these do not sound so very wonderful. But wait until you hear! The spear, which was named Gungnir, was bewitched, so that it made no difference if the person who held it was clumsy and careless. For it had this amazing quality, that no matter how badly it was aimed, or how unskillfully it was thrown, it was sure to go straight to the mark—which is a very obliging and convenient thing in one's weapon, as you will readily see.

And Skidbladnir—this was the harsh name of the ship—was even more wonderful. It could be taken to pieces and folded up so small that it would go into one's pocket. But when it was unfolded and put together, it would hold all the gods of Asgard for a sea-journey. Besides all this, when the sails were set, the ship was sure always to have a fair wind, which would make it skim along like a great bird, which was the best part of the charm, as any sailor will tell you.

Now Loki felt very proud of these three treasures, and left the hill cave stretching his neck and strutting like a great red turkey cock.

Outside the gate, however, he met Brock, the black dwarf, who was the brother of Sindri, the best workman in all the underworld.

"Hello! what have you there?" asked Brock of the big head, pointing at the bundles which Loki was carrying.

"The three finest gifts in the world," boasted Loki, hugging his treasures tight.

"Pooh!" said Brock, "I don't believe it. Did my brother Sindri make them?"

"No," answered Loki; "they were made by the black elves, the sons of Ivaldi. And they are the most precious gifts that ever were seen."

"Pooh!" again puffed Brock, wagging his long beard crossly. "Nonsense! Whatever they be, my brother Sindri can make three other gifts more precious; that I know."

"Can he, though?" laughed Loki. "I will give him my head if he can."

"Done!" shouted the dwarf. "Let me see your famous gifts." So Loki showed him the three wonders: the gold hair for Sif, the spear, and the ship. But again the dwarf said: "Pooh! These are nothing. I will show you what the master-smith can do, and you shall lose your bragging red head, my Loki."

Now Loki began to be a little uneasy. He followed Brock back to the smithy in the mountain, where they found Sindri at his forge. Oh,

"Loke [*sic*]." Illustrator unknown for Annie Klingensmith, *Old Norse Wonder Tales* (Chicago: A. Flanagan Company, 1923).

yes! He could beat the poor gifts of which Loki was so proud. But he would not tell what his own three gifts were to be.

First Sindri took a pig's skin and laid it on the fire. Then he went away for a little time; but he set Brock at the bellows and bade him blow—blow—blow the fire until Sindri should return. Now when Sindri was gone, Loki also stole away; for, as usual, he was up to mischief. He had the power of changing his shape and of becoming any creature he chose, which was often very convenient. Thus he turned himself into a huge biting fly. Then he flew back into the smithy where Brock was blow—blow—blowing. Loki buzzed about the dwarf's head, and finally lighted on his hand and stung him, hoping to make him let go the bellows. But no! Brock only cried out, "Oh-ee!" and kept on blowing for dear life. Now soon back came Sindri to the forge and took the pigskin from the fire. Wonder of wonders! It had turned into a hog with golden bristles; a live hog that shone like the sun. Brock was not satisfied, however.

"Well! I don't think much of that," he grumbled.

"Wait a little," said Sindri mysteriously. "Wait and see." Then he went on to make the second gift.

This time he put a lump of gold into the fire. And when he went away, as before, he bade Brock stand at the bellows to blow—blow—blow without stopping. Again, as before, in buzzed Loki the gadfly as soon as the master-smith had gone out. This time he settled on Brock's swarthy neck, and stung him so sorely that the blood came and the dwarf roared till the mountain trembled. Still Brock did not let go the handle of the bellows, but blew and howled—blew and howled with pain till Sindri returned. And this time the dwarf took from the fire a fine gold ring, round as roundness.

"Um! I don't think so much of that," said Brock, again disappointed, for he had expected some wonderful jewel. But Sindri wagged his head wisely.

"Wait a little," he said. "We shall see what we shall see." He heaved a great lump of iron into the fire to make the third gift. But this time when he went away, leaving Brock at the bellows, he charged him to blow—blow—blow without a minute's rest, or everything would be spoiled. For this was to be the best gift of all.

Brock planted himself wide-legged at the forge and blew—blew—blew. But for the third time Loki, winged as a fly, came buzzing into the smithy. This time he fastened viciously below Brock's bushy eyebrow, and stung him so cruelly that the blood trickled down, a red river, into his eyes and the poor dwarf was blinded. With a howl Brock raised his hand to wipe away the blood, and of course in that minute the bellows stood still. Then Loki buzzed away with a sound that seemed like a mocking laugh. At the same moment in rushed Sindri, panting with fright, for he had heard that sound and guessed what it meant.

"What have you done?" he cried. "You have let the bellows rest! You have spoiled everything!"

"Only a little moment, but one little moment," pleaded Brock, in a panic. "It has done no harm, has it?"

Sindri leaned anxiously over the fire, and out of the flames he drew the third gift—an enormous hammer.

"Oh!" said Brock, much disappointed, "only an old iron hammer! I don't think anything of that. Look how short the handle is, too."

"That is your fault, brother," returned the smith crossly. "If you had not let the bellows stand still, the handle would have been long enough. Yet as it is—we shall see, we shall see. I think it will at least win for you red Loki's head. Take the three gifts, brother, such as they are, and bear them to Asgard. Let all the gods be judges between you and Loki, which gifts are best, his or yours. But stay—I may as well tell you the secrets of your three treasures, or you will not know how to make them work. Your toy that is not wound up is of no use at all." Which is very true, as we all know. Then he bent over and whispered in Brock's ear. And what he said pleased Brock so much that he jumped straight up into the air and capered like one of Thor's goats.

"What a clever brother you are, to be sure!" he cried.

At that moment Loki, who had ceased to be a gadfly, came in grinning, with his three gifts. "Well, are you ready?" he asked. Then he caught sight of the three gifts which Brock was putting into his sack.

"Ho! A pig, a ring, and a stub-handled hammer!" he shouted. "Is that all you have? Fine gifts, indeed! I was really growing uneasy, but now I see that my head is safe. Let us start for Asgard immediately, where I promise you that I with my three treasures shall be thrice more welcome than you with your stupid pig, your ugly ring, and your half-made hammer."

So together they climbed to Asgard, and there they found the Aesir sitting in the great judgment hall on Ida Plain. There was Father Odin on his high throne, with his two ravens at his head and his two wolves at his feet. There was Queen Frigg by his side; and about them were Balder the beautiful, Frey and Freia, the fair brother and sister; the mighty Thor, with Sif, his crop-haired wife, and all the rest of the great Aesir who lived in the upper world above the homes of men.

"Brother Aesir," said Loki, bowing politely, for he was a smooth rascal, "we have come each with three gifts, the dwarf and I; and you shall judge which be the most worthy of praise. But if I lose,—I, your brother,—I lose my head to this crooked little dwarf." So he spoke, hoping to put the Aesir on his side from the first. For his head was a very handsome one, and the dwarf was indeed an ill-looking fellow. The gods, however, nodded gravely, and bade the two show what their gifts might be.

Then Loki stepped forward to the foot of Odin's throne. And first he pulled from his great wallet the spear Gungnir, which could not miss aim. This he gave to Odin, the all-wise. And Odin was vastly pleased, as you may imagine, to find himself thenceforth an unequaled marksman. So he smiled upon Loki kindly and said: "Well done, brother."

Next Loki took out the promised hair for Sif, which he handed Thor with a grimace. Now when the golden locks were set upon her head, they grew there like real hair, long and soft and curling—but still real gold. So that Sif was more beautiful than ever before, and more precious, too. You can fancy how pleased Thor was with Loki's gift. He kissed lovely Sif before all the gods and goddesses, and vowed that he forgave Loki for the mischief which he had done in the first place, since he had so nobly made reparation.

Then Loki took out the third gift, all folded up like a paper boat; and it was the ship Skidbladnir,—I am sorry they did not give it a prettier name. This he presented to Frey the peaceful. And you can guess whether or not Frey's blue eyes laughed with pleasure at such a gift.

Now when Loki stepped back, all the Aesir clapped their hands and vowed that he had done wondrous well.

"You will have to show us fine things, you dwarf," quoth Father Odin, "to better the gifts of red Loki. Come, what have you in the sack you bear upon your shoulders?"

Then the crooked little Brock hobbled forward, bent almost double under the great load which he carried. "I have what I have," he said.

First, out he pulled the ring Draupnir, round as roundness and shining of gold. This the dwarf gave to Odin, and though it seemed but little, yet it was much. For every ninth night out of this ring, he said, would drop eight other rings of gold, as large and as fair. Then Odin clapped his hands and cried: "Oh, wondrous gift! I like it even better than the magic spear which Loki gave." And all the other Aesir agreed with him.

Then out of the sack came grunting Goldbristle, the hog, all of gold. Brock gave him to Frey, to match the magic ship of Loki. This Goldbristle was so marvelously forged that he could run more swiftly than any horse, on air or water. Moreover, he was a living lantern. For on the darkest night he bristled with light like a million-pointed star, so that one riding on his back would light the air and the sea like a firefly, wherever he went. This idea pleased Frey mightily, for he was the merriest of the gods, and he laughed aloud.

"'Tis a wondrous fine gift," he said. "I like old Goldbristle even better than the compressible boat. For on this lusty steed I can ride about the world when I am tending the crops and the cattle of men and scattering the rain upon them. Master dwarf, I give my vote to you." And all the other Aesir agreed with him.

Then out of the sack Brock drew the third gift. It was the short-handled hammer named Miölnir. And this was the gift which Sindri had made for Thor, the mightiest of the gods; and it was the best gift of all. For with it Thor could burst the hardest metal and shatter the thickest mountain, and nothing could withstand its power. But it never could hurt Thor himself; and no matter how far or how hard it was thrown, it would always fly back into Thor's own hand. Last of all, whenever he so wished, the great hammer would become so small that he could put it in his pocket, quite out of sight. But Brock was sorry that the handle was so short—all owing to his fault, because he had let the bellows rest for that one moment.

When Thor had this gift in his hand, he jumped up with a shout of joy. "'Tis a wondrous fine gift," he cried, "with short handle or with long. And I prize it even more than I prize the golden hair of Sif which Loki gave. For with it I shall fight our enemies, the Frost Giants and the mischievous Trolls and the other monsters—Loki's friends. And all the Aesir will be glad of my gift when they see what deeds I shall do therewith. Now, if I may have my say, I judge that the three gifts made by Sindri the dwarf are the most precious that may be. So Brock has gained the prize of Loki's red head,—a sorry recompense indeed for gifts so masterly." Then Thor sat down. And all the other Aesir shouted that he had spoken well, and that they agreed with him.

So Loki was like to lose his head. He offered to pay instead a huge price, if Brock would let him go. But Brock refused. "The red head of Loki for my gift," he insisted, and the gods nodded that it must be so, since he had earned his wish.

But when Loki saw that the count was all against him, his eyes grew crafty. "Well, take me, then—if you can!" he shouted. And off he shot like an arrow from a bow. For Loki had on magic shoes, with which he could run over sea or land or sky; and the dwarf could never catch him in the world. Then Brock was furious. He stood stamping and chattering, tearing his long beard with rage.

"I am cheated!" he cried. "I have won—but I have lost." Then he turned to Thor, who was playing with his hammer, bursting a mountain or two and splitting a tree here and there. "Mighty Thor," begged the dwarf, "catch me the fellow who has broken his word. I have given you the best gift,—your wonderful hammer. Catch me, then, the boasting red head which I have fairly bought."

Then Thor stopped his game and set out in pursuit of Loki, for he was ever on the side of fairness. No one, however fleet, can escape when Thor follows, for his is the swiftness of a lightning flash. So he soon brought Loki back to Ida Plain, and gave him up a prisoner to the dwarf.

"I have you now, boaster," said Brock fiercely, "and I will cut off your red head in the twinkling of an eye." But just as he was about to do as he said, Loki had another sly idea.

"Hold, sirrah dwarf," he said. "It is true that you have won my head, but not the neck, not an inch of the neck." And all the gods agreed that this was so. Then Brock was puzzled indeed, for how could he cut off Loki's head without an inch of the neck, too? But this he must not do, or he knew the just Aesir would punish him with death. So he was forced to be content with stopping Loki's boasting in another way. He would sew up the bragging lips.

He brought a stout, strong thread and an awl to bore the holes. And in a twinkling he had stitched up the lips of the sly one, firm and fast. So for a time, at least, he put an end to Loki's boasting and his taunts and his lies.

It is a pity that those mischief-making lips were not fastened up forever; for that would have saved much of the trouble and sorrow which came after. But at last, after a long time, Loki got his lips free, and they made great sorrow in Asgard for the gods and on earth for men, as you shall hear.

Now this is the end of the tale which tells of the dwarf's gifts, and especially of Thor's hammer, which was afterwards to be of such service to him and such bane to the enemies of the Aesir. And that also you shall hear before all is done.

Week Two:

"The Nightingale and the Glow-worm"

A nightingale, that all day long
Had cheered the village with his song,
Nor yet at eve his note suspended,
Nor yet when eventide was ended,
Began to feel, as well he might,
The keen demands of appetite;
When, looking eagerly around,
He spied far off, upon the ground,
A something shining in the dark,
And knew the glow-worm by his spark;
So, stooping down from hawthorn top,
He thought to put him in his crop.
The worm, aware of his intent,
Harangued him thus, right eloquent:
"Did you admire my lamp," quoth he,

"As much as I your minstrelsy,
You would abhor to do me wrong,
As much as I to spoil your song;
For "twas the self-same power divine,
Taught you to sing and me to shine;
That you with music, I with light,
Might beautify and cheer the night."
The songster heard his short oration,
And warbling out his approbation,
Released him, as my story tells,
And found a supper somewhere else.

WILLIAM COWPER
(1731–1800)

Week Three:
How Arthur Became King
British Legend

Once upon a time, a thousand years before Columbus discovered America, and when Rome was still the greatest city in the world, there lived a brave and beautiful youth whose name was Arthur. His home was in England, near London; and he lived with the good knight Sir Hector, whom he always called father.

They dwelt in a great square castle of gray stone, with a round tower at each corner. It was built about a courtyard, and was surrounded by a moat, across which was a drawbridge that could be raised or lowered. When it was raised the castle was practically a little island and very hard for enemies to attack.

On one side of the moat was a large wood, and here Arthur spent a great deal of his time. He liked to lie under the trees and gaze up at the blue of the sky. All about him old oaks stood like giant guardians watching sturdily over the soil where they had grown for centuries. Arthur could look between the trunks and see rabbits and squirrels whisking about. Sometimes a herd of brown deer with shy dark eyes would pass, holding their graceful heads high in the air; sometimes a flock of pheasants with brilliant plumage rose from the bushes. Again there was no sound except the tapping of a bright-crested woodpecker, and no motion but the fluttering of leaves and the trembling of violets half buried in green moss.

At times, when it was dim and silent in the wood, Arthur would hear bursts of merry laughter, the tinkling of bells, and the jingling of spurs. Then he would know that knights and ladies were riding down the road which ran beside the trees. Soon the knights would appear on horses, brown, black, and white, with gaily ornamented saddles, and bridles from which hung silver bells. Often the saddles were made of ivory or ebony, set with rubies or emeralds. The knights wore helmets laced with slender gold chains, and coats of mail made of tiny links of steel, so fine and light that all together hardly weighed more than a coat of cloth. Usually the legs of the knights were sheathed in steel armor; and their spurs were steel, or even gold. The ladies sat on horses with long trappings of silk, purple, white, or scarlet, with ornamented saddles and swinging bells. The robes of the ladies were very beautiful, being made of velvet or silk trimmed with ermine. Arthur liked to watch them, flashing by; crimson, and gold, and blue, and rose-colored. Better still, he liked to see the pretty happy faces of the ladies, and hear their gay voices. In those troublous times, however, the roads were so insecure that such companies did not often pass.

Sometimes the knights and ladies came to visit Sir Hector. Then Arthur would hurry from the forest to the castle. Sir Hector would stand on the lowered drawbridge to greet his guests, and would lead them, with many expressions of pleasure, into the courtyard. Then he would take a huge hammer hanging from a post, and beat with it on a table which stood in a corner of the courtyard. Immediately from all parts of the castle the squires and servants would come running to take the horses of the knights and ladies. Sir Hector's wife and daughters would then appear, and with their own hands remove the armor of the knights. They would offer them golden basins of water, and towels for washing, and after that put velvet mantles upon their shoulders. Then the guests would be brought to the supper table.

But Arthur did not spend all his time dreaming in the woods or gazing at knights and ladies. For many hours of the day he practiced feats of arms in the courtyard. It was the custom in England to train boys of noble birth to be knights. As soon as they were old enough they were taught to ride. Later on, they lived much among the ladies and maidens, learning gentle manners. Under the care of the knights, they learned to hunt, to carry a lance properly, and to use the sword; and having gained this skill, they were made squires if they had shown themselves to be of good character.

Then, day by day, the squires practiced at the quintain. This was an upright post, on the top of which turned a crosspiece, having on one end a broad board, and on the other a bag of sand. The object was to ride up at full gallop, strike the board with a long lance, and get away without being hit by the sand bag.

Besides this, the squires had services to do for the knights, in order that they might learn to be useful in as many ways as possible, and to be always humble. For instance, they took care of the armor of the knights, carried letters and messages for them, accompanied them at joustings and tournaments, being ready with extra weapons or assistance; and in the castle they helped to serve the guests at table. After months of such service, they went through a beautiful ceremony and were made knights. In the country round about, Arthur, of all the squires, was the most famous for his skill in the use of the lance and the sword, for his keenness in the hunt, and for his courtesy to all people.

Now, at this time there was no ruler in England. The powerful Uther of Wales, who had governed England, was dead, and all the strong lords of the country were struggling to be king in his place. This gave rise to a great deal of quarreling and bloodshed.

There was in the land a wise magician named Merlin. He was so old that his beard was as white as snow, but his eyes were as clear as a little child's. He was very sorry to see all the fighting that was going on, because he feared that it would do serious harm to the kingdom.

In those days the great and good men who ruled in the church had power almost equal to that of the monarch. The kings and the great lords listened to their advice, and gave them much land, and money for themselves and for the poor. So Merlin went to the Archbishop of Canterbury, the churchman who in all England was the most beloved, and said:

"Sir, it is my advice that you send to all the great lords of the realm and bid them come to London by Christmas to choose a king."

The archbishop did as Merlin advised, and at Christmas all the great lords came to London. The largest church in the city stood not far from the north bank of the Thames. A churchyard surrounded it, filled with yew trees, the trunks of which were knotted with age. The powerful lords rode up in their clanking armor to the gate, where they dismounted, and giving their horses into the care of their squires, reverently entered the church.

There were so many of them that they quite filled the nave and side-aisles of the building. The good archbishop, from where he stood in the chancel, looked down on them all. Just behind him was the altar covered with a cloth of crimson and gold, and surmounted by a golden crucifix and ten burning candles. In front of him, kneeling under the gray arches which spanned the church, were the greatest men in the kingdom. He looked at their stern bronzed faces, their heavy beards, their broad shoulders, and their glittering armor, and prayed to God to make the best man in the land king.

Then began the service. At the close of the first prayer some of the knights looked out of the window, and there in the churchyard they saw a great square stone. In the middle of it was an anvil of steel a foot high, and fixed therein was a beautiful sword. On the sword was some writing set in with gold which said:

"Whosoever pulls this sword out of this stone and anvil is the real king of all England."

The knights who read this told the archbishop, but he said:

"I command you all to keep within the church and still pray to God. No man is to touch the sword until all the prayers are said."

After the service was over, the lords went into the churchyard. They each pulled at the sword, but none could stir it.

"The king is not here," said the archbishop, "but God will make him known. Meantime, let ten good knights keep watch over this sword."

The knights were soon chosen, and then the archbishop said that on a fixed day every man in the kingdom should try to pull the sword out of the anvil. He ordered that on New Year's day all the people should be brought together for a great tournament to be held on the south bank of the Thames, near London bridge. After a few days spent in jousting among the knights, each man should make the trial to find out whether or not he was to be king.

The brave youth Arthur did not know of the contest that was to be made for the sword. Sir Hector told him that he was to go to a tournament, but he did not tell him the reason for holding the tournament. So Arthur rode to London with Sir Hector; and Sir Kay, who was Sir Hector's oldest son, was with them.

Sir Hector and Sir Kay rode soberly in front. They were tall, stalwart men and rode black horses, their dark figures making shadows on the light snow that had fallen. Arthur, riding behind them, felt exhilarated by the crisp winter air which caused the blood to dance in his veins. Sometimes he stood up in his saddle and flicked with his sword the dead leaves on the oaks. Again he made his horse crush the thin crust of ice that had formed in tiny pools on the road. He was so happy in the thought of the tournament he was to see, that he could have sung for joy.

The road was not very wide, for few carts passed upon it, but it had been well worn by riders. Sometimes it wound through a bit of thick woods; again it rose up over a gently rolling hill. From the hilltops the riders could see London far in the distance. It looked at first like a gray haze; then, as the three came nearer, the buildings, large and small, grew plain to the sight. The castles and huts, barns and sheds, smithies, shops and mills, stood out in the keen sunlight. A high wall surrounded them, while on one side flowed the river Thames.

After they had entered the city, and had passed the churchyard, and had almost reached London bridge, Sir Kay discovered that he had left his sword at home.

"Will you go back for it?" he asked Arthur.

"That I will," said Arthur, glad of the chance to ride longer in the delightful air.

But when he reached their dwelling, he could not get in. The drawbridge was raised, and he could not make the warden hear his calling. Then Arthur was disturbed and said to himself:

"I will hasten to the churchyard we passed, and take the beautiful sword which I saw in the stone. It does not seem to belong to anyone, and my brother Kay must have a weapon."

So he rode on till he reached the churchyard, dismounted, and tied his horse to a sapling. The ten knights who guarded the sword had gone away to see the combats in the tournament. Arthur ran up and pulled lightly but eagerly at the sword. It came at once from the anvil. He hurried to Sir Kay, who was waiting for him on London bridge. Sir Kay knew that the weapon was the one that had been fixed fast in the stone, but he said nothing to Arthur, and the two soon overtook Sir Hector, who had ridden slowly to the field where the tournament was taking place. Sir Kay immediately told his father what had happened.

The good knight at once spoke with great respect to Arthur.

"Sir," he said, "you must be the king of this land."

"What mean you, sir?" asked Arthur.

Sir Hector told the wondering youth the reason why he was destined to be king. Then he said:

"Can you put this sword back in its place and pull it out again?"

"Easily," replied Arthur.

The three returned to the great stone, and Arthur put back the sword. Sir Hector tried to take it out, but failed.

"Now, you try," he said to Sir Kay.

But Sir Kay, in spite of great efforts, also failed. Then Arthur, at Sir Hector's bidding, tried, and at once pulled forth the sword. At that Sir Hector and Sir Kay knelt before Arthur.

"Alas," said Arthur, raising them from the ground, "my own dear father and my brother, why do you kneel to me?"

"Nay, my lord Arthur," said Sir Hector, "I am not your father. You are of higher blood than I am. Long ago, when you were a little baby,

Merlin brought you to me to take care of, telling me that you were to be the king."

"Then whose son am I?" cried Arthur.

"There are two stories: the one that Merlin tells, and the one that old Bleys, the master of Merlin, tells. Merlin brought you to me, saying that you were the son of King Uther and Yguerne his wife. But because the king was dead and the lords powerful and jealous, he told me to guard you in secrecy lest your life be taken. I did not know whether the story was true or false then, but you were a helpless child, and Merlin was a wise sage, and so I took you and brought you up as my own."

Arthur was so astonished that he did not ask to hear the tale that Bleys told. He stood gazing at Sir Hector, who said:

"And now, my gracious lord, will you be good to me and mine when you are king?"

"I will, indeed," replied Arthur, "for I am more beholden to you than to anyone else in the world, and also to my good lady and foster mother, your wife, who has reared me as if I were her own child. If it be God's will that I shall sometime become king, ask of me then what you will."

"Sir," said Sir Hector, "I ask that you make my son Sir Kay, your foster brother, the steward of all your lands."

"That shall be done," said Arthur, "and more. He shall have that office as long as I live."

Then the three went to the Archbishop of Canterbury and related to him the story of Merlin and all that had occurred. At his request they told no one else.

At the command of the archbishop on Twelfth day, which is the sixth of January, all the great lords assembled in the churchyard. Each tried to draw forth the sword, and each failed. Then the untitled people came and tried. Everyone failed until at last Arthur stepped forward. He hardly more than touched the sword when it came away in his hand.

At this many of the great lords were angry.

"He is but a boy," they said, "and not of high blood."

They refused to believe the story of his birth told by Merlin and Sir Hector. And because of all the quarreling, it was decided to have another trial at Candlemas, which fell in the month of February. Again Arthur was victorious. Then the great lords decreed that there should be another trial at Easter, and again Arthur succeeded. Next they decided to have a final trial at the feast of the Pentecost, which fell in May.

Meanwhile, Merlin advised the archbishop to see that Arthur had a bodyguard. So the archbishop selected several knights whom the former king, Uther, had trusted. These were Sir Ulfius and Sir Brastias and Sir Bedivere; Sir Geraint and Sir Hector and Sir Kay were also chosen. These brave men formed a bodyguard for Arthur until the feast of the Pentecost.At this time Arthur again drew out the sword from the anvil. Then the common people, who had so far let the lords have their will, cried out:

"We will have Arthur for our king, and we will have no more delay, for we see that it is God's will that he shall be our ruler."

Then all the people knelt down, high and low, rich and poor, and begged Arthur's pardon for the delay he had undergone. Arthur forgave them, and taking his sword, reverently placed it on the great altar beside which the archbishop stood. This was a sign that he meant to dedicate himself and his sword to God.

Afterward the crowning was held, and all the brave men and fair ladies in the land were present. The lords wore beautiful robes of velvet and ermine, with gold and jewels on their breast-plates. The ladies' robes were of purple and white and scarlet and gold and blue, and they wore many pearls and rubies and diamonds, so that all the place where they were assembled was glowing with light and color.

But Arthur, who wore a plain white robe, did not think of the beauty and richness. He was very grave, knowing that he was about to take a solemn oath. He bowed his head, while the archbishop set upon it the golden crown, which gleamed with jewels. Then he stood up before his people, and vowed that he would be a good king and always do justice. All the people uncovered their heads and vowed to serve and obey him; and when he smiled kindly on them as he rode slowly through the throng, they threw up their caps and shouted joyfully: "Long live King Arthur! Long live the King!"

King Arthur chose worthy men for his officers, making Sir Kay steward as he had promised; Sir Ulfius he made chamberlain, and Sir Brastias warden. Arthur gave offices also to Sir Hector and Sir Bedivere and Sir Geraint.

After his crowning the king set about righting all the wrongs that had been done since the death of King Uther. He gave back the lands and money that had been taken from widows and orphans, and would permit no unkindness to any of his subjects. Thus, at the very beginning of his reign, his people began to call him "Good King Arthur."

"Arthur and the Lady of the Lake." Illustration by Water J. Enright for Maude L. Radford, *King Arthur and His Knights* (Chicago, New York, London: Rand, McNally & Company, 1903). Project Gutenberg EBook.

Week Three:

EXCALIBUR

British Legend

Soon after the crowning of King Arthur, he was journeying through the land with Merlin, the wise old magician, when they met a knight who challenged Arthur to a combat. The two fought, and at last the knight wounded Arthur severely. In the end the king was victorious, but he had lost so much blood that he could go no farther. Merlin took him to a good hermit who healed his wound in three days. Then the king departed with Merlin, and as they were slowly riding along he said:

"I am still weak from the blood I have lost, and my sword is broken."

"Do not fear," said Merlin. "You shall lose no more blood and you shall have a good sword. Ride on trustfully with me."

They rode in silence until they came to a lake, large and quiet, and as beautiful in color as a pearl. While Arthur was looking at its beauty, he became suddenly aware of three tall women, with fair, sweet faces, standing on the bank.

"Who are they?" the king asked.

"Three queens who shall help you at your worst need," answered Merlin. "Now look out upon the lake again."

Arthur turned his eyes upon the lake and saw that in the distance a slight mist had arisen. Through it the figure of a lady glided over the surface of the water. Her robe appeared to be made of waves which streamed away in flowing curves from her body. Her head and shoulders seemed wrapped in foam tinted with the colors of the rainbow, and her arms glittered with sparkles which came from bubbles of water. She was so wonderful that Arthur looked at her for some time before he asked softly:

"Who is she?"

"She is the Lady of the Lake," said Merlin. "She lives in a rock in the middle of the lake. See, she is coming toward us. Look at what is beyond her in the water."

Arthur looked and saw rising above the surface of the water an arm clothed in pure white. This arm held a huge cross-hilted sword, so brilliant that Arthur's eyes were dazzled.

When the Lady of the Lake approached nearer, he said:

"Damsel, what sword is that? I wish it were mine, for I have none."

The lady smiled, saying:

"Step into yonder boat, row to the sword, and take it, together with the scabbard."

So Arthur entered a little boat that was tied to the shore, and rowed out to the sword. As he took it and the scabbard, all gleaming with jewels, the hand and arm vanished into the water. And when Arthur looked about, the three queens and the Lady of the Lake were also gone.

As Arthur, still gazing at the sword, rowed to shore, Merlin said to him:

"My lord Arthur, which pleases you more, sword or scabbard?"

"In truth, the sword," replied the king.

"Let me assure you," said Merlin, smiling gravely, "that the scabbard is worth ten of the sword. While you have it with you you shall never lose blood, no, no matter how sorely you are wounded. So see that you guard it well."

The king, who was looking at the sword, sighed.

"There is writing on the sword," he said.

"True, my lord, written in the oldest tongue in the world."

"*Take me* on one side," said Arthur, "and *Cast me away* on the other. I am glad to take the sword, but it saddens me to think of casting it away."

Merlin's face grew sad, too. He was so wise that he knew what was going to happen in the future, and he was well aware that when the time came to cast the sword away, much evil would have befallen the good King Arthur. But he knew that the time was yet very far off; so he said:

"You have taken the sword. Now use it to make justice and right prevail in all the land. Do not think of casting it away until you must."

Arthur grew joyful again as he felt the strength of the good sword in his hand, and the two rode cheerfully forward through the country.

Week Three:
"The Brook" (excerpt)

I chatter, chatter, as I flow
To join the brimming river;
For men may come and men
    may go,
But I go on forever.

I wind about, and in and out,
With here a blossom sailing,
And here and there a lusty trout,
And here and there a grayling.

I steal by lawns and grassy plots,
I slide by hazel covers;
I move the sweet forget-me-nots
For men may come and men may go,
But I go on forever.

That grow for happy lovers.
I slip, I slide, I gloom, I glance,
Among my skimming swallows;
I make the netted sunbeams
    dance
Against my sandy shallows.

I murmur under moon and stars
In brambly wildernesses;
I linger by my shingly bars;
I loiter round my cresses.

And out again I curve and flow
To join the brimming river;

Alfred, Lord Tennyson
(1809–1892)

Week Four:

How Arthur Fought with a Giant

British Legend

Once upon a time King Arthur and some of his knights were sailing in a ship. The king, being tired, went to sleep in his cabin, and began to dream. It seemed to him that he was sailing with his people when a great dragon flew out of the west. This dragon had a blue head and a gold back. Underneath he shone like a rainbow. Flames of fire rushed out of his mouth and covered land and sea.

As he flew, there came out of the east a great bear, very rough, and as black as coal, and with wings that flapped like windmills. The bear and the dragon roared loudly, and they began to fight and struggle till the sea was all red with blood. At last the dragon conquered.

When the king awoke from this dream he sent for Merlin and told him of it, and asked for an explanation.

"My lord," Merlin replied, "the dragon betokens yourself; the colors on its body are signs of your glory. The bear betokens some tyrant who torments the people and whom you will slay."

Soon after this, the ship in which the company was, came in sight of land. When they had anchored, the knights noticed on the beach a crowd of people who were weeping. Descending from the ship, Arthur asked one of the men what troubled them, and what was the name of their country.

"Good sir," returned the man, "this is the country of Brittany, and we weep because our county is desolated by a giant. He makes us bring him food. First, he ate up all the oxen we had, and then our horses. Next he demanded our children, and now there are no little ones in the land. To-day he took our good duchess of Brittany, and carried her off to his mountain."

"Alas!" said the king. "It grieves me to hear this, not only because a cruel deed has been done, but because the duchess of Brittany is my cousin's wife. I must save this lady. I will fight with the giant."

"Good sir," cried the people in amazement, "it is not possible! A whole company of us dare not attack him, and yet we account ourselves brave men."

"That may well be," replied Arthur, "and yet with my good sword and scabbard, I have no fear."

Then the men said:

"If you will go, my lord, yonder is the great mountain where the giant lives. At the top, two huge fires burn continually in front of a cave, and in that cave are greater treasures than you can dream of. They are all yours if you will but slay this monster."

Arthur replied nothing to them, but called Sir Kay and Sir Bedivere, and rode with them to the foot of the mountain. From that point he ascended alone. When he was nearly to the top he came upon a woman, clad all in black, who sat weeping by the side of a newly-made grave.

"Good woman, why do you weep?" asked Arthur.

"Hush, hush!" she cried, "or the giant will hear you and come and kill you. He can hear me, but the sound of weeping delights him, and therefore I need not restrain my grief."

"Why do you grieve?" the king asked.

"Alas! Because my good mistress, the duchess of Brittany, is dead. The giant has killed her."

At that Arthur gripped tightly the handle of his sword and said:

"I will kill this wretch before I am an hour older."

"Ah, my lord," said the woman, "the greatest kings in the country are afraid of him. He has a coat embroidered with the beards of fifteen of them. He demanded these beards as a sign that they acknowledged him as lord."

"There is at least one king who does not acknowledge him as lord," shouted Arthur, as he strode hastily forward.

When he reached the top he saw the giant asleep in front of the two great fires before the cave. He was taller than the tallest pine that ever grew. His arms were as big as the trunk of an oak tree. His mouth was as large as a cave, and from it and his nostrils came forth fire and flame like that from the mountain of Vesuvius. Although his huge eyes were closed, flashes of lightning seemed to shoot from beneath the lids. At his side was an iron club as large as a steeple. About him stood trembling old women fanning him as he slept.

King Arthur approached the monster, and said to him:

"Wretch, awake and fight, for your hour has come."

The giant, starting up, looked down scornfully upon the king and, laughing, threw his great club at Arthur. But the king leapt aside and the club fell harmlessly on the ground, making a hollow where it struck.

Then Arthur rushed toward the giant, waving his good sword Excalibur. The giant caught him in his arms, in order to squeeze him to death. The king's armor pressed closer and closer about him, and he began to lose his strength. But he kept his hand upon his scabbard, and so did not die.

In a few minutes the monster, making sure that Arthur was dead, dropped him to the ground. After the king had recovered himself, he sprang to his feet, and taking his sword, threw it at the giant. The good steel pierced his neck, and he sank to the ground, shouting so loudly that Sir Kay and Sir Bedivere at the foot of the mountain heard, and trembled for their master's safety.

Then the giant again seized Arthur in his arms, and the two began to roll down the mountain side. Whenever Arthur was able to, he struck at the giant with his dagger, wounding him sorely. At last, still struggling and rolling, they came to the spot where Sir Kay and Sir Bedivere were. These two loosed the giant's arms from the king, who then gave one last blow to the monster, killing him. Then he sent Sir Kay and Sir Bedivere for his sword Excalibur.

When the people on the seashore heard what Arthur had done, they fell on their knees and thanked him, offering him all the giant's treasure. He said, however, that he would leave it with them to divide among the poor people of the country. For himself, all he wanted was the giant's iron club.

The people sent fifty men to the top of the mountain to get it for him. As they had no horses, it was a long time before they could drag the club to the seashore. There they put it on a barge. It was so heavy that it pressed the barge down till the water came almost to the edge of the vessel. Then King Arthur bade the people good-by, and took ship with his knights. The grateful men of Brittany stood on the shore, and shouted and waved until the ship could no longer be seen.

Week Four:

How Lancelot Saved Guinevere

British Legend

One day in May Queen Guinevere invited ten ladies and ten knights to ride a-Maying with her the next morning in the woods. So at the appointed time they assembled, all dressed in green silk and green velvet, the color of young grass. The knights wore white plumes in their helmets, and the ladies wore white May-blossoms in their hair. They rode off very happily, telling the king that they would return before noon.

Now the good King Bagdemagus, for whom Sir Lancelot had fought, had a bad son named Sir Malgrace. For a long time he had wanted to capture the queen and carry her off to his castle. He had been afraid to try, however, because of her large bodyguard. All the young knights of the Round Table liked to ride with her and protect her. They took good care of all the ladies of the Court, but they loved the queen most.

When Sir Malgrace heard that the queen was out a-Maying with only a few knights, and these not fully armed, he determined to take her prisoner. So he called together eighty men-at-arms and a hundred archers, and set out. Soon he came upon her and her attendants. They were sitting on a little hill, with wreaths of flowers and leaves on their arms and necks. Before they could rise to their feet, Sir Malgrace and his men dashed upon them.

"Traitor!" cried the queen. "What would you do?"

"I will carry you to my castle, fair queen," he said. "And never again shall you go free."

"I will not go with you," said the queen.

Then the ten knights drew their swords and set on the hundred and eighty men of Sir Malgrace. They fought so well that they overthrew forty. Still, they could do little against such numbers, and soon all were wounded. When the queen saw this, she cried out:

"Sir Malgrace, do not slay my noble knights, and I will go with you. I would rather die than cause them further harm."

The knights said that they would rather perish than be prisoners to Sir Malgrace. However, upon an order from their lord, the archers tied up the wounds of the queen's followers, and put them on horseback. Then the whole company rode slowly towards the castle of Sir Malgrace.

Sir Malgrace kept close to the queen for fear she would escape. Once when they were in a thick part of the wood he rode ahead to break the branches so that they should not strike her face. Then the queen whispered to a little maiden who rode near her:

"If you can do so, slip away from the company. You are so small that perhaps they will not notice you. Take this ring and give it to our greatest knight, Sir Lancelot, and pray him to come and rescue me."

The little maid waited until she thought the time for escape had come, and rode off as quietly as she could. Sir Malgrace saw her go, and suspected that the queen had sent her. He ordered his archers to shoot at the child, but she escaped unhurt.

"Madam," said Sir Malgrace to the queen, "I know well that you have sent for Sir Lancelot, but you may be sure that hither he shall never come."

Then Sir Malgrace ordered his archers to stand guard on the road and shoot down any knight they saw.

"But if he should be Sir Lancelot," he said, "be sure that you do not venture very close to him, for he is hard to overcome."

Meantime the little maid reached Arthur's Court in safety. She found the king and his knights very anxious because the queen had not returned. She told her story, and gave the queen's ring to Sir Lancelot.

"Bring me my armor!" shouted Sir Lancelot. "I will rescue my good and dear queen before the night falls. I would rather see her safe here again than own all France."

He put on his armor and mounted his white horse and rode off without delay. The little maid led him to the place where the ten knights had fought with the hundred and eighty. From this point he traced them by the blood on the grass and on the road. At last he reached the archers.

"Turn back," they said. "No one may pass here."

"That I will not," said Sir Lancelot. "I am a Knight of the Round Table, and therefore have the right of way throughout the land."

At that they shot their arrows at him. He was wounded with many of them, and his white horse was killed. Sir Lancelot tried to reach the men, but there were so many hedges and ditches in the way that he could not. They hastened back to tell Sir Malgrace that a knight whom they had not succeeded in killing was coming to the castle.

Sir Lancelot tried to walk, but his armor was too heavy for him to carry in his wounded state. He dared not leave any of it behind, for he would need it all in fighting. Just as he was wondering what he could do, a carter passed him, driving a rough wagon.

"Carter," said Sir Lancelot, "let me ride in your wagon to the castle of Sir Malgrace."

The carter was amazed, for in that day a knight never entered into a cart unless he was a condemned man going to be hanged. Sir Lancelot, however, did not stop to explain. He jumped into the cart and told the driver to go quickly.

Some of the ladies of Queen Guinevere were looking out of their window, and one said to her:

"See, my queen, there is a poor knight going to be hanged."

The queen looked out of the window and recognized Sir Lancelot by the three lions blazoned upon his shield. She was overjoyed, and waved him a glad greeting as he came up to the castle gate.

Sir Lancelot beat on the gate with his shield, and cried:

"Come out, false traitor, Sir Malgrace; come out and fight. If you do not, you will be branded as a coward forever."

At first Sir Malgrace thought that he would keep his gates shut fast and not answer the challenge. But in those days it was a sign of great cowardice not to accept a challenge. Moreover, since Sir Lancelot had been able to reach the castle in spite of the archers, he was afraid other knights of the Round Table might do the same. Then they would besiege him and force him to surrender. Still he was afraid to fight. So he went to Queen Guinevere and said:

"Fair queen, remember how I saved your ten knights when I could have killed them. Now I am sorry I took you prisoner. I beg that you will go to Sir Lancelot and urge him not to fight. Then I will entertain him in this castle with the best I have, and to-morrow you shall all go back to the court."

Then the queen said:

"Peace is always better than war. I will do the best I can."

So she went down to Sir Lancelot, who still beat upon the gate, and besought him to come in peaceably, for Sir Malgrace was sorry for what he had done. Sir Lancelot was unwilling, for he knew that Sir Malgrace was a traitor, deserving punishment. Still, he could not refuse the queen anything she asked him, and, therefore, he entered the castle.

Sir Malgrace greeted him with politeness, and served to him and to the others of Arthur's Court, a great banquet. After that, to the surprise of everyone, he rose and accused the queen of treason. All the company was astonished. Sir Lancelot was very angry.

"If you say the queen is a traitress," he cried, "you shall fight with me, although you were afraid just now."

"I am not afraid to fight," said Sir Malgrace.

"When and where will you meet me in combat?" asked Sir Lancelot.

"In eight days," replied Sir Malgrace, "in the field near Westminster."

Sir Lancelot agreed to this. Then Queen Guinevere rose with all her attendants and went into the courtyard. Their horses were brought them and they mounted. Sir Lancelot was the last to pass out of the banquet hall. As he was going through the door he stepped upon a trap which Sir Malgrace had prepared for him. The trapdoor fell and dropped him into a dark dungeon.

When the queen and her knights and ladies had ridden out of the courtyard, they noticed that Sir Lancelot was not with them. They supposed, however, that he had ridden off by himself, as was often his custom, so they went without him to Camelot, and told the king what had happened. He was very angry at Sir Malgrace's accusation, but he was sure that Sir Lancelot would punish Sir Malgrace, and so vindicate Queen Guinevere.

Meantime, the unhappy Sir Lancelot lay bruised in the dungeon, feeling very sure that Sir Malgrace meant to starve him to death. He lay hungry and thirsty for nearly two days. Then Sir Malgrace peeped in to see if he were dead.

"Ah, traitor!" cried Sir Lancelot, "I shall overcome you yet."

At that Sir Malgrace shut the trapdoor hastily, as if he were afraid that Sir Lancelot could leap up ten feet in the air. That one look, however, cost the wicked knight dear, for the daughter of the porter saw him shutting the trapdoor, and was curious to know who was in the dungeon. So at night she opened the trapdoor and let herself down by a rope.

When she saw Sir Lancelot she was very sorry for him. He offered her much money if she would free him. At last she said:

"I will do it for love of Queen Guinevere and not for money."

She let him climb up by the rope, and took him out of the courtyard. He was so sick that he went to a hermit's hut and rested for several days. When next Sir Malgrace looked into the dungeon he heard no movement. Then he rejoiced greatly, for he thought Sir Lancelot was dead.

When the eighth day had come, all the knights of the Round Table assembled in the tournament field and waited for Sir Lancelot to appear. They all thought he would surely come. But Sir Malgrace rode jauntily about the field. Many of the knights wondered at his courage, not knowing the reason for his confidence.

The herald blew his trumpet once, but Sir Lancelot did not appear; twice, and still he did not come. Then up started several knights and begged the king to let them fight instead of Sir Lancelot.

"He has been trapped," they said, "or he would be here."

While the king was hesitating whom to choose, in rode Sir Lancelot. He dashed up to Sir Malgrace.

"Here I am, traitor," he said. "Now do your worst."

Then they fought, but at the first stroke Sir Malgrace fell to the earth.

"Mercy!" he cried, "I yield to you, Sir Knight. Do not slay me. I put myself in the king's hands and yours."

Sir Lancelot was much vexed. He wanted to kill Sir Malgrace for his treachery, and yet, since the man had asked for mercy, he could not. So he said:

"What, coward, would you stop already? Shame upon you! Get up and fight."

"I shall not rise unless you take me as one who has yielded," answered the knight.

Then Sir Lancelot said:

"Traitor, I make you this offer: I will take off my helmet, unarm my left side, and tie my left hand behind my back. In that way I will fight with you."

Upon hearing this, Sir Malgrace rose to his feet, sure now of killing Sir Lancelot.

"My lord King," cried Sir Malgrace, "you have heard this offer. I accept."

The king was very sorry that Sir Lancelot had made the offer. However, it was impossible to withdraw it. A squire came and disarmed

Sir Lancelot, so that his head and left side were without cover; and since he had only one arm to fight with, he could not use his shield.

Then Sir Malgrace dashed at him, aiming for his left side. Sir Lancelot waited till he was very near, and then lightly stepped aside. Before Sir Malgrace could turn, Sir Lancelot lifted his spear and struck his enemy such a blow that he broke his breastplate and pierced his heart.

The body of Sir Malgrace was carried off the field and taken to the castle of his good father; Queen Guinevere was proclaimed innocent of treason; and Sir Lancelot was honored more than ever by his king and his queen.

"Sir Launcelot [*sic*] greets Queen Guinevere." Written and illustrated by Howard Pyle, *The Story of the Champions of the Round Table* (New York: Charles Scribner's Sons, 1905).

(THIS PAGE AND NEXT)"My Shadow." Illustrations by Jessie Willcox Smith for Robert Louis Stevenson, *A Child's Garden of Verses* (New York: Charles Scribner's Sons, 1905).

Week Four:
"MY SHADOW"

I have a little shadow that goes in and out with me,
And what can be the use of him is more than I can see.
He is very, very like me from the heels up to the head;
And I see him jump before me, when I jump into my bed.

The funniest thing about him is the way he likes to grow—
Not at all like proper children, which is always very slow;
For he sometimes shoots up taller like an india-rubber ball,
And he sometimes gets so little that there's none of him at all.

He hasn't got a notion of how children ought to play,
And can only make a fool of me in every sort of way.
He stays so close beside me, he's a coward, you can see;
I'd think shame to stick to nursie as that shadow sticks to me!

One morning, very early, before the sun was up,
I rose and found the shining dew on every buttercup;
But my lazy little shadow, like an arrant sleepy-head,
Had stayed at home behind me and was fast asleep in bed.

ROBERT LOUIS STEVENSON
(1850–1894)

"Then it was a swan that beat its wings in her face." Written and illustrated by Katharine Pyle in *Wonder Tales Retold* (Boston: Little, Brown, c. 1905).

Week Five:

TAMLANE

From a Scottish Ballad

Young Tamlane was son of Earl Murray, and Burd Janet was daughter of Dunbar, Earl of March. And when they were young they loved one another and plighted their troth. But when the time came near for their marrying, Tamlane disappeared, and none knew what had become of him.

Many, many days after he had disappeared, Burd Janet was wandering in Carterhaugh Wood, though she had been warned not to go there. And as she wandered she plucked the flowers from the bushes. She came at last to a bush of broom and began plucking it. She had not taken more than three flowerets when by her side up started young Tamlane.

"Where come ye from, Tamlane, Tamlane?" Burd Janet said; "and why have you been away so long?"

"From Elfland I come," said young Tamlane. "The Queen of Elfland has made me her knight."

"But how did you get there, Tamlane?" said Burd Janet.

"I was hunting one day, and as I rode widershins round yon hill, a deep drowsiness fell upon me, and when I awoke, behold! I was in Elfland. Fair is that land and gay, and fain would I stop but for thee and one other thing. Every seven years the Elves pay their tithe to the Nether world, and for all the queen makes much of me, I fear it is myself that will be the tithe."

"Oh, can you not be saved? Tell me if aught I can do will save you, Tamlane?"

"One only thing is there for my safety. Tomorrow night is Hallowe'en, and the fairy court will then ride through England and Scotland, and if you would borrow me from Elfland you must take your stand by Miles Cross between twelve and one o'the night, and with holy water in your hand you must cast a compass all around you."

"But how shall I know you, Tamlane?" quoth Burd Janet, "amid so many knights I've ne'er seen before?"

"The first court of Elves that come by let pass. The next court you shall pay reverence to, but do naught nor say aught.

But the third court that comes by is the chief court of them, and at the head rides the Queen of all Elfland. And I shall ride by her side upon a milk-white steed with a star in my crown; they give me this honour as being a christened knight. Watch my hands, Janet, the right one will be gloved but the left one will be bare, and by that token you will know me."

"But how to save you, Tamlane?" quoth Burd Janet.

"You must spring upon me suddenly, and I will fall to the ground. Then seize me quick, and whatever change befall me, for they will exercise all their magic on me, cling hold to me till they turn me into

"Janet casts the flaming sword into the well." Illustration by John D. Batten for Joseph Jacobs, *More English Fairy Tales* (New York and London: G. P. Putnam's Sons, 1891).

red-hot iron. Then cast me into this pool and I will be turned back into a mother-naked man. Cast then your green mantle over me, and I shall be yours, and be of the world again."

So Burd Janet promised to do all for Tamlane, and next night at midnight she took her stand by Miles Cross and cast a compass round her with holy water.

Soon there came riding by the Elfin court, first over the mound went a troop on black steeds, and then another troop on brown. But in the third court, all on milk-white steeds, she saw the Queen of Elfland, and by her side a knight with a star in his crown, with right hand gloved and the left bare. Then she knew this was her own Tamlane, and springing forward she seized the bridle of the milk-white steed and pulled its rider down. And as soon as he had touched the ground she let go the bridle and seized him in her arms.

"He's won, he's won amongst us all," shrieked out the eldritch crew, and all came around her and tried their spells on young Tamlane.

First they turned him in Janet's arms like frozen ice, then into a huge flame of roaring fire. Then, again, the fire vanished and an adder was skipping through her arms, but still she held on; and then they turned him into a snake that reared up as if to bite her, and yet she held on. Then suddenly a dove was struggling in her arms, and almost flew away. Then they turned him into a swan, but all was in vain, till at last he was turned into a red-hot glaive, and this she cast into a well of water and then he turned back into a mother-naked man. She quickly cast her green mantle over him, and young Tamlane was Burd Janet's for ever.

Then sang the Queen of Elfland as the court turned away and began to resume its march:

> "She that has borrowed young Tamlane
>   Has gotten a stately groom,
> She's taken away my bonniest knight,
>   Left nothing in his room.

"But had I known, Tamlane, Tamlane,
    A lady would borrow thee,
I'd hae ta'en out thy two grey eyne,
    Put in two eyne of tree.

"Had I but known, Tamlane, Tamlane,
    Before we came from home,
I'd hae ta'en out thy heart o' flesh,
    Put in a heart of stone.

"Had I but had the wit yestreen
    That I have got today,
I'd paid the Fiend seven times his teind
    Ere you'd been won away."

And then the Elfin court rode away, and Burd Janet and young Tamlane went their way homewards and were soon after married after young Tamlane had again been sained by the holy water and made Christian once more.

Week Five:

Britomart and the Magic Mirror

English Fairy Tale

Long years ago there lived a beautiful princess whose name was Britomart.

When she was a little girl she did not care to play with dolls nor to sew, but she loved to ride and to play boys' games. And when she grew older she learned to fight with spears and swords like the knights at her father's court.

Now a great magician called Merlin had once given a wonderful gift to the king, Britomart's father.

It was a magic mirror, that looked like a ball of the clearest crystal.

When the king looked in this mirror he saw all that was going to happen to him, and which of his friends were false and which true. There was no hidden secret which that crystal ball could not tell.

One day Britomart went into her father's room and looked into his magic mirror.

"What shall I wish to see?" she asked of herself.

Then she thought, "Some day I shall marry. I should like the crystal ball to show me what my husband will be like."

Even as she thought this, she saw, like a moving picture, a knight riding across the crystal.

He was tall and broad and strong, and looked very brave. The front of his shining helmet was drawn up, and from under it looked out the handsome face that his friends loved and his foes feared. He wore beautiful armour, all inlaid with gold, and she knew what his name was, and that he had won this armour in a fight with another great knight, for on it was written:

"Achilles' armes which Artegall did win."

From that day Britomart could think of nothing but the knight whose picture had ridden across the mirror and vanished away.

She grew thoughtful and sad, and could not sleep, for she feared it was a dreadful thing to love a shadow.

Her old nurse slept in her room, and at night when she heard Britomart tossing about in bed and softly crying to herself, the old woman was very unhappy. Night after night she heard her, till she could bear it no longer. She asked Britomart what was wrong, and Britomart sobbingly told her.

"I should like the crystal ball to shew [*sic*] me what my husband will be like." Illustration by Rose Le Quesne for Jeanie Lang, *Stories from The Faerie Queen Told to the Children* (London: T. C. and E. C. Jack, Ltd; New York: E. P. Dutton & Co., 1905).

Then the good old nurse comforted Britomart. She said she was sure that Artegall must be a real man, and not just a shadow, and that she would find him. Then she tucked the bedclothes round Britomart, and put out the flickering lamp. When Britomart, much comforted, had fallen quietly asleep, her nurse sat and watched beside her, and dropped some tears because Britomart was no longer a little baby-girl for her to take care of, but a grown-up girl who loved a knight.

Next day the old nurse went to the woods and gathered all sorts of herbs. She boiled them down together, and mixed them with milk and other things, and put them in an earthen pot. Round the pot she bound three of her hairs plaited together. Then she said a charm over the pot, and made Britomart turn round and round and round about it. She thought that this charm would cure Britomart of loving the knight, and make her gay and happy again. But the old nurse's charm was no good. Britomart grew thin and sad and ill.

Then the old woman thought of Merlin, the magician who had made the mirror.

"It is all his fault that my princess is so sad," she said; "he must make her happy again."

So she dressed Britomart and herself in shabby old clothes, and went to seek Merlin.

The magician lived in a dark cave under a rock. The rock lay near a swift-rushing river that ran down between thickly wooded hills. Hollow, fearful sounds, and a clanking, as of chains, were always heard there.

When Britomart and her nurse reached the lonely cave, and heard the noise of moans and groans and clanking chains, they were too frightened at first to go in. But at length they plucked up courage and entered the cave, and found Merlin writing magic words on the dark floor. He knew very well, although they wore shabby old clothes, that his visitors were the Princess Britomart and the princess's nurse. But he pretended that he did not know them, and asked them what they wanted.

"Three moons have come and gone," said the nurse, "since this fair maid first turned ill. I do not know what ails her, but if you cannot cure her, she will die."

Merlin smiled.

"If that is all you want," he said, "you had better take her to a doctor."

"If any doctor could have done her good," said the nurse, "I should not have troubled you. But I fear that a witch or a wicked fairy must have bewitched her."

Then Merlin burst out laughing.

"Why do you go on pretending to me?" he said. "I know all about it. This is the beautiful Princess Britomart, and you are her nurse."

At that Britomart blushed rosy red, but the nurse said:

"If you know all our grief, then have pity on us, and give us your help."

Then Merlin told Britomart not to be sad, for Artegall was a real living knight, and one of the bravest and noblest that lived. His home was in Fairyland, but he was a king's son that the fairies had stolen away when he was a baby.

"You shall marry Artegall," said the magician, "and bring him back from Fairyland to his own country, where he shall be king."

Then he gave her much advice, and told her of the great things that should be done in the days to come by the sons that were to be hers and Artegall's.

And Britomart and her nurse, with happy hearts, came away from the magician's gloomy cave.

"But how shall we seek my knight?" asked Britomart of her nurse. "How shall we find him?"

The nurse said: "Let us dress ourselves in some of the armour that your father has taken from his enemies. You shall be a knight, and I will be your squire. Together we will ride to Fairyland and find Artegall."

When Britomart was dressed in shining armour of silver and gold, she looked a very handsome, tall, young knight. Her nurse dressed her as carefully as she had dressed her long ago in her baby-clothes, and, when all her armour was on, she put into her hand a long spear. It was a magic spear, and there had never yet been born a knight who could sit on his saddle when it struck him.

In the silent night they got on their horses and rode away, no longer a princess and her nurse, but a gallant knight and a little old squire, who seemed to find his big shield much too heavy for him.

Before Britomart and her nurse had ridden very far, they saw two knights riding towards them. These were Guyon and the Red Cross Knight.

Guyon rode furiously at Britomart, but Britomart rode as furiously at him with her magic spear. And, for the first time in his life, Guyon found himself thrown from his horse and sitting heavily down on the ground. He was very much ashamed and very angry, and would have rushed at Britomart with his sword. But the old palmer, who was with him, calmed his rage, and he made friends with Britomart. And for some time Britomart and those two brave knights rode on together, and shared fights and adventures.

One day as they rode together, Britomart asked the Red Cross Knight if he knew a wicked knight called Artegall.

"He is not a wicked knight," said the Red Cross Knight angrily. "He is one of the bravest and the best."

Britomart was so glad to hear him say this of Artegall, that she could scarcely hide her joy. But she went on pretending that she thought Artegall bad and cruel, just that she might hear his friend praise him.

"There is no knight more brave than Artegall," said the Red Cross Knight. "Ladies who suffer wrong, and little children who have none to care for them, are always sure of having Artegall to fight for them. He is as good as he is brave, and as brave as he is good."

Britomart loved the Red Cross Knight because he was so true to his friend, and more than ever she loved Artegall, the knight of the Mirror.

Presently her way and that of the Red Cross Knight parted, and she rode on with her squire until they came to the sea-shore.

The sea was beating against the rocks, and moaning as it cast itself against the high crags.

Britomart made her old nurse unlace her helmet, and sat down and watched the cold grey waves.

"I feel like a little boat beaten about by the sea," she said. "When shall I ever reach my harbour, and find the knight I seek?"

For a long time she sat, sadly thinking. But at last she saw a knight cantering along the sand, and quickly put on her helmet and leaped on her horse, and rode to meet him.

He was a bold knight, and told her to fly, or he would kill her.

"Fly!" proudly said Britomart. "Words only frighten babies. I will not fly. I will fight you!"

Then they fought, and with her spear Britomart gave the knight a terrible wound, and rode away, leaving him lying senseless on the shore.

Many other fights had Britomart as she sought Artegall, and always her magic spear made her the winner.

One day she came to a place where a great many knights were having a tournament.

A beautiful golden girdle, sparkling with jewels, was to be the prize for the knight that fought the best.

For three days they had fought and fought, until the ground was strewed with broken spears and swords.

On the last day of the tournament a stranger knight had appeared. His armour did not shine with silver and gold like those of the other knights, but looked like an old tree all overgrown with moss. His horse was decked with oak-leaves, and he carried a battered old shield.

"The Savage Knight," the others called him, and they would have laughed at him and his shabby armour, had he not fought so well. All day long he fought, and one knight after another he threw wounded or dead on the ground. At sunset they feared him as they might have feared a fierce lion, and none dared stand against him.

Just then Britomart rode up with her golden armour gleaming against the sunset sky.

She couched her spear and rode at the Savage Knight, and threw him to the ground.

The other knights then all rode at her, but them, too, she threw down with her magic spear.

So they had to own that Britomart was the victor, and had won the golden girdle.

Now the Savage Knight was not really a savage knight. He was no other than Artegall, the knight of the Crystal Ball.

Artegall was so ashamed, and so angry with Britomart for having thrown him from his horse, that when the tournament was over, he rode away to a wood, through which he knew that Britomart must pass.

"The stranger knight with his magic spear shall fight me once again," he angrily said, "and this time he shall not be the victor."

Presently, as he sat under the trees, and watched his horse grazing, he saw Britomart riding up, brave and fearless, in her golden armour.

Artegall sprang on his horse, and furiously rode at Britomart with his steel-headed lance. But, in the twinkling of an eye, he found himself lying on the turf, again unseated by the magic spear.

He rushed at Britomart then with his sword, and cut and thrust at her so savagely that her horse backed away from him. At last he struck a great blow at her head, and the sword, glancing down her armour, struck her horse with such force on its back that it fell to the ground, and Britomart had to jump off. She threw aside her spear and furiously smote Artegall with her sword. She cut his armour through, and wounded him so deeply that blood from his wound streamed to the ground. The blows from Artegall's sword fell on her like hail, but she struck him as fiercely as he struck her. The grass got trampled down and stained with blood, yet still they smote and thrust and smote again.

At last Artegall grew very tired, and Britomart was more tired still. When Artegall saw how tired she was, he gathered up all his strength and struck her a terrific blow, hoping to kill her quite. But the blow only sheared off the front part of her helmet, and left her face uncovered.

And as Artegall's arm rose again for another deadly stroke, it stopped short in the air. For instead of the grim face of the fierce knight he thought he was fighting, there looked out a face that Artegall thought was the loveliest he had ever seen.

Britomart's cheeks were hot and pink, and her hair, that was so long that it reached her feet, had burst from its band and framed her fair face like a golden frame.

The sword slipped from Artegall's fingers to the ground. He knelt at Britomart's feet and begged her to forgive him for having treated her so roughly.

But Britomart was still angry with him for that last fierce stroke of his.

"Rise!" she said, "or I shall kill you!" and she held her sword over his head.

But Artegall would not rise, but only prayed her the more earnestly to forgive him.

Then the old nurse drew near and begged Britomart to have a truce.

"Rest yourself for a little," she said, "and let the Savage Knight rest too."

Britomart agreed, and the knight raised the front of his helmet that he might breathe more freely.

When Britomart saw his face, so handsome and so brave, she knew at once that the Savage Knight that she had tried to kill was Artegall, the knight of the Mirror.

Her arm dropped, and her sword fell from her hand.

She tried to speak roughly to him, but her tongue would not say the words.

Together they rode off to a castle, where they stayed till they were rested and their wounds were healed.

And each day that they were together Artegall loved Britomart more and more, until at last he could stay no longer silent, but told her that he loved her more than all the world.

So it was that the beautiful princess Britomart found her husband, the gallant knight of the Magic Mirror.

Week Five:

"The Tournament"

I.

Bright shone the lists, blue bent the skies,
 And the knights still hurried amain
To the tournament under the ladies' eyes,
 Where the jousters were Heart and Brain.

II.

Flourished the trumpets, entered Heart,
 A youth in crimson and gold;
Flourished again; Brain stood apart,
 Steel-armoured, dark and cold.

III.

Heart's palfrey caracoled gaily round,
 Heart tra-li-ra'd merrily;
But Brain sat still, with never a sound,
 So cynical-calm was he.

IV.

Heart's helmet-crest bore favours three
 From his lady's white hand caught;
While Brain wore a plumeless casque; not he
 Or favour gave or sought.

V.

The trumpet blew; Heart shot a glance
 To catch his lady's eye.
But Brain gazed straight ahead, his lance
 To aim more faithfully.

VI.

They charged, they struck; both fell, both bled;
 Brain rose again, ungloved;
Heart, dying, smiled and faintly said,
 "My love to my beloved."
   Sidney Lanier (1842–1881)

"The aged Palmer gives young David of Doncaster news of Will Stutely." Written and illustrated by Howard Pyle, *The Merry Adventures of Robin Hood of Great Renown in Nottinghamshire* (New York: Charles Scribner's Sons, 1883).

Week Six:

WINNING THE SHERIFF'S GOLDEN ARROW

English Folklore

It was very pleasant in Sherwood Forest to those who did not fear hardship, and Robin Hood and his men came to love every tree that grew and every bird that sang there. They did not mind that they had no houses to live in. They made themselves shelters of bark and logs to keep the rain off, and mostly they stayed in the open. They did not sigh for soft beds or fine tables and furnishings. They put down rushes and spread deer skins over them to lie on, and slept under the stars. They cooked over a great fire built beside a big tree, and they sat and ate on the ground.

More than a hundred men were in Robin Hood's band; every one was devoted to him and obeyed his slightest word. They were the best archers, the best wrestlers, the best runners and the best wielders of cudgel and quarter-staff in all the country, and they grew better continually, for they practiced these things every day.

Robin Hood was the best archer in all the land. Even the king had heard of his wonderful marksmanship, and even though he knew him an outlaw, he had an admiring and almost kindly feeling for this bold outlaw who shot so marvelously well. But the greedy lords and churchmen who oppressed the people hated Robin Hood; and the sheriff of Nottingham hated him most of all, and wished above all things to hang him on the gallows.

He was a cruel, hard man with no kindness in his bosom, and all his spite was turned against Robin Hood, because every time that he tried to catch him, Robin outwitted him. Now he was especially angered, for he had sent a messenger with a warrant to take Robin Hood and the merry Robin had met the messenger and feasted him, and then, while he was asleep after the feast, stolen the very warrant out of his pocket so that he had to go back to the sheriff without man or warrant either. So the sheriff of Nottingham used all his wits to get another plan to take Robin Hood. It was plainly of no use to send men, no matter how stout, with warrants after him. He must be coaxed into their clutches.

"I have it," said the sheriff of Nottingham at last, with a very sour look on his grim face. "I'll catch him by craft. I'll proclaim a great archery festival, and get all the best archers in England to come here to shoot. I'll offer for the prize an arrow of beaten gold. That will be sure to fetch Robin Hood and his men here, and then I'll catch them and hang them."

Now Robin Hood and his men did come to the archery contest. But they did not come in the suits of Lincoln green that they wore as men of the forest. Each man dressed himself up to seem somebody else. Some appeared as barefoot friars, some as traveling tinkers or tradesmen, some as beggars, and some as rustic peasants. Robin Hood was the hardest to recognize of all.

"Don't go, master," his men had begged. "This archery contest is just a trap to catch you. The sheriff of Nottingham and his men will be looking for you and they will know you by your hair and eyes and face and height, even if you wear different clothes. The sheriff has made this festival just to lure you to death. Don't go."

But Robin Hood laughed merrily.

"Why, as to my yellow hair, I can stain that with walnut stain. As to my eyes, I can cover one of them with a patch and then my face will not be recognized. I would scorn to be afraid, and if an adventure is somewhat dangerous, I like it all the better."

So Robin Hood went, clad from top to toe in tattered scarlet, the raggedest beggarman that had ever been seen in Nottingham. The field where the contest was to be held was a splendid sight. Rows and rows of benches had been built on it for the gentlefolk to sit on, and they wore their best clothes and were gayer than birds of paradise. As for the sheriff and his wife, they wore velvet, the sheriff purple and his lady blue. Their rich garments were trimmed with ermine. They wore broad gold chains around their necks, and the sheriff had shoes with wondrously pointed toes that were fastened to his gold-embroidered garters by golden chains. Oh! they were dressed very splendidly, and if their faces had been kind, they would have looked beautiful. But their faces were full of pride and hate. The sheriff was looking everywhere with spiteful glances for Robin Hood, and very cross he was that he did not see Robin there.

But Robin was there, though the sheriff did not see him. There he stood in his ragged beggar's garments, not ten feet away from the sheriff.

The targets were placed eighty yards from where the archers were to stand. Pace that off, and see what a great distance it is. There were a great number of archers to shoot and each was to have one shot. Then the ten who shot best were to shoot two arrows each; and the three who shot best out of the ten were to shoot three arrows apiece. The one who came nearest to the center of the target was to get a prize.

The sheriff looked gloweringly at the ten.

"I was sure that Robin Hood would be among them," he said to the man-at-arms at his side. "Could no one of these ten be Robin Hood in disguise?"

"No," answered the man-at-arms. "Six of these I know well. They are the best archers in England. There is Gill o' the Red Cap, Diccon Cruikshank, Adam o' the Dell, William o' Leslie, Hubert o' Cloud, and Swithin o'Hertford. Of the four beside, one is too tall and one too short and one not broad-shouldered enough to be Robin Hood. There remains only this ragged beggar, and his hair and beard are much too dark to be Robin Hood's, and beside, he is blind in one eye. Robin Hood is safe in Sherwood Forest."

Even as he spoke, the man-at-arms was glad, for he was but a common soldier, and he loved Robin Hood and wished no harm to come to him. One reason why Robin Hood got away from the sheriff so many times was that the common people, even among the sheriff's own men, were friendly to him and helped him all they could. The gatekeepers shut their eyes when Robin Hood went through the gates that they might say they had not seen him enter. Hardly any one would betray him, and many, when they knew of evil being planned against him, sent warning to him. But even the man-at-arms who loved him did not recognize Robin Hood today.

The ten made wonderful shots. Not one arrow failed to come within the circles that surrounded the center. But when the three shot, it was more wonderful still. Gill o' the Red Cap's first arrow struck only a finger's breadth from the center, and his second was nearer still. But the beggar's arrow struck in the very center. Adam o' the Dell, who had one more shot, unstrung his bow when he saw it.

"Fourscore years and more have I shot shaft, and beaten many competitors, but I can never better that," he said.

The prize of the golden arrow belonged to the tattered beggar, but the sheriff's face was very sour as he gave it to him. He tried to induce him to enter his service, promising great wages.

"You are the best archer I have ever seen," he said. "I trow you shoot even better than that rascal and coward of a Robin Hood who dared not show his face here today. Will you join my service?"

"No, I will not," answered the scarlet-clad stranger, and then the sheriff looked at him so spitefully that he knew it was well to get away. As he walked toward Sherwood Forest, the sheriff's words rankled.

"I cannot bear to have even my enemy think that I am a coward," he said to Little John. "I wish there was a way to tell the sheriff that it was Robin Hood that won his golden arrow."

And they found a way. That evening the sheriff sat at supper, and though the supper was a fine one, his face was gloomy.

"I thought I could catch that rascal Robin Hood by means of this archery contest," he said to his wife, "but he was too much of a coward to show his face here."

Just then something came through the window and fell rattling among the dishes on the table. It was a blunted gray goose quill with a bit of writing tied to it. The sheriff unfolded the writing. It told that it was Robin Hood who had won the golden arrow. When the sheriff read it, even his wife thought best to slip away, for he was the crossest man in Nottingham.

"Little John caught the horse by the bridle." Illustration by Patten Wilson for M. I. Ebbutt M.A., *Hero-Myths & Legends of the British Race* (Kingsway, London: George G. Harrap & Company, 1910).

Week Six:

How Little John
Joined Robin Hood

English Folklore

This is the story of how Robin gained his right hand man and dearest friend, Little John. Little John was one of the tallest and strongest youths that ever walked through a forest. When Robin Hood first saw him, he was walking in the edge of the forest and came to a narrow bridge across a stream. The bridge was so narrow that but one could go across it at once, and it chanced that Robin Hood stepped upon it from one side just as Little John stepped on the other end.

"Go back, and let the better man cross before you," called Robin Hood, not because he cared a bit but rather with a mirthful wish to see what the tall youth would do.

"Stand back yourself. I am the better man," cried the stranger.

"Let us fight for it," said Robin Hood, who loved a good bout more than his dinner.

"With all my heart," answered the stranger.

Then Robin cut him a stick of oak to serve as a quarter-staff, for he would have held it a shame to use his bow and arrows when the other had no such weapon, and they met as joyously as two boys wrestling for sport.

"The one who can knock the other into the water is the better man," said Robin. Then the fight with the staves began. What a fight it was! They struck again and again, but so skilful was each one in warding off blows that neither could knock the other down. Many hard blows each one took, until there were sore bones and bumps, and black and blue spots in plenty, but neither thought of stopping for that. A whole hour they fought there on the bridge, and neither could get the better of the other, then another hour. At last Robin gave the stranger a terrible whack that made him stagger, but the stranger returned with a crack on the crown that made the blood flow. Robin whacked back at him savagely, but the stranger avoided the blow and gave one to Robin that tumbled him fairly into the water.

He lay there looking up and laughing, for Robin Hood never bore any malice.

"You have a right sturdy hand with the cudgel. Never have I been beaten before," he laughed. He splashed ashore and seized the stranger's hand.

"I like you well," he said. "Now watch, and I will show you something."

He put his horn to his lips and blew, and up came two score of Robin Hood's followers, all clothed in Lincoln green, and bearing bows and arrows and swords.

"How is this, master?" said the foremost. "You are all bruised and wet to the skin."

"Yon sturdy fellow has given me a drubbing and tumbled me into the water," he said.

"Then he shall get a ducking and a drubbing himself," said Will Stutely, starting forth angrily, followed by half a dozen, all eager to carry out his threat. But Robin Hood ordered him back.

"No," he said, "it was a fair fight, and he won. I would not have you hurt him for anything. But he is a right brave and lusty youth and I would fain have him in our band. Will you join yourself to my men?" he asked of the wondering stranger. "I am Robin Hood, and my band is the finest in all England."

Hardly a man in the country but would have trembled at the name. But John Little, the strange youth, was afraid of no man.

"If there is any man among you who can shoot a better shaft than I, I will," he said.

"Well, I will try," said Robin. He sent Will Stutely to set up a piece of white bark four fingers in breadth on an oak eighty yards away.

"Now choose any of our bows and arrows to shoot with," he said.

The stranger chose the very stoutest bow. Then he aimed his arrow carefully and sent it down the path and it struck the very center of the mark. All Robin Hood's followers caught their breaths in amaze.

"That is a fine shot indeed," said Robin Hood heartily. "No one could better it; but perhaps I may mar it."

Then he shot an arrow; and so true and swift it sped that it struck the stranger's arrow and splintered it into pieces. And all who saw it cried out that there never was such shooting before.

"Now, will you not come into my band?" said Robin Hood with a smile.

"With all my heart," answered the stranger; and from that minute he loved Robin as his dearest friend.

"What is your name?" said Will Stutely, taking out a tablet as though he would enroll it.

"John Little," answered the stranger youth.

"I like not the name," said merry Will. "This fellow is too small to be called John Little. Let us christen him over, Little John."

And so they had a christening and great sport; and from that day Little John was Robin's right hand man and second in command over the band. True and faithfully did he serve Robin for many years and loved him better with every year.

Week Six:
"The Months"

January brings the snow,
Makes our feet and fingers glow.

February brings the rain,
Thaws the frozen lake again.

March brings breezes loud and
shrill,
Stirs the dancing daffodil.

April brings the primrose sweet,
Scatters daisies at our feet.

May brings flocks of pretty
lambs,
Skipping by their fleecy dams.

June brings tulips, lilies, roses,
Fills the children's hands with
posies.

Hot July brings cooling showers,
Apricots and gilliflowers.

August brings the sheaves of
corn,
Then the harvest home is borne.

Warm September brings the
fruit,
Sportsmen the begin to shoot.

Fresh October brings the
pheasant,
Then to gather nuts is pleasant.

Dull November brings the blast,
Then the leaves are whirling fast.

Chill December brings the sleet,
Blazing fire, and Christmas
treat.

SARA COLERIDGE
(1802–1852)

"Welcome be thou to Greenwood,
Gentle Knight, and free;
My master hath abiden you fasting,
Sir, all these hours three."

"Welcome be thou to Greenwood." Illustration by A. G. Walker, A.R.A. for Mary MacLeod, *A Book of Ballad Stories* (London: Wells Gardner, Darton & Co. Ltd., c. 1880).

Week Seven:

Robin Hood and the Sorrowful Knight

English Folklore

e have had no guests for a long time," said Robin Hood one day. "Let us go out and look for some. Little John, you go to the east and I will go to the west, and we will see if we do not find passing a greedy noble, or fat churchman who carries too much of this world's goods with him, and needs to be relieved for the good of the poor."

Now when Robin Hood and his men robbed a man—and they never molested any but the rich who had made their wealth by grinding down the poor—they brought him into the forest and made a feast for him. Then, after he had feasted, they told him he must pay his reckoning, and they took his goods or gold that he carried and divided these into three piles. One-third they gave back to him; one-third they kept for themselves; and the other third they distributed to the poor. The rich and grasping shuddered at the very mention of Robin Hood's feasts, but the poor breathed blessings on his name whenever they thought of them.

So Little John and his part of the band went to the east; and they were lucky, for they brought in the rich bishop of Hereford with five sumpter mules loaded with goods. But Robin Hood and his half found only a sorrowful knight who sighed as he rode along and seemed too sad to notice anything. Robin Hood laid his hand on his bridle, stopping his horse.

"Hold," he said. "I would speak with you."

"Now who are you who would stop a peaceful traveler on the king's highway?" asked the knight.

"Some call me an honest man and some call me a robber," answered Robin Hood. "At any rate, I and my men have an inn in the forest where we want you to stop and feast. But we let you know that we count upon our guests paying their reckoning."

"I take your meaning," answered the knight, "but I am no guest for you, for I have no money. Indeed, I am in great sorrow by reason of this very thing. Having great need of money to save the life of my son, I mortgaged my estate to the prior of Emmet and, though I could raise the money if he would give me more time, he will not give me a day, but means to seize the estate and turn me out a beggar."

"How much money did you borrow of him?" asked Robin Hood.

"Only four hundred pounds. The estate is worth many times that but he will show no mercy."

"Have you no friends who could lend you the money?" asked Robin Hood.

"Alas, no," answered the knight. "When I was fortunate I had many friends who crowded around me, but now that I have come to trouble they have all deserted me."

"Well, the men who are in trouble always have friends in Sherwood Forest," answered Robin Hood. "Come with me as a free guest and we will find a way to help you."

So they went on until they came to the great tree where Friar Tuck and half a dozen others were preparing the feast around a huge fire. And there in the light of the flames sat the bishop of Hereford under guard, with his sumpter mules with their loaded packs tied to the trees around.

"Have mercy," he whined. But Robin Hood answered sternly.

"What mercy have you ever shown to the poor? Men, open his packs!"

So they opened the packs, which were full of rich goods and divided them into three parts. Beside the packs of goods there was a box that held fifteen hundred pounds in gold. Robin Hood took up the portion divided out for the poor and gave it to the sorrowful knight.

"Since the churchmen have despoiled you, the churchmen shall help you," he said.

"Oh, I thank you," cried the knight, his sorrowful face lighting up for the first time that day. "But I will not take it as a gift but as a loan. I will pay it back to the bishop or to you."

The bishop nodded and opened his mouth to say "That is well," but Robin Hood interrupted him shortly.

"Pay it to me," he said. "I will help the poor with it. The bishop would but crowd it into his own coffers, and use it to gain more money."

So the knight who had been so sorrowful departed with all his troubles cleared away. Sorely disappointed was the prior of Emmet for he had made sure by cheating and craft that the poor knight who had fallen into his clutches could not get the money to redeem his lands anywhere, and he counted them already in his grasp. But he had to give them up; and that is a story too, but we have not room to tell it here.

"'Smite on boldly,' said Robin,
'J give thee large leave ;'
Anon our King, with that word,
He folds up his sleeve.

"'Smite on boldly,' said Robin." Illustration by A. G. Walker, A.R.A. for Mary MacLeod, *A Book of Ballad Stories* (London: Wells Gardner, Darton & Co. Ltd., c. 1880).

Week Seven:
ROBIN HOOD AND THE KING
English Folklore

J wish I could see Robin Hood," said King Richard. "I wish I could see him and his men shoot and wrestle and go through all the feats in which they have such wondrous skill. But if they heard that the king was coming, they would think it was only to arrest them, and they would flee deep into the forest and I should never get a glimpse of them."

King Richard spoke kindly, for he was a king who loved all manly sports and those who excelled in them.

"I would give a hundred pounds to see Robin Hood and his men in the greenwood," he said.

"I'll tell you how you can see him without a doubt," spoke up one of the king's trusty companions with a laugh. "Put on the robes of a fat abbot and ride through Sherwood Forest with the hundred pounds in your pouch, and you will be sure to see him and be feasted by him."

"I'll do it," cried bluff King Richard, slapping his knee. "It will be a huge joke."

So he and seven of his followers dressed themselves as an abbot and seven black friars and rode out along the highway toward Sherwood Forest. And Robin Hood and his men took them and brought them to the Trystal Tree, and there they searched them and took the pouch of gold. But they gave half the gold back to the king, for it was not their custom to leave any man in need. They were pleased with these travelers because they did not resist nor rail at them.

"Now we shall give you a feast that will be worth fifty pounds," said Robin Hood.

"I have a good appetite for a feast," said the pretended abbot, "but even more do I desire to see the archery and wrestling and play with the quarter-staff and all those things in which I am told you excel."

"You shall see the very best we can do," answered Robin Hood. "But, I pray you, holy father, lay aside your cowl that you may enjoy this sweet evening air."

"No," answered the mock abbot. "It may not be, for I and my brothers have vowed not to let our faces be seen during this journey."

"Very well, then," said Robin Hood. "I interfere with no man's vows." And he never dreamed that it was the king.

They gave them a splendid feast of roasted venison and pheasant and fish and wild fowls, all done to a turn over the roaring fire, and the best of drink. Then they arranged the sports.

The target was a garland of leaves and flowers that was hung six score paces distant upon a stake. It was a mark that only the best of archers could hit at all.

"Now shoot!" said Robin Hood. "You shall each of you have three shots, and every one who fails to place his arrows within the garland shall forfeit the arrow and receive beside a box on the side of the head as stout as can be given."

"Can any one hit inside that little garland at such a distance?" asked the king in amaze.

"Look and see," answered Robin Hood proudly.

First, David of Doncaster shot, and lodged all three arrows within the garland, while the king looked on, astonished. Then Midge, the miller's son, and he also placed all his arrows inside of the garland. Then Wat the Tinker drew his bow; but he was unlucky, for one of his arrows missed the mark by the breadth of two fingers.

"Come here and take your punishment," called Robin Hood. The king supposed that, since he had missed by so little, he would receive but a light tap, but he got a blow that knocked him spinning across the grass, heels over head.

"Ha, ha, ha!" laughed his comrades, and "O ho!" thought King Richard, "I am glad I am not in this." But he was much impressed with the way Robin Hood's men obeyed him.

"They are better to follow his commands than my servants are to follow mine," he thought.

The shooting went on, and most of the men shot their arrows within the garland, but a few missed and received tremendous buffets.

Last Robin Hood shot. His first shaft split off a piece of the stake on which the garland was hung. His second lodged a scant inch from the first. But the last arrow he shot was feathered faultily, and it swerved to one side, and smote an inch outside of the garland.

Then all the company roared with good-natured laughter, for it was seldom indeed that they saw their master miss.

"Go and take your punishment, master," said Midge, the miller's son. "I hope it will be as heavy as Wat's."

"Well," said Robin Hood, "I will forfeit my arrow to our guest and take my buffet from him."

Now the merry Robin was somewhat crafty in this, for, though he did not mind hard knocks at all, he did not like the thought of being sent sprawling before his band. The hands of churchmen were soft, and their strongest blows but feeble, for they did not work nor use their muscles much. But the pretended abbot bared an arm so stout and muscular that it made the yeomen stare. Robin Hood placed himself fairly in front of him and he struck a blow that would have felled an ox. Down went Robin Hood on the ground rolling over and over, and his men fairly shouted with laughter.

"Well," said Robin Hood, sitting up, half dazed, "I did not think that there was an arm in England that could strike such a blow. Who are you, man? I'll warrant you are no churchman as you seem."

Then Richard threw his cowl, and Robin knew his king. If he had been a disloyal man as well as an outlaw, he would have trembled then.

But, though he knelt at the king's feet and signalled all his men to kneel, his voice was not ashamed.

"Your majesty," he said, "you have no subjects in all England more loyal to you than I and my merry men. We have done no evil except to certain of the greedy and rich who oppressed your subjects. We crave your pardon if we have done wrong, and we beg for your protection, and swear that we will ever serve you faithfully."

Then the king looked down in amazement that an outlaw should speak so. But he knew men, and he knew what people said of Robin Hood. And he knew, too, that he was the best archer in all England and he wanted him in his own train.

"I will forgive all your law-breaking," he said, "if you will come with me to my court and serve me there. You shall take Little John and Will Scarlet and Allen-a-Dale, who is the sweetest singer I ever heard; and the rest of your men I will make into royal rangers, since I judge that they can protect Sherwood Forest better than any others."

So Robin Hood left the greenwood and went to the king's court and he served King Richard well. But he did not like the confinement of the court and could not abide the gaieties and jealousies of the courtiers. After King Richard died, his brother John took the throne, and he was one of the worst kings that ever ruled England. Then Robin Hood went back to the forest and his merry men gathered around him once more, and again they became outlaws. And there in the forest he lived till he died.

Week Seven:

"WHO HAS SEEN THE WIND?"

Who has seen the wind?
Neither I nor you.
But when the leaves hang trembling,
The wind is passing through.
Who has seen the wind?
Neither you nor I.
But when the trees bow down their heads,
The wind is passing by.

CHRISTINA ROSSETTI
(1830–1894)

"The Wind." Illustration by Jessie Willcox Smith for Robert Louis Stevenson,
A Child's Garden of Verses (New York: Charles Scribner's Sons, 1905).

"Ferdinand and Miranda." Illustration by Max Bihn for E. Nesbit, *Beautiful Stories from Shakespeare* (Chicago: D. E. Cunningham, 1907).

Week Eight:
THE TEMPEST
William Shakespeare, English

Prospero, the Duke of Milan, was a learned and studious man, who lived among his books, leaving the management of his dukedom to his brother Antonio, in whom indeed he had complete trust. But that trust was ill-rewarded, for Antonio wanted to wear the duke's crown himself, and, to gain his ends, would have killed his brother but for the love the people bore him. However, with the help of Prospero's great enemy, Alonso, King of Naples, he managed to get into his hands the dukedom with all its honor, power, and riches. For they took Prospero to sea, and when they were far away from land, forced him into a little boat with no tackle, mast, or sail. In their cruelty and hatred they put his little daughter, Miranda (not yet three years old), into the boat with him, and sailed away, leaving them to their fate.

But one among the courtiers with Antonio was true to his rightful master, Prospero. To save the duke from his enemies was impossible, but much could be done to remind him of a subject's love. So this worthy lord, whose name was Gonzalo, secretly placed in the boat some fresh water, provisions, and clothes, and what Prospero valued most of all, some of his precious books.

The boat was cast on an island, and Prospero and his little one landed in safety. Now this island was enchanted, and for years had lain under the spell of a fell witch, Sycorax, who had imprisoned in the trunks of trees all the good spirits she found there. She died shortly before Prospero was cast on those shores, but the spirits, of whom Ariel was the chief, still remained in their prisons.

Prospero was a great magician, for he had devoted himself almost entirely to the study of magic during the years in which he allowed his brother to manage the affairs of Milan. By his art he set free the imprisoned spirits, yet kept them obedient to his will, and they were more truly his subjects than his people in Milan had been. For he treated them kindly as long as they did his bidding, and he exercised his power over them wisely and well. One creature alone he found it necessary to treat with harshness: this was Caliban, the son of the wicked old witch, a hideous, deformed monster, horrible to look on, and vicious and brutal in all his habits.

When Miranda was grown up into a maiden, sweet and fair to see, it chanced that Antonio and Alonso, with Sebastian, his brother, and Ferdinand, his son, were at sea together with old Gonzalo, and their ship came near Prospero's island. Prospero, knowing they were there, raised by his art a great storm, so that even the sailors on board gave themselves up for lost; and first among them all Prince Ferdinand leaped into the sea, and, as his father thought in his grief, was drowned. But Ariel brought him safe ashore; and all the rest of the crew, although they were washed overboard, were landed unhurt in different parts of the island, and the good ship herself, which they all thought had been wrecked, lay at anchor in the harbor whither Ariel had brought her. Such wonders could Prospero and his spirits perform.

While yet the tempest was raging, Prospero showed his daughter the brave ship laboring in the trough of the sea, and told her that it was filled with living human beings like themselves. She, in pity of their lives, prayed him who had raised this storm to quell it. Then her father bade her to have no fear, for he intended to save every one of them. Then, for the first time, he told her the story of his life and hers, and that he had caused this storm to rise in order that his enemies, Antonio and Alonso, who were on board, might be delivered into his hands.

When he had made an end of his story he charmed her into sleep, for Ariel was at hand, and he had work for him to do. Ariel, who longed for his complete freedom, grumbled to be kept in drudgery, but on being threateningly reminded of all the sufferings he had undergone when Sycorax ruled in the land, and of the debt of gratitude he owed to the master who had made those sufferings to end, he ceased to complain, and promised faithfully to do whatever Prospero might command.

"Do so," said Prospero, "and in two days I will discharge thee."

Then he bade Ariel take the form of a water nymph and sent him in search of the young prince. And Ariel, invisible to Ferdinand, hovered near him, singing the while—

> *"Come unto these yellow sands*
> *And then take hands:*
> *Court'sied when you have, and kiss'd*
> *(The wild waves whist),*
> *Foot it featly here and there;*
> *And, sweet sprites, the burden bear!"*

And Ferdinand followed the magic singing, as the song changed to a solemn air, and the words brought grief to his heart, and tears to his eyes, for thus they ran—

> *"Full fathom five thy father lies;*
> *Of his bones are coral made.*
> *Those are pearls that were his eyes,*
> *Nothing of him that doth fade,*
> *But doth suffer a sea-change*
> *Into something rich and strange.*
> *Sea-nymphs hourly ring his knell.*
> *Hark! now I hear them,— ding dong bell!"*

And so singing, Ariel led the spell-bound prince into the presence of Prospero and Miranda. Then, behold! all happened as Prospero desired. For Miranda, who had never, since she could first remember, seen any human being save her father, looked on the youthful prince with reverence in her eyes, and love in her secret heart.

"I might call him," she said, "a thing divine, for nothing natural I ever saw so noble!"

And Ferdinand, beholding her beauty with wonder and delight, exclaimed—

"Most sure the goddess on whom these airs attend!"

Nor did he attempt to hide the passion which she inspired in him, for scarcely had they exchanged half a dozen sentences, before he vowed to make her his queen if she were willing. But Prospero, though secretly delighted, pretended wrath.

"You come here as a spy," he said to Ferdinand. "I will manacle your neck and feet together, and you shall feed on fresh water mussels, withered roots and husk, and have sea-water to drink. Follow."

"No," said Ferdinand, and drew his sword. But on the instant Prospero charmed him so that he stood there like a statue, still as stone; and Miranda in terror prayed her father to have mercy on her lover. But he harshly refused her, and made Ferdinand follow him to his cell. There he set the Prince to work, making him remove thousands of heavy logs of timber and pile them up; and Ferdinand patiently obeyed, and thought his toil all too well repaid by the sympathy of the sweet Miranda.

She in very pity would have helped him in his hard work, but he would not let her, yet he could not keep from her the secret of his love, and she, hearing it, rejoiced and promised to be his wife.

Then Prospero released him from his servitude, and glad at heart, he gave his consent to their marriage.

"Take her," he said, "she is thine own."

In the meantime, Antonio and Sebastian in another part of the island were plotting the murder of Alonso, the King of Naples, for Ferdinand being dead, as they thought, Sebastian would succeed to the throne on Alonso's death. And they would have carried out their wicked purpose while their victim was asleep, but that Ariel woke him in good time.

Many tricks did Ariel play them. Once he set a banquet before them, and just as they were going to fall to, he appeared to them amid thunder and lightning in the form of a harpy, and immediately the banquet disappeared. Then Ariel upbraided them with their sins and vanished too.

Prospero by his enchantments drew them all to the grove without his cell, where they waited, trembling and afraid, and now at last bitterly repenting them of their sins.

Prospero determined to make one last use of his magic power, "And then," said he, "I'll break my staff and deeper than did ever plummet sound I'll drown my book."

So he made heavenly music to sound in the air, and appeared to them in his proper shape as the Duke of Milan. Because they repented, he forgave them and told them the story of his life since they had cruelly committed him and his baby daughter to the mercy of wind and waves. Alonso, who seemed sorriest of them all for his past crimes, lamented the loss of his heir. But Prospero drew back a curtain and showed them Ferdinand and Miranda playing at chess. Great was Alonso's joy to greet his loved son again, and when he heard that the fair maid with whom Ferdinand was playing was Prospero's daughter, and that the young folks had plighted their troth, he said—

"Give me your hands, let grief and sorrow still embrace his heart that doth not wish you joy."

So all ended happily. The ship was safe in the harbor, and next day they all set sail for Naples, where Ferdinand and Miranda were to be married. Ariel gave them calm seas and auspicious gales; and many were the rejoicings at the wedding.

Then Prospero, after many years of absence, went back to his own dukedom, where he was welcomed with great joy by his faithful subjects. He practiced the arts of magic no more, but his life was happy, and not only because he had found his own again, but chiefly because, when his bitterest foes who had done him deadly wrong lay at his mercy, he took no vengeance on them, but nobly forgave them.

As for Ariel, Prospero made him free as air, so that he could wander where he would, and sing with a light heart his sweet song—

> *"Where the bee sucks, there suck I:*
> *In a cowslip's bell I lie;*
> *There I couch when owls do cry.*
> *On the bat's back I do fly*
> *After summer, merrily:*
> *Merrily, merrily, shall I live now,*
> *Under the blossom that hangs on the bough."*

Week Eight:

A MIDSUMMER NIGHT'S DREAM

William Shakespeare, English

Hermia and Lysander were lovers; but Hermia's father wished her to marry another man, named Demetrius.

Now, in Athens, where they lived, there was a wicked law, by which any girl who refused to marry according to her father's wishes, might be put to death. Hermia's father was so angry with her for refusing to do as he wished, that he actually brought her before the Duke of Athens to ask that she might be killed, if she still refused to obey him. The Duke gave her four days to think about it, and, at the end of that time, if she still refused to marry Demetrius, she would have to die.

Lysander of course was nearly mad with grief, and the best thing to do seemed to him for Hermia to run away to his aunt's house at a place beyond the reach of that cruel law; and there he would come to her and marry her. But before she started, she told her friend, Helena, what she was going to do.

Helena had been Demetrius' sweetheart long before his marriage with Hermia had been thought of, and being very silly, like all jealous people, she could not see that it was not poor Hermia's fault that Demetrius wished to marry her instead of his own lady, Helena. She knew that if she told Demetrius that Hermia was going, as she was, to the wood outside Athens, he would follow her, "and I can follow him, and at least I shall see him," she said to herself. So she went to him, and betrayed her friend's secret.

Now this wood where Lysander was to meet Hermia, and where the other two had decided to follow them, was full of fairies, as most woods are, if one only had the eyes to see them, and in this wood on this night were the King and Queen of the fairies, Oberon and Titania. Now fairies are very wise people, but now and then they can be quite as foolish as mortal folk. Oberon and Titania, who might have been as happy as the days were long, had thrown away all their joy in a foolish quarrel. They never met without saying disagreeable things to each other, and scolded each other so dreadfully that all their little fairy followers, for fear, would creep into acorn cups and hide them there.

So, instead of keeping one happy Court and dancing all night through in the moonlight as is fairies' use, the King with his attendants wandered through one part of the wood, while the Queen with hers kept state in another. And the cause of all this trouble was a little Indian boy whom Titania had taken to be one of her followers. Oberon wanted the child to follow him and be one of his fairy knights; but the Queen would not give him up.

On this night, in a mossy moonlit glade, the King and Queen of the fairies met.

"Ill met by moonlight, proud Titania," said the King.

"What! jealous, Oberon?" answered the Queen. "You spoil everything with your quarreling. Come, fairies, let us leave him. I am not friends with him now."

"It rests with you to make up the quarrel," said the King.

"Give me that little Indian boy, and I will again be your humble servant and suitor."

"Set your mind at rest," said the Queen. "Your whole fairy kingdom buys not that boy from me. Come, fairies."

And she and her train rode off down the moonbeams.

"Well, go your ways," said Oberon. "But I'll be even with you before you leave this wood."

Then Oberon called his favorite fairy, Puck. Puck was the spirit of mischief. He used to slip into the dairies and take the cream away, and get into the churn so that the butter would not come, and turn the beer sour, and lead people out of their way on dark nights and then laugh at them, and tumble people's stools from under them when they were going to sit down, and upset their hot ale over their chins when they were going to drink. "Now," said Oberon to this little sprite, "fetch me the flower called Love-in-idleness. The juice of that little purple flower laid on the eyes of those who sleep will make them, when they wake, to love the first thing they see. I will put some of the juice of that flower on my Titania's eyes, and when she wakes she will love the first thing she sees, were it lion, bear, or wolf, or bull, or meddling monkey, or a busy ape."

While Puck was gone, Demetrius passed through the glade followed by poor Helena, and still she told him how she loved him and reminded him of all his promises, and still he told her that he did not and could not love her, and that his promises were nothing. Oberon was sorry for poor Helena, and when Puck returned with the flower, he bade him follow Demetrius and put some of the juice on his eyes, so that he might love Helena when he woke and looked on her, as much as she loved him. So Puck set off, and wandering through the wood found, not Demetrius, but Lysander, on whose eyes he put the juice; but when Lysander woke, he saw not his own Hermia, but Helena, who was walking through the wood looking for the cruel Demetrius; and directly he saw her he loved her and left his own lady, under the spell of the purple flower.

"Puck." Illustrator unknown for Robert R. Raymond, A.M. (editor) *Shakespeare for the Young Folk* (New York: Fords, Howard, & Hulbert, 1881.)

When Hermia woke she found Lysander gone, and wandered about the wood trying to find him. Puck went back and told Oberon what he had done, and Oberon soon found that he had made a mistake, and set about looking for Demetrius, and having found him, put some of the juice on his eyes. And the first thing Demetrius saw when he woke was also Helena. So now Demetrius and Lysander were both following her through the wood, and it was Hermia's turn to follow her lover as Helena had done before. The end of it was that Helena and Hermia began to quarrel, and Demetrius and Lysander went off to fight. Oberon was very sorry to see his kind scheme to help these lovers turn out so badly. So he said to Puck—

"These two young men are going to fight. You must overhang the night with drooping fog, and lead them so astray, that one will never find the other. When they are tired out, they will fall asleep. Then drop this other herb on Lysander's eyes. That will give him his old sight and his old love. Then each man will have the lady who loves him, and they will all think that this has been only a Midsummer Night's Dream. Then when this is done, all will be well with them."

So Puck went and did as he was told, and when the two had fallen asleep without meeting each other, Puck poured the juice on Lysander's eyes, and said:—

> "*When thou wakest,*
> *Thou takest*
> *True delight*
> *In the sight*
> *Of thy former lady's eye:*
> *Jack shall have Jill;*
> *Nought shall go ill.*"

Meanwhile Oberon found Titania asleep on a bank where grew wild thyme, oxlips, and violets, and woodbine, musk-roses and eglantine. There Titania always slept a part of the night, wrapped in the enameled skin of a snake. Oberon stooped over her and laid the juice on her eyes, saying:—

> "*What thou seest when thou wake,*
> *Do it for thy true love take.*"

Now, it happened that when Titania woke the first thing she saw was a stupid clown, one of a party of players who had come out into the wood to rehearse their play. This clown had met with Puck, who had clapped an ass's head on his shoulders so that it looked as if it grew there. Directly Titania woke and saw this dreadful monster, she said, "What angel is this? Are you as wise as you are beautiful?"

"If I am wise enough to find my way out of this wood, that's enough for me," said the foolish clown.

"Do not desire to go out of the wood," said Titania. The spell of the love-juice was on her, and to her the clown seemed the most beautiful and delightful creature on all the earth. "I love you," she went on. "Come with me, and I will give you fairies to attend on you."

So she called four fairies, whose names were Peaseblossom, Cobweb, Moth, and Mustardseed.

"You must attend this gentleman," said the Queen. "Feed him with apricots and dewberries, purple grapes, green figs, and mulberries. Steal honey-bags for him from the bumble-bees, and with the wings of painted butterflies fan the moonbeams from his sleeping eyes."

"I will," said one of the fairies, and all the others said, "I will."

"Now, sit down with me," said the Queen to the clown, "and let me stroke your dear cheeks, and stick musk-roses in your smooth, sleek head, and kiss your fair large ears, my gentle joy."

"Where's Peaseblossom?" asked the clown with the ass's head. He did not care much about the Queen's affection, but he was very proud of having fairies to wait on him. "Ready," said Peaseblossom.

"Scratch my head, Peaseblossom," said the clown. "Where's Cobweb?" "Ready," said Cobweb.

"*Titania*. 'O, how I love thee! how I dote on thee!'" Illustrator unknown for Robert R. Raymond, A.M. (editor) *Shakespeare for the Young Folk* (New York: Fords, Howard, & Hulbert, 1881.)

"Kill me," said the clown, "the red bumble-bee on the top of the thistle yonder, and bring me the honey-bag. Where's Mustardseed?"

"Ready," said Mustardseed.

"Oh, I want nothing," said the clown. "Only just help Cobweb to scratch. I must go to the barber's, for methinks I am marvelous hairy about the face."

"Would you like anything to eat?" said the fairy Queen.

"I should like some good dry oats," said the clown—for his donkey's head made him desire donkey's food—"and some hay to follow."

"Shall some of my fairies fetch you new nuts from the squirrel's house?" asked the Queen.

"I'd rather have a handful or two of good dried peas," said the clown. "But please don't let any of your people disturb me; I am going to sleep."

Then said the Queen, "And I will wind thee in my arms."

And so when Oberon came along he found his beautiful Queen lavishing kisses and endearments on a clown with a donkey's head.

And before he released her from the enchantment, he persuaded her to give him the little Indian boy he so much desired to have. Then he took pity on her, and threw some juice of the disenchanting flower on her pretty eyes; and then in a moment she saw plainly the donkey-headed clown she had been loving, and knew how foolish she had been.

Oberon took off the ass's head from the clown, and left him to finish his sleep with his own silly head lying on the thyme and violets.

Thus all was made plain and straight again. Oberon and Titania loved each other more than ever. Demetrius thought of no one but Helena, and Helena had never had any thought of anyone but Demetrius.

As for Hermia and Lysander, they were as loving a couple as you could meet in a day's march, even through a fairy wood.

So the four mortal lovers went back to Athens and were married; and the fairy King and Queen live happily together in that very wood at this very day.

"The Merchant of Venice." Illustration by Mrs. Laura Valentine for William Shakespeare, *The Merchant of Venice* (New York: McLaughlin Brothers, 1882).

Week Eight:

"The Quality of Mercy" (Selections from Shakespeare)

MERCHANT OF VENICE, ACT IV., SCENE I.

The quality of mercy is not strained;
It droppeth as the gentle rain from heaven
Upon the place beneath; it is twice blessed;
It blesseth him that gives, and him that takes.
'Tis mightiest in the mightiest; it becomes
The thronèd monarch better than his crown;
His sceptre shows the force of temporal power,
The attribute to awe and majesty,
Wherein doth sit the dread and fear of kings:
But mercy is above the sceptred sway:
It is enthroned in the hearts of kings,
It is an attribute of God himself:
And earthly power doth then show likest God's,
When mercy seasons justice. Therefore,
Jew, though justice be thy plea, consider this,—
That, in the course of justice, none of us
Should see salvation; we do pray for mercy;
And that same prayer doth teach us all to render
The deeds of mercy.

WILLIAM SHAKESPEARE
(1564–1616)

"*Friar Laurence*. 'Here comes the lady.'" Illustration by Maude Adams for William
Shakespeare, *Shakespeare's Tragedy of Romeo and Juliet* (New York: H. M. Caldwell
Company, 1900).

Week Nine:

ROMEO AND JULIET

William Shakespeare, English

Once upon a time there lived in Verona two great families named Montagu and Capulet. They were both rich, and I suppose they were as sensible, in most things, as other rich people. But in one thing they were extremely silly. There was an old, old quarrel between the two families, and instead of making it up like reasonable folks, they made a sort of pet of their quarrel, and would not let it die out. So that a Montagu wouldn't speak to a Capulet if he met one in the street—nor a Capulet to a Montagu—or if they did speak, it was to say rude and unpleasant things, which often ended in a fight. And their relations and servants were just as foolish, so that street fights and duels and uncomfortablenesses of that kind were always growing out of the Montagu-and-Capulet quarrel.

Now Lord Capulet, the head of that family, gave a party—a grand supper and a dance—and he was so hospitable that he said anyone

"Verona." Illustrator unknown for William J. Rolfe and William Shakespeare, *Shakespeare's Tragedy of Romeo and Juliet* (New York, Cincinnati, Chicago: American Book Company, 1904 and 1907).

might come to it except (of course) the Montagues. But there was a young Montagu named Romeo, who very much wanted to be there, because Rosaline, the lady he loved, had been asked. This lady had never been at all kind to him, and he had no reason to love her; but the fact was that he wanted to love somebody, and as he hadn't seen the right lady, he was obliged to love the wrong one. So to the Capulet's grand party he came, with his friends Mercutio and Benvolio.

Old Capulet welcomed him and his two friends very kindly—and young Romeo moved about among the crowd of courtly folk dressed in their velvets and satins, the men with jeweled sword hilts and collars, and the ladies with brilliant gems on breast and arms, and stones of price set in their bright girdles. Romeo was in his best too, and though he wore a black mask over his eyes and nose, everyone could see by his mouth and his hair, and the way he held his head, that he was twelve times handsomer than anyone else in the room.

Presently amid the dancers he saw a lady so beautiful and so lovable that from that moment he never again gave one thought to that Rosaline whom he had thought he loved. And he looked at this other fair lady, as she moved in the dance in her white satin and pearls, and all the world seemed vain and worthless to him compared with her. And he was saying this, or something like it, when Tybalt, Lady Capulet's nephew, hearing his voice, knew him to be Romeo. Tybalt, being very angry, went at once to his uncle, and told him how a Montagu had come uninvited to the feast; but old Capulet was too fine a gentleman to be discourteous to any man under his own roof, and he bade Tybalt be quiet. But this young man only waited for a chance to quarrel with Romeo.

In the meantime Romeo made his way to the fair lady, and told her in sweet words that he loved her, and kissed her. Just then her mother sent for her, and then Romeo found out that the lady on whom he had set his heart's hopes was Juliet, the daughter of Lord Capulet, his sworn foe. So he went away, sorrowing indeed, but loving her none the less.

Then Juliet said to her nurse:

"Who is that gentleman that would not dance?"

"His name is Romeo, and a Montagu, the only son of your great enemy," answered the nurse.

Then Juliet went to her room, and looked out of her window, over the beautiful green-grey garden, where the moon was shining. And Romeo was hidden in that garden among the trees—because he could not bear to go right away without trying to see her again. So she—not knowing him to be there—spoke her secret thought aloud, and told the quiet garden how she loved Romeo.

And Romeo heard and was glad beyond measure. Hidden below, he looked up and saw her fair face in the moonlight, framed in the blossoming creepers that grew round her window, and as he looked and listened, he felt as though he had been carried away in a dream, and set down by some magician in that beautiful and enchanted garden.

"Ah—why are you called Romeo?" said Juliet. "Since I love you, what does it matter what you are called?"

"Call me but love, and I'll be new baptized—henceforth I never will be Romeo," he cried, stepping into the full white moonlight from the shade of the cypresses and oleanders that had hidden him.

"The 'Measure.'" Illustrator unknown for William J. Rolfe and William Shakespeare, *Shakespeare's Tragedy of Romeo and Juliet* (New York, Cincinnati, Chicago: American Book Company, 1904 and 1907). Project Gutenberg EBook.

She was frightened at first, but when she saw that it was Romeo himself, and no stranger, she too was glad, and, he standing in the garden below and she leaning from the window, they spoke long together, each one trying to find the sweetest words in the world, to make that pleasant talk that lovers use. And the tale of all they said, and the sweet music their voices made together, is all set down in a golden book, where you children may read it for yourselves some day.

And the time passed so quickly, as it does for folk who love each other and are together, that when the time came to part, it seemed as though they had met but that moment—and indeed they hardly knew how to part.

"I will send to you to-morrow," said Juliet.

And so at last, with lingering and longing, they said good-bye.

Juliet went into her room, and a dark curtain bid her bright window. Romeo went away through the still and dewy garden like a man in a dream.

The next morning, very early, Romeo went to Friar Laurence, a priest, and, telling him all the story, begged him to marry him to Juliet without delay. And this, after some talk, the priest consented to do.

So when Juliet sent her old nurse to Romeo that day to know what he purposed to do, the old woman took back a message that all was well, and all things ready for the marriage of Juliet and Romeo on the next morning.

The young lovers were afraid to ask their parents' consent to their marriage, as young people should do, because of this foolish old quarrel between the Capulets and the Montagues.

And Friar Laurence was willing to help the young lovers secretly, because he thought that when they were once married their parents might soon be told, and that the match might put a happy end to the old quarrel.

So the next morning early, Romeo and Juliet were married at Friar Laurence's cell, and parted with tears and kisses. And Romeo promised to come into the garden that evening, and the nurse got ready a rope-ladder to let down from the window, so that Romeo could climb up and talk to his dear wife quietly and alone.

But that very day a dreadful thing happened.

Tybalt, the young man who had been so vexed at Romeo's going to the Capulet's feast, met him and his two friends, Mercutio and Benvolio, in the street, called Romeo a villain, and asked him to fight. Romeo had no wish to fight with Juliet's cousin, but Mercutio drew his sword, and he and Tybalt fought. And Mercutio was killed. When Romeo saw that this friend was dead, he forgot everything except anger at the man who had killed him, and he and Tybalt fought till Tybalt fell dead.

So, on the very day of his wedding, Romeo killed his dear Juliet's cousin, and was sentenced to be banished. Poor Juliet and her young husband met that night indeed; he climbed the rope-ladder among the flowers, and found her window, but their meeting was a sad one, and they parted with bitter tears and hearts heavy, because they could not know when they should meet again.

Now Juliet's father, who, of course, had no idea that she was married, wished her to wed a gentleman named Paris, and was so angry when she refused, that she hurried away to ask Friar Laurence what she should do. He advised her to pretend to consent, and then he said:

"I will give you a draught that will make you seem to be dead for two days, and then when they take you to church it will be to bury you, and not to marry you. They will put you in the vault thinking you are dead, and before you wake up Romeo and I will be there to take care of you. Will you do this, or are you afraid?"

"I will do it; talk not to me of fear!" said Juliet. And she went home and told her father she would marry Paris. If she had spoken out and told her father the truth . . . well, then this would have been a different story.

Lord Capulet was very much pleased to get his own way, and set about inviting his friends and getting the wedding feast ready. Everyone stayed up all night, for there was a great deal to do, and very little time to do it in. Lord Capulet was anxious to get Juliet married because he saw she was very unhappy. Of course she was really fretting about her husband Romeo, but her father thought she was grieving for the death of her cousin Tybalt, and he thought marriage would give her something else to think about.

Early in the morning the nurse came to call Juliet, and to dress her for her wedding; but she would not wake, and at last the nurse cried out suddenly—

"Alas! alas! help! help! my lady's dead! Oh, well-a-day that ever I was born!"

Lady Capulet came running in, and then Lord Capulet, and Lord Paris, the bridegroom. There lay Juliet cold and white and lifeless, and all their weeping could not wake her. So it was a burying that day instead of a marrying. Meantime Friar Laurence had sent a messenger to Mantua with a letter to Romeo telling him of all these things; and all would have been well, only the messenger was delayed, and could not go.

But ill news travels fast. Romeo's servant who knew the secret of the marriage, but not of Juliet's pretended death, heard of her funeral, and hurried to Mantua to tell Romeo how his young wife was dead and lying in the grave.

"Is it so?" cried Romeo, heart-broken. "Then I will lie by Juliet's side to-night."

And he bought himself a poison, and went straight back to Verona. He hastened to the tomb where Juliet was lying. It was not a grave, but a vault. He broke open the door, and was just going down the stone steps that led to the vault where all the dead Capulets lay, when he heard a voice behind him calling on him to stop.

It was the Count Paris, who was to have married Juliet that very day.

"How dare you come here and disturb the dead bodies of the Capulets, you vile Montagu?" cried Paris.

Poor Romeo, half mad with sorrow, yet tried to answer gently.

"You were told," said Paris, "that if you returned to Verona you must die."

"I must indeed," said Romeo. "I came here for nothing else. Good, gentle youth—leave me! Oh, go—before I do you any harm! I love you better than myself—go—leave me here—"

Then Paris said, "I defy you, and I arrest you as a felon," and Romeo, in his anger and despair, drew his sword. They fought, and Paris was killed.

As Romeo's sword pierced him, Paris cried—

"Oh, I am slain! If thou be merciful, open the tomb, and lay me with Juliet!"

And Romeo said, "In faith I will."

And he carried the dead man into the tomb and laid him by the dear Juliet's side. Then he kneeled by Juliet and spoke to her, and held her in his arms, and kissed her cold lips, believing that she was dead, while all the while she was coming nearer and nearer to the time of her awakening. Then he drank the poison, and died beside his sweetheart and wife.

Now came Friar Laurence when it was too late, and saw all that had happened—and then poor Juliet woke out of her sleep to find her husband and her friend both dead beside her.

The noise of the fight had brought other folks to the place too, and Friar Laurence, hearing them, ran away, and Juliet was left alone. She saw the cup that had held the poison, and knew how all had happened, and since no poison was left for her, she drew her Romeo's dagger and thrust it through her heart—and so, falling with her head on her Romeo's breast, she died. And here ends the story of these faithful and most unhappy lovers.

And when the old folks knew from Friar Laurence of all that had befallen, they sorrowed exceedingly, and now, seeing all the mischief their wicked quarrel had wrought, they repented them of it, and over the bodies of their dead children they clasped hands at last, in friendship and forgiveness.

"Prince Florizel and Perdita." Illustration by Max Bihn for E. Nesbit, *Beautiful Stories from Shakespeare* (Chicago: D. E. Cunningham, 1907).

Week Nine:
THE WINTER'S TALE
William Shakespeare, English

Leontes was the King of Sicily, and his dearest friend was Polixenes, King of Bohemia. They had been brought up together, and only separated when they reached man's estate and each had to go and rule over his kingdom. After many years, when each was married and had a son, Polixenes came to stay with Leontes in Sicily.

Leontes was a violent-tempered man and rather silly, and he took it into his stupid head that his wife, Hermione, liked Polixenes better than she did him, her own husband. When once he had got this into his head, nothing could put it out; and he ordered one of his lords, Camillo, to put a poison in Polixenes' wine. Camillo tried to dissuade him from this wicked action, but finding he was not to be moved, pretended to consent. He then told Polixenes what was proposed against him, and they fled from the Court of Sicily that night, and returned to Bohemia, where Camillo lived on as Polixenes' friend and counselor.

Leontes threw the Queen into prison; and her son, the heir to the throne, died of sorrow to see his mother so unjustly and cruelly treated.

While the Queen was in prison she had a little baby, and a friend of hers, named Paulina, had the baby dressed in its best, and took it to show the King, thinking that the sight of his helpless little daughter would soften his heart towards his dear Queen, who had never done him any wrong, and who loved him a great deal more than he deserved; but the King would not look at the baby, and ordered Paulina's husband to take it away in a ship, and leave it in the most desert and dreadful place he could find, which Paulina's husband, very much against his will, was obliged to do.

Then the poor Queen was brought up to be tried for treason in preferring Polixenes to her King; but really she had never thought of anyone except Leontes, her husband. Leontes had sent some messengers to ask the god, Apollo, whether he was not right in his cruel thoughts of the Queen. But he had not patience to wait till they came back, and so it happened that they arrived in the middle of the trial. The Oracle said—

"Hermione is innocent, Polixenes blameless, Camillo a true subject, Leontes a jealous tyrant, and the King shall live without an heir, if that which is lost be not found."

Then a man came and told them that the little Prince was dead. The poor Queen, hearing this, fell down in a fit; and then the King saw how wicked and wrong he had been. He ordered Paulina and the ladies who were with the Queen to take her away, and try to restore her. But Paulina came back in a few moments, and told the King that Hermione was dead.

Now Leontes' eyes were at last opened to his folly. His Queen was dead, and the little daughter who might have been a comfort to him he had sent away to be the prey of wolves and kites. Life had nothing

left for him now. He gave himself up to his grief, and passed many sad years in prayer and remorse.

The baby Princess was left on the seacoast of Bohemia, the very kingdom where Polixenes reigned. Paulina's husband never went home to tell Leontes where he had left the baby; for

"The King would not look." Illustration by Max Bihn for E. Nesbit, *Beautiful Stories from Shakespeare* (Chicago: D. E. Cunningham, 1907). Project Gutenberg EBook.

as he was going back to the ship, he met a bear and was torn to pieces. So there was an end of him.

But the poor deserted little baby was found by a shepherd. She was richly dressed, and had with her some jewels, and a paper was pinned to her cloak, saying that her name was Perdita, and that she came of noble parents.

The shepherd, being a kind-hearted man, took home the little baby to his wife, and they brought it up as their own child. She had no more teaching than a shepherd's child generally has, but she inherited from her royal mother many graces and charms, so that she was quite different from the other maidens in the village where she lived.

One day Prince Florizel, the son of the good King of Bohemia, was bunting near the shepherd's house and saw Perdita, now grown up to a charming woman. He made friends with the shepherd, not telling him that he was the Prince, but saying that his name was Doricles, and that he was a private gentleman; and then, being deeply in love with the pretty Perdita, he came almost daily to see her.

The King could not understand what it was that took his son nearly every day from home; so he set people to watch him, and then found out that the heir of the King of Bohemia was in love with Perdita, the pretty shepherd girl. Polixenes, wishing to see whether this was true, disguised himself, and went with the faithful Camillo, in disguise too, to the old shepherd's house. They arrived at the feast of sheep-shearing, and, though strangers, they were made very welcome. There was dancing going on, and a peddler was selling ribbons and laces and gloves, which the young men bought for their sweethearts.

Florizel and Perdita, however, were taking no part in this gay scene, but sat quietly together talking. The King noticed the charming manners and great beauty of Perdita, never guessing that she was the daughter of his old friend, Leontes. He said to Camillo—

"This is the prettiest low-born lass that ever ran on the green-sward. Nothing she does or seems but smacks of something greater than herself—too noble for this place."

And Camillo answered, "In truth she is the Queen of curds and cream."

But when Florizel, who did not recognize his father, called upon the strangers to witness his betrothal with the pretty shepherdess, the King made himself known and forbade the marriage, adding that if ever she saw Florizel again, he would kill her and her old father, the shepherd; and with that he left them. But Camillo remained behind, for he was charmed with Perdita, and wished to befriend her.

Camillo had long known how sorry Leontes was for that foolish madness of his, and he longed to go back to Sicily to see his old master. He now proposed that the young people should go there and claim the protection of Leontes. So they went, and the shepherd went with them, taking Perdita's jewels, her baby clothes, and the paper he had found pinned to her cloak.

Leontes received them with great kindness. He was very polite to Prince Florizel, but all his looks were for Perdita. He saw how much she was like the Queen Hermione, and said again and again—

"Such a sweet creature my daughter might have been, if I had not cruelly sent her from me."

When the old shepherd heard that the King had lost a baby daughter, who had been left upon the coast of Bohemia, he felt sure that Perdita, the child he had reared, must be the King's daughter, and when he told his tale and showed the jewels and the paper, the King perceived that Perdita was indeed his long-lost child. He welcomed her with joy, and rewarded the good shepherd.

Polixenes had hastened after his son to prevent his marriage with Perdita, but when he found that she was the daughter of his old friend, he was only too glad to give his consent.

Yet Leontes could not be happy. He remembered how his fair Queen, who should have been at his side to share his joy in his daughter's happiness, was dead through his unkindness, and he could say nothing for a long time but—

"Oh, thy mother! thy mother!" and ask forgiveness of the King of Bohemia, and then kiss his daughter again, and then the Prince

Florizel, and then thank the old shepherd for all his goodness.

Then Paulina, who had been high all these years in the King's favor, because of her kindness to the dead Queen Hermione, said—"I have a statue made in the likeness of the dead Queen, a piece many years in doing, and performed by the rare Italian master, Giulio Romano. I keep it in a private house apart, and there, ever since you lost your Queen, I have gone twice or thrice a day. Will it please your Majesty to go and see the statue?"

So Leontes and Polixenes, and Florizel and Perdita, with Camillo and their attendants, went to Paulina's house where there was a heavy purple curtain screening off an alcove; and Paulina, with her hand on the curtain, said—

"She was peerless when she was alive, and I do believe that her dead likeness excels whatever yet you have looked upon, or that the hand of man hath done. Therefore I keep it lonely, apart. But here it is—behold, and say, 'tis well."

And with that she drew back the curtain and showed them the statue. The King gazed and gazed on the beautiful statue of his dead wife, but said nothing.

"I like your silence," said Paulina; "it the more shows off your wonder. But speak, is it not like her?"

"It is almost herself," said the King, "and yet, Paulina, Hermione was not so much wrinkled, nothing so old as this seems."

"Oh, not by much," said Polixenes.

"Al," said Paulina, "that is the cleverness of the carver, who shows her to us as she would have been had she lived till now."

"Leontes receiving Florizel and Perdita." Illustration by Max Bihn for E. Nesbit, *Beautiful Stories from Shakespeare* (Chicago: D. E. Cunningham, 1907). Project Gutenberg EBook.

And still Leontes looked at the statue and could not take his eyes away.

"If I had known," said Paulina, "that this poor image would so have stirred your grief, and love, I would not have shown it to you."

But he only answered, "Do not draw the curtain."

"No, you must not look any longer," said Paulina, "or you will think it moves."

"Let be! let be!" said the King. "Would you not think it breathed?"

"I will draw the curtain," said Paulina; "you will think it lives presently."

"Ah, sweet Paulina," said Leontes, "make me to think so twenty years together."

"If you can bear it," said Paulina, "I can make the statue move, make it come down and take you by the hand. Only you would think it was by wicked magic."

"Whatever you can make her do, I am content to look on," said the King.

And then, all folks there admiring and beholding, the statue moved from its pedestal, and came down the steps and put its arms round the King's neck, and he held her face and kissed her many times, for this was no statue, but the real living Queen Hermione herself. She had lived hidden, by Paulina's kindness, all these years, and would not discover herself to her husband, though she knew he had repented, because she could not quite forgive him till she knew what had become of her little baby.

Now that Perdita was found, she forgave her husband everything, and it was like a new and beautiful marriage to them, to be together once more.

Florizel and Perdita were married and lived long and happily.

To Leontes his many years of suffering were well paid for in the moment when, after long grief and pain, he felt the arms of his true love around him once again.

Week Nine:
"THE MOON"

The moon has a face like the clock in the hall;
She shines on thieves on the garden wall,
On streets and field and harbour quays,
And birdies asleep in the forks of the trees.

The squalling cat and the squeaking mouse,
The howling dog by the door of the house,
The bat that lies in bed at noon,
All love to be out by the light of the moon.

But all of the things that belong to the day
Cuddle to sleep to be out of her way;
And flowers and children close their eyes
Till up in the morning the sun shall arise.

ROBERT LOUIS STEVENSON
(1850–1894)

"The Moon." Illustrations by Jessie Willcox Smith for Robert Louis Stevenson, *A Child's Garden of Verses,* Verse 142 (New York: Charles Scribner's Sons, 1905).

"'My good old lady,' said the princess, 'what are you doing?'" Illustrator unknown for Wilhelm Grimm, *Grimm's Fairy Tales: Retold in One-Syllable Words* (New York: McLoughlin Brothers, 1899). University of North Carolina at Chapel Hill.

Week Ten:
BRIAR ROSE
Grimm's Fairy Tale

A king and queen once upon a time reigned in a country a great way off, where there were in those days fairies. Now this king and queen had plenty of money, and plenty of fine clothes to wear, and plenty of good things to eat and drink, and a coach to ride out in every day: but though they had been married many years they had no children, and this grieved them very much indeed. But one day as the queen was walking by the side of the river, at the bottom of the garden, she saw a poor little fish, that had thrown itself out of the water, and lay gasping and nearly dead on the bank. Then the queen took pity on the little fish, and threw it back again into the river; and before it swam away it lifted its head out of the water and said, "I know what your wish is, and it shall be fulfilled, in return for your kindness to me—you will soon have a daughter." What the little fish had foretold soon came to pass; and the queen had a little girl, so very beautiful that the king could not cease looking on it for joy, and said he would hold a great feast and make merry, and show the child to all the land. So he asked his kinsmen, and nobles, and friends, and neighbours. But the queen said, "I will have the fairies also, that they might be kind and good to our little daughter." Now there were thirteen fairies in the kingdom; but as the king and queen had only twelve golden dishes for them to eat out of, they were forced to leave one of the fairies without asking her. So twelve fairies came, each with a high red cap on her head, and red shoes with high heels on her feet, and a long white wand in her hand: and after the feast was over they gathered round in a ring and gave all their best gifts to the little princess. One gave her goodness, another beauty, another riches, and so on till she had all that was good in the world.

Just as eleven of them had done blessing her, a great noise was heard in the courtyard, and word was brought that the thirteenth fairy was come, with a black cap on her head, and black shoes on her feet, and a broomstick in her hand: and presently up she came into the dining-hall. Now, as she had not been asked to the feast she was very angry, and scolded the king and queen very much, and set to work to take her revenge. So she cried out, "The king's daughter shall, in her fifteenth year, be wounded by a spindle, and fall down dead." Then the twelfth of the friendly fairies, who had not yet given her gift, came forward, and said that the evil wish must be fulfilled, but that she could soften its mischief; so her gift was, that the king's daughter, when the spindle wounded her, should not really die, but should only fall asleep for a hundred years.

However, the king hoped still to save his dear child altogether from the threatened evil; so he ordered that all the spindles in the kingdom should be bought up and burnt. But all the gifts of the first eleven fairies were in the meantime fulfilled; for the princess was so beautiful, and well behaved, and good, and wise, that everyone who knew her loved her.

It happened that, on the very day she was fifteen years old, the king and queen were not at home, and she was left alone in the palace. So she roved about by herself, and looked at all the rooms and chambers, till at last she came to an old tower, to which there was a narrow staircase ending with a little door. In the door there was a golden key, and when she turned it the door sprang open, and there sat an old lady spinning away very busily. "Why, how now, good mother," said the princess; "what are you doing there?" "Spinning," said the old lady, and nodded her head, humming a tune, while buzz! went the wheel. "How prettily that little thing turns round!" said the princess, and took

BRIAR ROSE

the spindle and began to try and spin. But scarcely had she touched it, before the fairy's prophecy was fulfilled; the spindle wounded her, and she fell down lifeless on the ground.

However, she was not dead, but had only fallen into a deep sleep; and the king and the queen, who had just come home, and all their court, fell asleep too; and the horses slept in the stables, and the dogs in the court, the pigeons on the house-top, and the very flies slept upon it for the king's dinner stood still; and the cook, who was at that moment pulling the kitchen-boy by the hair to give him a box on the ear forsomething he had done amiss, let him go, and both fell asleep; the butler, who was slyly tasting the ale, fell asleep with the jug at his lips: and thus everything stood still, and slept soundly.

A large hedge of thorns soon grew round the palace, and every year it became higher and thicker; till at last the old palace was surrounded and hidden, so that not even the roof or the chimneys could be seen. But there went a report through all the land of the beautiful sleeping

"There was the princess fast asleep." Illustrator unknown for Edna Henry Lee Turpin, *Grimm's Fairy Tales* (New York: Maynard, Merrill, & Co., 1903). Harvard University.

Briar Rose (for so the king's daughter was called): so that, from time to time, several kings' sons came, and tried to break through the thicket into the palace. This, however, none of them could ever do; for the thorns and bushes laid hold of them, as it were with hands; and there they stuck fast, and died wretchedly.

After many, many years there came a king's son into that land: and an old man told him the story of the thicket of thorns; and how a beautiful palace stood behind it, and how a wonderful princess, called Briar Rose, lay in it asleep, with all her court. He told, too, how he had heard from his grandfather that many, many princes had come, and had tried to break through the thicket, but that they had all stuck fast in it, and died. Then the young prince said, "All this shall not frighten me; I will go and see this Briar Rose." The old man tried to hinder him, but he was bent upon going.

Now that very day the hundred years were ended; and as the prince came to the thicket he saw nothing but beautiful flowering shrubs, through which he went with ease, and they shut in after him as thick as ever. Then he came at last to the palace, and there in the court lay the dogs asleep; and the horses were standing in the stables; and on the roof sat the pigeons fast asleep, with their heads under their wings. And when he came into the palace, the flies were sleeping on the walls; the spit was standing still; the butler had the jug of ale at his lips, going to drink a draught; the maid sat with a fowl in her lap ready to be plucked; and the cook in the kitchen was still holding up her hand, as if she was going to beat the boy.

Then he went on still farther, and all was so still that he could hear every breath he drew; till at last he came to the old tower, and opened the door of the little room in which Briar Rose was; and there she lay, fast asleep on a couch by the window. She looked so beautiful that he could not take his eyes off her, so he stooped down and gave her a kiss. But the moment he kissed her she opened her eyes and awoke, and smiled upon him; and they went out together; and soon the king and queen also awoke, and all the court, and gazed on each other with great wonder. And the horses shook themselves, and the dogs jumped up and barked; the pigeons took their heads from under their wings, and looked about and flew into the fields; the flies on the walls buzzed again; the fire in the kitchen blazed up; round went the jack, and round went the spit, with the goose for the king's dinner upon it; the butler finished his draught of ale; the maid went on plucking the fowl; and the cook gave the boy the box on his ear.

And then the prince and Briar Rose were married, and the wedding feast was given; and they lived happily together all their lives long.

"Rapunzel." Illustration by J. B. Grueller for Jacob Grimm, *Grimm's Fairy Stories* (New York: Cupples and Leon Company, 1922). Library of Congress.

Week Ten:
RAPUNZEL
Grimm's Fairy Tale

There were once a man and a woman who had long in vain wished for a child. At length the woman hoped that God was about to grant her desire. These people had a little window at the back of their house from which a splendid garden could be seen, which was full of the most beautiful flowers and herbs. It was, however, surrounded by a high wall, and no one dared to go into it because it belonged to an enchantress, who had great power and was dreaded by all the world. One day the woman was standing by this window and looking down into the garden, when she saw a bed which was planted with the most beautiful rampion (rapunzel), and it looked so fresh and green that she longed for it, she quite pined away, and began to look pale and miserable. Then her husband was alarmed, and asked: "What ails you, dear wife?"

"Ah," she replied, "if I can't eat some of the rampion, which is in the garden behind our house, I shall die."

The man, who loved her, thought: "Sooner than let your wife die, bring her some of the rampion yourself, let it cost what it will." At twilight, he clambered down over the wall into the garden of the enchantress, hastily clutched a handful of rampion, and took it to his wife. She at once made herself a salad of it, and ate it greedily. It tasted so good to her—so very good, that the next day she longed for it three times as much as before. If he was to have any rest, her husband must once more descend into the garden. In the gloom of evening therefore, he let himself down again; but when he had clambered down the wall he was terribly afraid, for he saw the enchantress standing before him.

"How can you dare," said she with angry look, "descend into my garden and steal my rampion like a thief? You shall suffer for it!"

"Ah," answered he, "let mercy take the place of justice, I only made up my mind to do it out of necessity. My wife saw your rampion from the window, and felt such a longing for it that she would have died if she had not got some to eat."

Then the enchantress allowed her anger to be softened, and said to him: "If the case be as you say, I will allow you to take away with you as much rampion as you will, only I make one condition, you must give me the child which your wife will bring into the world; it shall be well treated, and I will care for it like a mother."

The man in his terror consented to everything, and when the woman was brought to bed, the enchantress appeared at once, gave the child the name of Rapunzel, and took it away with her.

Rapunzel grew into the most beautiful child under the sun. When she was twelve years old, the enchantress shut her into a tower, which lay in a forest, and had neither stairs nor door, but quite at the top was a little window. When the enchantress wanted to go in, she placed herself beneath it and cried:

> *"Rapunzel, Rapunzel,*
> *Let down your hair to me."*

Rapunzel had magnificent long hair, fine as spun gold, and when she heard the voice of the enchantress she unfastened her braided tresses, wound them round one of the hooks of the window above, and then the hair fell twenty ells down, and the enchantress climbed up by it.

After a year or two, it came to pass that the king's son rode through the forest and passed by the tower. Then he heard a song, which was so charming that he stood still and listened. This was Rapunzel, who in her solitude passed her time in letting her sweet voice resound. The

king's son wanted to climb up to her, and looked for the door of the tower, but none was to be found. He rode home, but the singing had so deeply touched his heart, that every day he went out into the forest and listened to it. Once when he was thus standing behind a tree, he saw that an enchantress came there, and he heard how she cried:

> *"Rapunzel, Rapunzel,*
> *Let down your hair to me."*

Then Rapunzel let down the braids of her hair, and the enchantress climbed up to her. "If that is the ladder by which one mounts, I too will try my fortune," said he, and the next day when it began to grow dark, he went to the tower and cried:

> *"Rapunzel, Rapunzel,*
> *Let down your hair to me."*

"Rapunzel." Illustration by R. Emmett Owen for Jacob Grimm, *Grimm's Fairy Tales* (New York: Cupples and Leon Company, 1922). Library of Congress.

Immediately the hair fell down and the king's son climbed up.

At first Rapunzel was terribly frightened when a man, such as her eyes had never yet beheld, came to her; but the king's son began to talk to her quite like a friend, and told her that his heart had been so stirred that it had let him have no rest, and he had been forced to see her. Then Rapunzel lost her fear, and when he asked her if she would take him for her husband, and she saw that he was young and handsome, she thought: "He will love me more than old Dame Gothel does"; and she said yes, and laid her hand in his. She said: "I will willingly go away with you, but I do not know how to get down. Bring with you a skein of silk every time that you come, and I will weave a ladder with it, and when that is ready I will descend, and you will take me on your horse." They agreed that until that time he should come to her every evening, for the old woman came by day. The enchantress remarked nothing of this, until once Rapunzel said to her: "Tell me, Dame Gothel, how it happens that you are so much heavier for me to draw up than the young king's son—he is with me in a moment." "Ah! you wicked child," cried the enchantress. "What do I hear you say! I thought I had separated you from all the world, and yet you have deceived me!" In her anger she clutched Rapunzel's beautiful tresses, wrapped them twice round her left hand, seized a pair of scissors with the right, and snip, snap, they were cut off, and the lovely braids lay on the ground. And she was so pitiless that she took poor Rapunzel into a desert where she had to live in great grief and misery.

On the same day that she cast out Rapunzel, however, the enchantress fastened the braids of hair, which she had cut off, to the hook of the window, and when the king's son came and cried:

> "*Rapunzel, Rapunzel,*
> *Let down your hair to me,*"

she let the hair down. The king's son ascended, but instead of finding his dearest Rapunzel, he found the enchantress, who gazed at him with wicked and venomous looks. "Aha!" she cried mockingly, "you would fetch your dearest, but the beautiful bird sits no longer singing in the nest; the cat has got it, and will scratch out your eyes as well. Rapunzel is lost to you; you will never see her again." The king's son was beside himself with pain, and in his despair he leapt down from the tower. He escaped with his life, but the thorns into which he fell pierced his eyes. Then he wandered quite blind about the forest, ate nothing but roots and berries, and did naught but lament and weep over the loss of his dearest wife. Thus he roamed about in misery for some years, and at length came to the desert where Rapunzel, with the twins to which she had given birth, a boy and a girl, lived in wretchedness. He heard a voice, and it seemed so familiar to him that he went towards it, and when he approached, Rapunzel knew him and fell on his neck and wept. Two of her tears wetted his eyes and they grew clear again, and he could see with them as before. He led her to his kingdom where he was joyfully received, and they lived for a long time afterwards, happy and contented.

Week Ten:
"MONDAY'S CHILD"

Monday's child is fair in face,
Tuesday's child is full of grace,
Wednesday's child is full of woe,
Thursday's child has far to go,

Friday's child is loving and giving,
Saturday's child works hard for its living;
And a child that's born on a Christmas day,
Is fair and wise, good and gay.

ANONYMOUS

"The Frog Prince." Illustration by Walter Crane, *Beauty and the Beast Picture Book* (New York: Dodd, Mead and Company, 1911).

Week Eleven:
THE FROG PRINCE
Grimm's Fairy Tale

One fine evening a young princess put on her bonnet and clogs, and went out to take a walk by herself in a wood; and when she came to a cool spring of water, that rose in the midst of it, she sat herself down to rest a while. Now she had a golden ball in her hand, which was her favourite plaything; and she was always tossing it up into the air, and catching it again as it fell. After a time she threw it up so high that she missed catching it as it fell; and the ball bounded away, and rolled along upon the ground, till at last it fell down into the spring. The princess looked into the spring after her ball, but it was very deep, so deep that she could not see the bottom of it. Then she began to bewail her loss, and said, "Alas! if I could only get my ball again, I would give all my fine clothes and jewels, and everything that I have in the world."

Whilst she was speaking, a frog put its head out of the water, and said, "Princess, why do you weep so bitterly?" "Alas!" said she, "what can you do for me, you nasty frog? My golden ball has fallen into the spring." The frog said, "I want

"The Frog Prince." Illustrator unknown for Wilhelm Grimm, *Grimm's Fairy Tales Retold in One-Syllable Words* (New York: McLoughlin Brothers, 1899).

not your pearls, and jewels, and fine clothes; but if you will love me, and let me live with you and eat from off your golden plate, and sleep upon your bed, I will bring you your ball again." "What nonsense," thought the princess, "this silly frog is talking! He can never even get out of the spring to visit me, though he may be able to get my ball for me, and therefore I will tell him he shall have what he asks." So she said to the frog, "Well, if you will bring me my ball, I will do all you ask." Then the frog put his head down, and dived deep under the water; and after a little while he came up again, with the ball in his mouth, and threw it on the edge of the spring. As soon as the young princess saw her ball, she ran to pick it up; and she was so overjoyed to have it in her hand again, that she never thought of the frog, but ran home with it as fast as she could. The frog called after her, "Stay, princess, and take me with you as you said." But she did not stop to hear a word.

The next day, just as the princess had sat down to dinner, she heard a strange noise—tap, tap—plash, plash—as if something was coming up the marble staircase: and soon afterwards there was a gentle knock at the door, and a little voice cried out and said:

> "*Open the door, my princess dear,*
> *Open the door to thy true love here!*
> *And mind the words that thou and I said*
> *By the fountain cool, in the greenwood shade.*"

Then the princess ran to the door and opened it, and there she saw the frog, whom she had quite forgotten. At this sight she was sadly frightened, and shutting the door as fast as she could came back

"The Frog Prince." Illustrator unknown for Edna Henry Lee Turpin, *Grimm's Fairy Tales* (New York: Maynard, Merrill, & Co., 1903). Harvard University.

to her seat. The king, her father, seeing that something had frightened her, asked her what was the matter. "There is a nasty frog," said she, "at the door, that lifted my ball for me out of the spring this morning: I told him that he should live with me here, thinking that he could never get out of the spring; but there he is at the door, and he wants to come in."

While she was speaking the frog knocked again at the door, and said:

> *"Open the door, my princess dear,*
> *Open the door to thy true love here!*
> *And mind the words that thou and I said*
> *By the fountain cool, in the greenwood shade."*

Then the king said to the young princess, "As you have given your word you must keep it; so go and let him in." She did so, and the frog hopped into the room, and then straight on—tap, tap—plash, plash—from the bottom of the room to the top, till he came up close to the table where the princess sat. "Pray lift me upon chair," said he to the princess, "and let me sit next to you." As soon as she had done this, the frog said, "Put your plate nearer to me, that I may eat out of it." This she did, and when he had eaten as much as he could, he said, "Now I am tired; carry me upstairs, and put me into your bed." And the princess, though very unwilling, took him up in her hand, and put him upon the pillow of her own bed, where he slept all night long. As soon as it was light he jumped up, hopped downstairs, and went out of the house. "Now, then," thought the princess, "at last he is gone, and I shall be troubled with him no more."

But she was mistaken; for when night came again she heard the same tapping at the door; and the frog came once more, and said:

> *"Open the door, my princess dear,*
> *Open the door to thy true love here!*
> *And mind the words that thou and I said*
> *By the fountain cool, in the greenwood shade."*

And when the princess opened the door the frog came in, and slept upon her pillow as before, till the morning broke. And the third night he did the same. But when the princess awoke on the following morning she was astonished to see, instead of the frog, a handsome prince, gazing on her with the most beautiful eyes she had ever seen, and standing at the head of her bed.

He told her that he had been enchanted by a spiteful fairy, who had changed him into a frog; and that he had been fated so to abide till some princess should take him out of the spring, and let him eat from her plate, and sleep upon her bed for three nights. "You," said the prince, "have broken his cruel charm, and now I have nothing to wish for but that you should go with me into my father's kingdom, where I will marry you, and love you as long as you live."

The young princess, you may be sure, was not long in saying "Yes" to all this; and as they spoke a gay coach drove up, with eight beautiful horses, decked with plumes of feathers and a golden harness; and behind the coach rode the prince's servant, faithful Heinrich, who had bewailed the misfortunes of his dear master during his enchantment so long and so bitterly, that his heart had well-nigh burst.

They then took leave of the king, and got into the coach with eight horses, and all set out, full of joy and merriment, for the prince's kingdom, which they reached safely; and there they lived happily a great many years.

Week Eleven:
THE VALIANT LITTLE TAILOR
Grimm's Fairy Tale

One summer's morning a little tailor was sitting on his table by the window; he was in good spirits, and sewed with all his might. Then came a peasant woman down the street crying: "Good jams, cheap! Good jams, cheap!" This rang pleasantly in the tailor's ears; he stretched his delicate head out of the window, and called: "Come up here, dear woman; here you will get rid of your goods." The woman came up the three steps to the tailor with her heavy basket, and he made her unpack all the pots for him. He inspected each one, lifted it up, put his nose to it, and at length said: "The jam seems to me to be good, so weigh me out four ounces, dear woman, and if it is a quarter of a pound that is of no consequence." The woman who had hoped to find a good sale, gave him what he desired, but went away quite angry and grumbling. "Now, this jam shall be blessed by God," cried the little tailor, "and give me health and strength"; so he brought the bread out of the cupboard, cut himself a piece right across the loaf and spread the jam over it. "This won't taste bitter," said he, "but I will just finish the jacket before I take a bite." He laid the bread near him, sewed on, and in his joy, made bigger and bigger stitches. In the meantime the smell of the sweet jam rose to where the flies were sitting in great numbers, and they were attracted and descended on it in hosts. "Hi! who invited you?" said the little tailor, and drove the unbidden guests away. The flies, however, who understood no German, would not be turned away,

"The Valiant Little Tailor." Illustrator unknown for Jacob and Wilhelm Grimm, *Children's and Household Fairy Tales [Kinder-und Hausmärchen Gesammelt Durch die Brüder Jacob und Wilhelm Grimm]* (Gütersloh, Bertelsmann, 1889).

but came back again in ever-increasing companies. The little tailor at last lost all patience, and drew a piece of cloth from the hole under his work-table, and saying: "Wait, and I will give it to you," struck it mercilessly on them. When he drew it away and counted, there lay before him no fewer than seven, dead and with legs stretched out. "Are you a fellow of that sort?" said he, and could not help admiring his own bravery. "The whole town shall know of this!" And the little tailor hastened to cut himself a girdle, stitched it, and embroidered on it in large letters: "Seven at one stroke!" "What, the town!" he continued, "the whole world shall hear of it!" and his heart wagged with joy like a lamb's tail. The tailor put on the girdle, and resolved to go forth into the world, because he thought his workshop was too small for his valour. Before he went away, he sought about in the house to see if there was anything which he could take with him; however, he found nothing but an old cheese, and that he put in his pocket. In front of the door he observed a bird which had caught itself in the thicket. It had to go into his pocket with the cheese. Now he took to the road boldly, and as he was light and nimble, he felt no fatigue. The road led him up a mountain, and when he had reached the highest point of it, there sat a powerful giant looking peacefully about him. The little tailor went bravely up, spoke to him, and said: "Good day, comrade, so you are sitting there overlooking the wide-spread world! I am just on my way thither, and want to try my luck. Have you any inclination to go with me?" The giant looked contemptuously at the tailor, and said: "You ragamuffin! You miserable creature!"

"Oh, indeed?" answered the little tailor, and unbuttoned his coat, and showed the giant the girdle, "there may you read what kind of a man I am!" The giant read: "Seven at one stroke," and thought that they had been men whom the tailor had killed, and began to feel a little respect for the tiny fellow. Nevertheless, he wished to try him first, and took a stone in his hand and squeezed it together so that water dropped out of it. "Do that likewise," said the giant, "if you have strength." "Is that all?" said the tailor, "that is child's play with us!" and put his hand into his pocket, brought out the soft cheese, and pressed it until the liquid ran out of it. "Faith," said he, "that was a little better, wasn't it?" The giant did not know what to say, and could not believe it of the little man. Then the giant picked up a stone and threw it so high that the eye could scarcely follow it. "Now, little mite of a man, do that likewise," "Well thrown," said the tailor, "but after all the stone came down to earth again; I will throw you one which shall never come back at all," and he put his hand into his pocket, took out the bird, and threw it into the air. The bird, delighted with its liberty, rose, flew away and did not come back. "How does that shot please you, comrade?" asked the tailor. "You can certainly throw," said the giant, "but now we will see if you are able to carry anything properly." He took the little tailor to a mighty oak tree which lay there felled on the ground, and said: "If you are strong enough, help me to carry the tree out of the forest." "Readily," answered the little man; "take you the trunk on your shoulders, and I will raise up the branches and twigs; after all, they are the heaviest." The giant took the trunk on his shoulder, but the tailor seated himself on a branch, and the giant, who could not look round, had to carry away the whole tree, and the little tailor into the bargain: he behind, was quite merry and happy, and whistled the song: "Three tailors rode forth from the gate," as if carrying the tree were child's play. The giant, after he had dragged the heavy burden part of the way, could go no further, and cried: "Hark you, I shall have to let the tree fall!" The tailor sprang nimbly down, seized the tree with both arms as if he had been carrying it, and said to the giant: "You are such a great fellow, and yet cannot even carry the tree!"

They went on together, and as they passed a cherry-tree, the giant laid hold of the top of the tree where the ripest fruit was hanging, bent it down, gave it into the tailor's hand, and bade him eat. But the little tailor was much too weak to hold the tree, and when the giant let it go, it sprang back again, and the tailor was tossed into the air with it. When he had fallen down again without injury, the giant said: "What is this? Have you not strength enough to hold the weak twig?" "There is no lack of strength," answered the little tailor. "Do you think that could be anything to a man who has struck down seven at one blow? I leapt over the tree because the huntsmen are shooting down there in the thicket. Jump as I did, if you can do it." The giant made the attempt but he could not get over the tree, and remained hanging in the branches, so that in this also the tailor kept the upper hand.

The giant said: "If you are such a valiant fellow, come with me into our cavern and spend the night with us." The little tailor was willing, and followed him. When they went into the cave, other giants were sitting there by the fire, and each of them had a roasted sheep in his hand and was eating it. The little tailor looked round and thought: "It is much more spacious here than in my workshop." The giant showed him a bed, and said he was to lie down in it and sleep. The bed, however, was too big for the little tailor; he did not lie down in it, but crept into a corner. When it was midnight, and the giant thought that the little tailor was lying in a sound sleep, he got up, took a great iron bar, cut through the bed with one blow, and thought he had finished off the grasshopper for good. With the earliest dawn the giants went into the forest, and had quite forgotten the little tailor, when all at once he walked up to them quite merrily and boldly. The giants were terrified, they were afraid that he would strike them all dead, and ran away in a great hurry.

The little tailor went onwards, always following his own pointed nose. After he had walked for a long time, he came to the courtyard of a royal palace, and as he felt weary, he lay down on the grass and fell asleep. Whilst he lay there, the people came and inspected him on all sides, and read on his girdle: "Seven at one stroke." "Ah!" said they, "what does the great warrior want here in the midst of peace? He must be a mighty lord." They went and announced him to the king, and gave it as their opinion that if war should break out, this would be a weighty and useful man who ought on no account to be allowed to depart. The counsel pleased the king, and he sent one of his courtiers to the little tailor to offer him military service when he awoke. The ambassador remained standing by the sleeper, waited until he stretched his limbs and opened his eyes, and then conveyed to him this proposal. "For this very reason have I come here," the tailor replied, "I am ready to enter the king's service." He was therefore honourably received, and a special dwelling was assigned him.

The soldiers, however, were set against the little tailor, and wished him a thousand miles away. "What is to be the end of this?" they said among themselves. "If we quarrel with him, and he strikes about him, seven of us will fall at every blow; not one of us can stand against him." They came therefore to a decision, betook themselves in a body to the king, and begged for their dismissal. "We are not prepared," said they, "to stay with a man who kills seven at one stroke." The king was sorry that for the sake of one he should lose all his faithful servants, wished that he had never set eyes on the tailor, and would willingly have been rid of him again. But he did not venture to give him his dismissal, for he dreaded lest he should strike him and all his people dead, and place himself on the royal throne. He thought about it for a long time, and at last found good counsel. He sent to the little tailor and caused him to be informed that as he was a great warrior, he had one request to make to him. In a forest of his country lived two giants, who caused great mischief with their robbing, murdering, ravaging, and burning, and no one could approach them without putting himself in danger of death.

"The Valiant Little Tailor." Illustration by R. Emmett Owen for Jacob Grimm, *Grimm's Fairy Stories* (New York: Cupples and Leon Company, 1922). Library of Congress.

If the tailor conquered and killed these two giants, he would give him his only daughter to wife, and half of his kingdom as a dowry, likewise one hundred horsemen should go with him to assist him. "That would indeed be a fine thing for a man like me!" thought the little tailor. "One is not offered a beautiful princess and half a kingdom every day of one's life!" "Oh, yes," he replied, "I will soon subdue the giants, and do not require the help of the hundred horsemen to do it; he who can hit seven with one blow has no need to be afraid of two."

The little tailor went forth, and the hundred horsemen followed him. When he came to the outskirts of the forest, he said to his followers: "Just stay waiting here, I alone will soon finish off the giants." Then he bounded into the forest and looked about right and left. After a while he perceived both giants. They lay sleeping under a tree, and snored so that the branches waved up and down. The little tailor, not idle, gathered two pocketsful of stones, and with these climbed up the tree. When he was halfway up, he slipped down by a branch, until he sat just above the sleepers, and then let one stone after another fall on the breast of one of the giants. For a long time the giant felt nothing, but at last he awoke, pushed his comrade, and said: "Why are you knocking me?" "You must be dreaming," said the other, "I am not knocking you." They laid themselves down to sleep again, and then the tailor threw a stone down on the second. "What is the meaning of this?" cried the other "Why are you pelting me?" "I am not pelting you," answered the first, growling. They disputed about it for a time, but as they were weary they let the matter rest, and their eyes closed once more. The little tailor began his game again, picked out the biggest stone, and threw it with all his might on the breast of the first giant. "That is too bad!" cried he, and sprang up like a madman, and pushed his companion against the tree until it shook. The other paid him back in the same coin, and they got into such a rage that they tore up trees and belaboured each other so long, that at last they both fell down dead on the ground at the same time. Then the little tailor leapt down. "It is a lucky thing," said he, "that they did not tear up the tree on which I was sitting, or I should have had to sprint on to another like a squirrel; but we tailors are nimble."

He drew out his sword and gave each of them a couple of thrusts in the breast, and then went out to the horsemen and said: "The work is done; I have finished both of them off, but it was hard work! They tore up trees in their sore need, and defended themselves with them, but all that is to no purpose when a man like myself comes, who can kill seven at one blow." "But are you not wounded?" asked the horsemen. "You need not concern yourself about that," answered the tailor, "they have not bent one hair of mine." The horsemen would not believe him, and rode into the forest; there they found the giants swimming in their blood, and all round about lay the torn-up trees.

The little tailor demanded of the king the promised reward; he, however, repented of his promise, and again bethought himself how he could get rid of the hero. "Before you receive my daughter, and the half of my kingdom," said he to him, "you must perform one more heroic deed. In the forest roams a unicorn which does great harm, and you must catch it first." "I fear one unicorn still less than two giants. Seven at one blow, is my kind of affair." He took a rope and an axe with him, went forth into the forest, and again bade those who were sent with him to wait outside. He had not long to seek. The unicorn soon came towards him, and rushed directly on the tailor, as if it would gore him with its horn without more ado. "Softly, softly; it can't be done as quickly as that," said he, and stood still and waited until the animal was quite close, and then sprang nimbly behind the tree. The unicorn ran against the tree with all its strength, and stuck its horn so fast in the trunk that it had not the strength enough to draw it out again, and thus it was caught. "Now, I have got the bird," said the tailor, and came out from behind the tree and put the rope round its neck, and then with his axe he hewed the horn out of the tree, and when all was ready he led the beast away and took it to the king.

Still the King didn't want to give him the promised reward and made a third demand. The tailor was to catch a wild boar for him that did a great deal of harm in the wood; and he might have the huntsmen to help him. "Willingly" said the tailor; "that's mere child's play." But he didn't take the huntsmen into the wood with him, and they were well enough pleased to remain behind, for the wild boar had often received them in a manner which did not make them desire its further acquaintance. As soon as the boar perceived the tailor it ran at him with foaming mouth and gleaming teeth, and tried to knock him down; but our alert little friend ran into a chapel that stood near, and got out of the window again with a jump. The boar pursued him into the church, but the tailor skipped round to the door, and closed it securely. So the raging beast was caught, for it was far too heavy and unwieldy to spring out of the window. The little tailor summoned the huntsmen together, that they might see the prisoner with their own eyes. Then the hero betook himself to the King, who was obliged now, whether he liked it or not, to keep his promise, and hand him over his daughter and half his kingdom. Had he known that no hero-warrior, but only a little tailor stood before him, it would have gone even more to his heart. So the wedding was celebrated with much splendor and little joy, and the tailor became a king.

After a time the Queen heard her husband saying one night in his sleep: "My lad, make that waistcoat and patch these trousers, or I'll box your ears." Thus she learned in what rank the young gentleman had been born, and next day she poured forth her woes to her father, and begged him to help her to get rid of a husband who was nothing more nor less than a tailor. The King comforted her, and said: "Leave your bedroom door open to-night, my servants shall stand outside, and when your husband is fast asleep they shall enter, bind him fast, and carry him on to a ship, which shall sail away out into the wide ocean." The Queen was well satisfied with the idea, but the armor-bearer, who had overheard everything, being much attached to his young master, went straight to him and revealed the whole plot. "I'll soon put a stop to the business," said the tailor. That night he and his wife went to bed at the usual time; and when she thought he had fallen asleep she got up, opened the door, and then lay down again. The little tailor, who had only pretended to be asleep, began to call out in a clear voice: "My lad, make that waistcoat and patch those trousers, or I'll box your ears. I have killed seven at a blow, slain two giants, led a unicorn captive, and caught a wild boar, then why should I be afraid of those men standing outside my door?" The men, when they heard the tailor saying these words, were so terrified that they fled as if pursued by a wild army, and didn't dare go near him again. So the little tailor was and remained a king all the days of his life.

Week Eleven:
"A Boy's Song"

Where the pools are bright and deep,
Where the gray trout lies asleep,
Up the river and o'er the lea,
That's the way for Billy and me.

Where the blackbird sings the latest,
Where the hawthorn blooms the sweetest,
Where the nestlings chirp and flee,
That's the way for Billy and me.

Where the mowers mow the cleanest,
Where the hay lies thick and greenest,
There to trace the homeward bee,
That's the way for Billy and me.

Where the hazel bank is steepest,
Where the shadow falls the deepest,
Where the clustering nuts fall free,
That's the way for Billy and me.

Why the boys should drive away,
Little sweet maidens from the play,
Or love to banter and fight so well,
That's the thing I never could tell.

But this I know, I love to play,
Through the meadow, among the hay;
Up the water and o'er the lea,
That's the way for Billy and me.

JAMES HOGG
(1770–1835)

"Hansel and Grethel [*sic*] follow the white bird." Illustrator unknown for Wilhelm Grimm, *Grimm's Fairy Tales Retold in One-Syllable Words* (New York: McLoughlin Brothers, 1899).

Week Twelve:

HANSEL AND GRETEL
Grimm's Fairy Tale

ard by a great forest dwelt a poor wood-cutter with his wife and his two children. The boy was called Hansel and the girl Gretel. He had little to bite and to break, and once when great dearth fell on the land, he could no longer procure even daily bread. Now when he thought over this by night in his bed, and tossed about in his anxiety, he groaned and said to his wife: "What is to become of us? How are we to feed our poor children, when we no longer have anything even for ourselves?" "I'll tell you what, husband," answered the woman, "early tomorrow morning we will take the children out into the forest to where it is the thickest; there we will light a fire for them, and give each of them one more piece of bread, and then we will go to our work and leave them alone. They will not find the way home again, and we shall be rid of them." "No, wife," said the man, "I will not do that; how can I bear to leave my children alone in the forest?—the wild animals would soon come and tear them to pieces." "O, you fool!" said she, "then we must all four die of hunger, you may as well plane the planks for our coffins," and she left him no peace until he consented. "But I feel very sorry for the poor children, all the same," said the man.

The two children had also not been able to sleep for hunger, and had heard what their stepmother had said to their father. Gretel wept bitter tears, and said to Hansel: "Now all is over with us." "Be quiet, Gretel," said Hansel, "do not distress yourself, I will soon find a way to help us." And when the old folks had fallen asleep, he got up, put on his little coat, opened the door below, and crept outside. The moon shone brightly, and the white pebbles which lay in front of the house glittered like real silver pennies. Hansel stooped and stuffed the little pocket of his coat with as many as he could get in. Then he went back and said to Gretel: "Be comforted, dear little sister, and sleep in peace, God will not forsake us," and he lay down again in his bed. When day dawned, but before the sun had risen, the woman came and awoke the two children, saying: "Get up, you sluggards! we are going into the forest to fetch wood." She gave each a little piece of bread, and said: "There is something for your dinner, but do not eat it up before then, for you will get nothing else." Gretel took the bread under her apron, as Hansel had the pebbles in his pocket. Then they all set out together on the way to the forest. When they had walked a short time, Hansel stood still and peeped back at the house, and did so again and again. His father said: "Hansel, what are you looking at there and staying behind for? Pay attention, and do not forget how to use your legs." "Ah, father," said Hansel, "I am looking at my little white cat, which is sitting up on the roof, and wants to say goodbye to me." The wife said: "Fool, that is not your little cat, that is the morning sun which is shining on the chimneys." Hansel, however, had not been looking back at the cat, but had been constantly throwing one of the white pebble-stones out of his pocket on the road.

When they had reached the middle of the forest, the father said: "Now, children, pile up some wood, and I will light a fire that you may not be cold." Hansel and Gretel gathered brushwood together, as high as a little hill. The brushwood was lighted, and when the flames were burning very high, the woman said: "Now, children, lay yourselves down by the fire and rest, we will go into the forest and cut some wood. When we have done, we will come back and fetch you away."

Hansel and Gretel sat by the fire, and when noon came, each ate a little piece of bread, and as they heard the strokes of the wood-axe they believed that their father was near. It was not the axe, however, but a branch which he had fastened to a withered tree which the wind was blowing backwards and forwards. And as they had been sitting such a long time, their eyes closed with fatigue, and they fell fast asleep. When at last they awoke, it was already dark night. Gretel began to cry and said: "How are we to get out of the forest now?" But Hansel comforted her and said: "Just wait a little, until the moon has risen, and then we will soon find the way." And when the full moon had risen, Hansel took his little sister by the hand, and followed the pebbles which shone like newly-coined silver pieces, and showed them the way.

They walked the whole night long, and by break of day came once more to their father's house. They knocked at the door, and when the woman opened it and saw that it was Hansel and Gretel, she said: "You naughty children, why have you slept so long in the forest?—we thought you were never coming back at all!" The father, however, rejoiced, for it had cut him to the heart to leave them behind alone.

Not long afterwards, there was once more great dearth throughout the land, and the children heard their mother saying at night to their father: "Everything is eaten again,

"Hansel and Grethel [*sic*]." Illustration by R. Emmett Owen for Jacob Grimm, *Grimm's Fairy Stories* (New York: Cupples and Leon Company, 1922). Library of Congress.

we have one half loaf left, and that is the end. The children must go, we will take them farther into the wood, so that they will not find their way out again; there is no other means of saving ourselves!" The man's heart was heavy, and he thought: "It would be better for you to share the last mouthful with your children." The woman, however, would listen to nothing that he had to say, but scolded and reproached him. He who says A must say B, likewise, and as he had yielded the first time, he had to do so a second time also.

The children, however, were still awake and had heard the conversation. When the old folks were asleep, Hansel again got up, and wanted to go out and pick up pebbles as he had done before, but the woman had locked the door, and Hansel could not get out. Nevertheless he comforted his little sister, and said: "Do not cry, Gretel, go to sleep quietly, the good God will help us."

Early in the morning came the woman, and took the children out of their beds. Their piece of bread was given to them, but it was

"Hansel and Grethel [*sic*]." Illustration by R. Emmett Owen for Jacob Grimm, *Grimm's Fairy Stories* (New York: Cupples and Leon Company, 1922). Library of Congress.

still smaller than the time before. On the way into the forest Hansel crumbled his in his pocket, and often stood still and threw a morsel on the ground. "Hansel, why do you stop and look round?" said the father, "go on." "I am looking back at my little pigeon which is sitting on the roof, and wants to say goodbye to me," answered Hansel. "Fool!" said the woman, "that is not your little pigeon, that is the morning sun that is shining on the chimney." Hansel, however little by little, threw all the crumbs on the path.

The woman led the children still deeper into the forest, where they had never in their lives been before. Then a great fire was again made, and the mother said: "Just sit there, you children, and when you are tired you may sleep a little; we are going into the forest to cut wood, and in the evening when we are done, we will come and fetch you away." When it was noon, Gretel shared her piece of bread with Hansel, who had scattered his by the way. Then they fell asleep and evening passed, but no one came to the poor children. They did not awake until it was dark night, and Hansel comforted his little sister and said: "Just wait, Gretel, until the moon rises, and then we shall see the crumbs of bread which I have strewn about, they will show us our way home again." When the moon came they set out, but they found no crumbs, for the many thousands of birds which fly about in the woods and fields had picked them all up. Hansel said to Gretel: "We shall soon find the way," but they did not find it. They walked the whole night and all the next day too from morning till evening, but they did not get out of the forest, and were very hungry, for they had nothing to eat but two or three berries, which grew on the ground. And as they were so weary that their legs would carry them no longer, they lay down beneath a tree and fell asleep.

It was now three mornings since they had left their father's house. They began to walk again, but they always came deeper into the forest, and if help did not come soon, they must die of hunger and weariness. When it was mid-day, they saw a beautiful snow-white bird sitting on a bough, which sang so delightfully that they stood still and listened to it. And when its song was over, it spread its wings and flew away before them, and they followed it until they reached a little house, on the roof of which it alighted; and when they approached the little house they saw that it was built of bread and covered with cakes, but that the windows were of clear sugar. "We will set to work on that," said Hansel, "and have a good meal. I will eat a bit of the roof, and you Gretel, can eat some of the window, it will taste sweet." Hansel reached up above, and broke off a little of the roof to try how it tasted, and Gretel leant against the window and nibbled at the panes. Then a soft voice cried from the parlour:

> *"Nibble, nibble, gnaw,*
> *Who is nibbling at my little house?"*

The children answered:

> *"The wind, the wind,*
> *The heaven-born wind,"*

and went on eating without disturbing themselves. Hansel, who liked the taste of the roof, tore down a great piece of it, and Gretel pushed out the whole of one round window-pane, sat down, and enjoyed herself with it. Suddenly the door opened, and a woman as old as the hills, who supported herself on crutches, came creeping out. Hansel and Gretel were so terribly frightened that they let fall what they had in their hands. The old woman, however, nodded her head, and said: "Oh, you dear children, who has brought you here? Do come in, and stay with me. No harm shall happen to you." She took them both by the hand, and led them into her little house. Then good food was set before them, milk and pancakes, with sugar, apples, and nuts. Afterwards two pretty little beds were covered with clean white linen, and Hansel and Gretel lay down in them, and thought they were in heaven.

The old woman had only pretended to be so kind; she was in reality a wicked witch, who lay in wait for children, and had only built the little house of bread in order to entice them there. When a child fell into her power, she killed it, cooked and ate it, and that was a feast day with her. Witches have red eyes, and cannot see far, but they have a keen scent like the beasts, and are aware when human beings draw near. When Hansel and Gretel came into her neighbourhood, she laughed with malice, and said mockingly: "I have them, they shall not escape me again!" Early in the morning before the children were awake, she was already up, and when she saw both of them sleeping and looking so pretty, with their plump and rosy cheeks she muttered to herself: "That will be a dainty mouthful!" Then she seized Hansel with her shrivelled hand, carried him into a little stable, and locked him in behind a grated door. Scream as he might, it would not help him. Then she went to Gretel, shook her till she awoke, and cried: "Get up, lazy thing, fetch some water, and cook something good for your brother, he is in the stable outside, and is to be made fat. When he is fat, I will eat him." Gretel began to weep bitterly, but it was all in vain, for she was forced to do what the wicked witch commanded.

And now the best food was cooked for poor Hansel, but Gretel got nothing but crab-shells. Every morning the woman crept to the little stable, and cried: "Hansel, stretch out your finger that I may feel if you will soon be fat." Hansel, however, stretched out a little bone to her, and the old woman, who had dim eyes, could not see it, and thought it was Hansel's finger, and was astonished that there was no way of fattening him. When four weeks had gone by, and Hansel still remained thin, she was seized with impatience and would not wait any longer. "Now, then, Gretel," she cried to the girl, "stir yourself, and bring some water. Let Hansel be fat or lean, tomorrow I will kill him, and cook him." Ah, how the poor little sister did lament when she had to fetch the water, and how her tears did flow down her cheeks! "Dear God, do help us," she cried. "If the wild beasts in the forest had but devoured us, we should at any rate have died together." "Just keep your noise to yourself," said the old woman, "it won't help you at all."

Early in the morning, Gretel had to go out and hang up the cauldron with the water, and light the fire. "We will bake first," said the

old woman, "I have already heated the oven, and kneaded the dough."
She pushed poor Gretel out to the oven, from which flames of fire were
already darting. "Creep in," said the witch, "and see if it is properly
heated, so that we can put the bread in." And once Gretel was inside,
she intended to shut the oven and let her bake in it, and then she would
eat her, too. But Gretel saw what she had in mind, and said: "I do not
know how I am to do it; how do I get in?" "Silly goose," said the old
woman. "The door is big enough; just look, I can get in myself!" and
she crept up and thrust her head into the oven. Then Gretel gave her a
push that drove her far into it, and shut the iron door, and fastened the
bolt. Oh! then she began to howl quite horribly, but Gretel ran away
and the godless witch was miserably burnt to death.

Gretel, however, ran like lightning to Hansel, opened his little
stable, and cried: "Hansel, we are saved! The old witch is dead!" Then
Hansel sprang like a bird from its cage when the door is opened. How
they did rejoice and embrace each other, and dance about and kiss each
other! And as they had no longer any need to fear her, they went into
the witch's house, and in every corner there stood chests full of pearls
and jewels. "These are far better than pebbles!" said Hansel, and thrust
into his pockets whatever could be got in, and Gretel said: "I, too, will
take something home with me," and filled her pinafore full. "But now
we must be off," said Hansel, "that we may get out of the witch's forest."

When they had walked for two hours, they came to a great stretch
of water. "We cannot cross," said Hansel, "I see no foot-plank, and no
bridge." "And there is also no ferry," answered Gretel, "but a white duck
is swimming there: if I ask her, she will help us over." Then she cried:

> *"Little duck, little duck, dost thou see,*
> *Hansel and Gretel are waiting for thee?*
> *There's never a plank, or bridge in sight,*
> *Take us across on thy back so white."*

The duck came to them, and Hansel seated himself on its back,
and told his sister to sit by him. "No," replied Gretel, "that will be too

heavy for the little duck; she shall take us across, one after the other."
The good little duck did so, and when they were once safely across and
had walked for a short time, the forest seemed to be more and more
familiar to them, and at length they saw from afar their father's house.
Then they began to run, rushed into the parlour, and threw themselves
round their father's neck. The man had not known one happy hour
since he had left the children in the forest; the woman, however, was
dead. Gretel emptied her pinafore until pearls and precious stones ran
about the room, and Hansel threw one handful after another out of his
pocket to add to them. Then all anxiety was at an end, and they lived
together in perfect happiness. My tale is done, there runs a mouse;
whosoever catches it, may make himself a big fur cap out of it.

"'Perhaps,' said she, 'your name is Rumpelstiltskin?'" Illustration by Rie Cramer for Frances Jenkins Olcott (editor), *Grimm's Fairy Tales* (Philadelphia: The Penn Publishing Company, 1905).

Week Twelve:

RUMPELSTILTSKIN

Grimm's Fairy Tale

y the side of a wood, in a country a long way off, ran a fine stream of water; and upon the stream there stood a mill. The miller's house was close by, and the miller, you must know, had a very beautiful daughter. She was, moreover, very shrewd and clever; and the miller was so proud of her, that he one day told the king of the land, who used to come and hunt in the wood, that his daughter could spin gold out of straw. Now this king was very fond of money; and when he heard the miller's boast his greediness was raised, and he sent for the girl to be brought before him. Then he led her to a chamber in his palace where there was a great heap of straw, and gave her a spinning-wheel, and said, "All this must be spun into gold before morning, as you love your life." It was in vain that the poor maiden said that it was only a silly boast of her father, for that she could do no such thing as spin straw into gold: the chamber door was locked, and she was left alone.

She sat down in one corner of the room, and began to bewail her hard fate; when on a sudden the door opened, and a droll-looking little man hobbled in, and said, "Good morrow to you, my good lass; what are you weeping for?" "Alas!" said she, "I must spin this straw into gold, and I know not how." "What will you give me," said the hobgoblin, "to do it for you?" "My necklace," replied the maiden. He took her at her word, and sat himself down to the wheel, and whistled and sang:

> *"Round about, "round about,*
>   *Lo and behold!*
> *Reel away, reel away,*
>   *Straw into gold!"*

And round about the wheel went merrily; the work was quickly done, and the straw was all spun into gold.

When the king came and saw this, he was greatly astonished and pleased; but his heart grew still more greedy of gain, and he shut up the poor miller's daughter again with a fresh task. Then she knew not what to do, and sat down once more to weep; but the dwarf soon opened the door, and said, "What will you give me to do your task?" "The ring on my finger," said she. So her little friend took the ring, and began to work at the wheel again, and whistled and sang:

> *"Round about, "round about,*
>   *Lo and behold!*
> *Reel away, reel away,*
>   *Straw into gold!"*

till, long before morning, all was done again.

The king was greatly delighted to see all this glittering treasure; but still he had not enough: so he took the miller's daughter to a yet larger heap, and said, "All this must be spun tonight; and if it is, you shall be my queen." As soon as she was alone that dwarf came in, and said, "What will you give me to spin gold for you this third time?" "I have nothing left," said she. "Then say you will give me," said the little man, "the first little child that you may have when you are queen." "That may never be," thought the miller's daughter: and as she knew no other way to get her task done, she said she would do what he asked. Round went the wheel again to the old song, and the manikin once more spun the heap into gold. The king came in the morning, and, finding all he wanted, was forced to keep his word; so he married the miller's daughter, and she really became queen.

At the birth of her first little child she was very glad, and forgot the dwarf, and what she had said. But one day he came into her room, where she was sitting playing with her baby, and put her in mind of it. Then she grieved sorely at her misfortune, and said she would give him all the wealth of the kingdom if he would let her off, but in vain; till at last her tears softened him, and he said, "I will give you three days' grace, and if during that time you tell me my name, you shall keep your child."

Now the queen lay awake all night, thinking of all the odd names that she had ever heard; and she sent messengers all over the land to find out new ones. The next day the little man came, and she began with TIMOTHY, ICHABOD, BENJAMIN, JEREMIAH, and all the names she could remember; but to all and each of them he said, "Madam, that is not my name."

The second day she began with all the comical names she could hear of, BANDY-LEGS, HUNCHBACK, CROOK-SHANKS, and so on; but the little gentleman still said to every one of them, "Madam, that is not my name."

The third day one of the messengers came back, and said, "I have travelled two days without hearing of any other names; but yesterday, as I was climbing a high hill, among the trees of the forest where the fox and the hare bid each other good night, I saw a little hut; and before the hut burnt a fire; and round about the fire a funny little dwarf was dancing upon one leg, and singing:

> *"Merrily the feast I'll make.*
> *Today I'll brew, tomorrow bake;*
> *Merrily I'll dance and sing,*
> *For next day will a stranger bring.*
> *Little does my lady dream*
> *Rumpelstiltskin is my name!"*

When the queen heard this she jumped for joy, and as soon as her little friend came she sat down upon her throne, and called all her court round to enjoy the fun; and the nurse stood by her side with the baby in her arms, as if it was quite ready to be given up. Then the little man began to chuckle at the thought of having the poor child, to take home with him to his hut in the woods; and he cried out, "Now, lady, what is my name?" "Is it JOHN?" asked she. "No, madam!" "Is it TOM?" "No, madam!" "Is it JEMMY?" "It is not." "Can your name be RUMPELSTILTSKIN?" said the lady slyly. "Some witch told you that!—some witch told you that!" cried the little man, and dashed his right foot in a rage so deep into the floor, that he was forced to lay hold of it with both hands to pull it out.

Then he made the best of his way off, while the nurse laughed and the baby crowed; and all the court jeered at him for having had so much trouble for nothing, and said, "We wish you a very good morning, and a merry feast, Mr. RUMPELSTILTSKIN!"

"Rumpelstiltskin." Illustration by R. Emmett Owen for Jacob Grimm, *Grimm's Fairy Stories* (New York: Cupples and Leon Company, 1922). Library of Congress.

Week Twelve:
"CAROL"

When the herds were watching
   In the midnight chill,
Came a spotless lambkin
   From the heavenly hill.

Snow was on the mountains,
   And the wind was cold,
When from God's own garden
   Dropped a rose of gold.

When "twas bitter winter,
   Houseless and forlorn
In a star-lit stable
   Christ the Babe was born.

Welcome, heavenly lambkin;
   Welcome, golden rose;
Alleluia, Baby,
   In the swaddling clothes!

WILLIAM CANTON
(1845–1926)

"Tom Thumb." Illustration by R. Emmett Owen for Jacob Grimm, *Grimm's Fairy Stories* (New York: Cupples and Leon Company, 1922). Library of Congress.

Week Thirteen:
TOM THUMB
English Fairy Tale

A poor woodman sat in his cottage one night, smoking his pipe by the fireside, while his wife sat by his side spinning. "How lonely it is, wife," said he, as he puffed out a long curl of smoke, "for you and me to sit here by ourselves, without any children to play about and amuse us while other people seem so happy and merry with their children!" "What you say is very true," said the wife, sighing, and turning round her wheel; "how happy should I be if I had but one child! If it were ever so small—nay, if it were no bigger than my thumb—I should be very happy, and love it dearly." Now—odd as you may think it—it came to pass that this good woman's wish was fulfilled, just in the very way she had wished it; for, not long afterwards, she had a little boy, who was quite healthy and strong, but was not much bigger than my thumb. So they said, "Well, we cannot say we have not got what we wished for, and, little as he is, we will love him dearly." And they called him Thomas Thumb.

They gave him plenty of food, yet for all they could do he never grew bigger, but kept just the same size as he had been when he was born. Still, his eyes were sharp and sparkling, and he soon showed himself to be a clever little fellow, who always knew well what he was about.

One day, as the woodman was getting ready to go into the wood to cut fuel, he said, "I wish I had someone to bring the cart after me, for I want to make haste." "Oh, father," cried Tom, "I will take care of that; the cart shall be in the wood by the time you want it." Then the woodman laughed, and said, "How can that be? You cannot reach up to the horse's bridle." "Never mind that, father," said Tom; "if my mother will only harness the horse, I will get into his ear and tell him which way to go." "Well," said the father, "we will try for once."

When the time came the mother harnessed the horse to the cart, and put Tom into his ear; and as he sat there the little man told the beast how to go, crying out, "Go on!" and "Stop!" as he wanted: and thus the horse went on just as well as if the woodman had driven it himself into the wood. It happened that as the horse was going a little too fast, and Tom was calling out, "Gently! gently!" two strangers came up. "What an odd thing that is!" said one: "there is a cart going along, and I hear a carter talking to the horse, but yet I can see no one." "That is queer, indeed," said the other; "let us follow the cart, and see where it goes." So they went on into the wood, till at last they came to the place where the woodman was. Then Tom Thumb, seeing his father, cried out, "See, father, here I am with the cart, all right and safe! Now take me down!" So his father took hold of the horse with one hand, and with the other took his son out of the horse's ear, and put him down upon a straw, where he sat as merry as you please.

The two strangers were all this time looking on, and did not know what to say for wonder. At last one took the other aside, and said, "That little urchin will make our fortune, if we can get him, and carry him about from town to town as a show; we must buy him." So they went up to the woodman, and asked him what he would take for the little man. "He will be better off," said they, "with us than with you." "I won't sell him at all," said the father; "my own flesh and blood is dearer to me than all the silver and gold in the world." But Tom, hearing of the bargain they wanted to make, crept up his father's coat to his shoulder and whispered in his ear, "Take the money, father, and let them have me; I'll soon come back to you."

So the woodman at last said he would sell Tom to the strangers for a large piece of gold, and they paid the price. "Where would you like to sit?" said one of them. "Oh, put me on the rim of your hat; that will be a nice gallery for me; I can walk about there and see the country as we go along." So they did as he wished; and when Tom had taken leave of his father they took him away with them.

They journeyed on till it began to be dusky, and then the little man said, "Let me get down, I'm tired." So the man took off his hat, and put him down on a clod of earth, in a ploughed field by the side of the road. But Tom ran about amongst the furrows, and at last slipped into an old mouse-hole. "Good night, my masters!" said he, "I'm off! Mind and look sharp after me the next time." Then they ran at once to the place, and poked the ends of their sticks into the mouse-hole, but all in vain; Tom only crawled farther and farther in; and at last it became quite dark, so that they were forced to go their way without their prize, as sulky as could be.

When Tom found they were gone, he came out of his hiding-place. "What dangerous walking it is," said he, "in this ploughed field! If I were to fall from one of these great clods, I should undoubtedly break my neck." At last, by good luck, he found a large empty snail-shell. "This is lucky," said he, "I can sleep here very well"; and in he crept.

Just as he was falling asleep, he heard two men passing by, chatting together; and one said to the other, "How can we rob that rich parson's house of his silver and gold?" "I'll tell you!" cried Tom. "What noise was that?" said the thief, frightened; "I'm sure I heard someone speak."

"Tom Thumb." Illustration by R. Emmett Owen for Jacob Grimm, *Grimm's Fairy Stories* (New York: Cupples and Leon Company, 1922). Library of Congress.

They stood still listening, and Tom said, "Take me with you, and I'll soon show you how to get the parson's money." "But where are you?" said they. "Look about on the ground," answered he, "and listen where the sound comes from." At last the thieves found him out, and lifted him up in their hands. "You little urchin!" they said, "what can you do for us?" "Why, I can get between the iron window-bars of the parson's house, and throw you out whatever you want." "That's a good thought," said the thieves; "come along, we shall see what you can do."

When they came to the parson's house, Tom slipped through the window-bars into the room, and then called out as loud as he could bawl, "Will you have all that is here?" At this the thieves were frightened, and said, "Softly, softly! Speak low, that you may not awaken anybody." But Tom seemed as if he did not understand them, and bawled out again, "How much will you have? Shall I throw it all out?" Now the cook lay in the next room; and hearing a noise she raised herself up in her bed and listened. Meantime the thieves were frightened, and ran off a little way; but at last they plucked up their hearts, and said, "The little urchin is only trying to make fools of us." So they came back and whispered softly to him, saying, "Now let us have no more of your roguish jokes; but throw us out some of the money." Then Tom called out as loud as he could, "Very well! hold your hands! here it comes."

The cook heard this quite plain, so she sprang out of bed, and ran to open the door. The thieves ran off as if a wolf was at their tails: and the maid, having groped about and found nothing, went away for a light. By the time she came back, Tom had slipped off into the barn; and when she had looked about and searched every hole and corner, and found nobody, she went to bed, thinking she must have been dreaming with her eyes open.

The little man crawled about in the hay-loft, and at last found a snug place to finish his night's rest in; so he laid himself down, meaning to sleep till daylight, and then find his way home to his father and mother. But alas! how woefully he was undone! What crosses and sorrows happen to us all in this world! The cook got up early, before daybreak, to feed the cows; and going straight to the hay-loft, carried away a large bundle of hay, with the little man in the middle of it, fast asleep. He still, however, slept on, and did not awake till he found himself in the mouth of the cow; for the cook had put the hay into the cow's rick, and the cow had taken Tom up in a mouthful of it. "Good lack-a-day!" said he, "How came I to tumble into the mill?" But he soon found out where he really was; and was forced to have all his wits about him, that he might not get between the cow's teeth, and so be crushed to death. At last down he went into her stomach. "It is rather dark," said he; "they forgot to build windows in this room to let the sun in; a candle would be no bad thing."

Though he made the best of his bad luck, he did not like his quarters at all; and the worst of it was, that more and more hay was always coming down, and the space left for him became smaller and smaller. At last he cried out as loud as he could, "Don't bring me any more hay! Don't bring me any more hay!"

The maid happened to be just then milking the cow; and hearing someone speak, but seeing nobody, and yet being quite sure it was the same voice that she had heard in the night, she was so frightened that she fell off her stool, and overset the milk-pail. As soon as she could pick herself up out of the dirt, she ran off as fast as she could to her master the parson, and said, "Sir, sir, the cow is talking!" But the parson said, "Woman, thou art surely mad!" However, he went with her into the cow-house, to try and see what was the matter.

Scarcely had they set foot on the threshold, when Tom called out, "Don't bring me any more hay!" Then the parson himself was frightened; and thinking the cow was surely bewitched, told his man to kill her on the spot. So the cow was killed, and cut up; and the stomach, in which Tom lay, was thrown out upon a dunghill.

Tom soon set himself to work to get out, which was not a very easy task; but at last, just as he had made room to get his head out, fresh ill-luck befell him. A hungry wolf sprang out, and swallowed up the whole stomach, with Tom in it, at one gulp, and ran away.

Tom, however, was still not disheartened; and thinking the wolf would not dislike having some chat with him as he was going along, he called out, "My good friend, I can show you a famous treat." "Where's that?" said the wolf. "In such and such a house," said Tom, describing his own father's house. "You can crawl through the drain into the kitchen and then into the pantry, and there you will find cakes, ham, beef, cold chicken, roast pig, apple-dumplings, and everything that your heart can wish."

The wolf did not want to be asked twice; so that very night he went to the house and crawled through the drain into the kitchen, and then into the pantry, and ate and drank there to his heart's content. As soon as he had had enough he wanted to get away; but he had eaten so much that he could not go out by the same way he came in.

This was just what Tom had reckoned upon; and now he began to set up a great shout, making all the noise he could. "Will you be easy?" said the wolf; "you'll awaken everybody in the house if you make such a clatter." "What's that to me?" said the little man; "you have had your frolic, now I've a mind to be merry myself'; and he began, singing and shouting as loud as he could.

The woodman and his wife, being awakened by the noise, peeped through a crack in the door; but when they saw a wolf was there, you may well suppose that they were sadly frightened; and the woodman ran for his axe, and gave his wife a scythe. "Do you stay behind," said the woodman, "and when I have knocked him on the head you must rip him up with the scythe." Tom heard all this, and cried out, "Father, father! I am here, the wolf has swallowed me." And his father said, "Heaven be praised! We have found our dear child again'; and he told his wife not to use the scythe for fear she should hurt him. Then he aimed a great blow, and struck the wolf on the head, and killed him on the spot! And when he was dead they cut open his body, and set Tommy free. "Ah!" said the father, "what fears we have had for you!" "Yes, father," answered he; "I have travelled all over the world, I think, in one way or other, since we parted; and now I am very glad to come home and get fresh air again." "Why, where have you been?" said his father. "I have been in a mouse-hole—and in a snail-shell—and down a cow's throat—and in the wolf's belly; and yet here I am again, safe and sound."

"Well," said they, "you are come back, and we will not sell you again for all the riches in the world."

Then they hugged and kissed their dear little son, and gave him plenty to eat and drink, for he was very hungry; and then they fetched new clothes for him, for his old ones had been quite spoiled on his journey. So Master Thumb stayed at home with his father and mother, in peace; for though he had been so great a traveller, and had done and seen so many fine things, and was fond enough of telling the whole story, he always agreed that, after all, there's no place like HOME!

"The elves began to stitch, sew, and hammer." Illustration by Rie Cramer for Frances Jenkins Olcott (editor), *Grimm's Fairy Tales* (Philadelphia: The Penn Publishing Company, 1905).

Week Thirteen:

THE ELVES AND THE SHOEMAKER

Grimm's Fairy Tale

There was once a shoemaker, who worked very hard and was very honest: but still he could not earn enough to live upon; and at last all he had in the world was gone, save just leather enough to make one pair of shoes.

Then he cut his leather out, all ready to make up the next day, meaning to rise early in the morning to his work. His conscience was clear and his heart light amidst all his troubles; so he went peaceably to bed, left all his cares to Heaven, and soon fell asleep. In the morning after he had said his prayers, he sat himself down to his work; when, to his great wonder, there stood the shoes all ready made, upon the table. The good man knew not what to say or think at such an odd thing happening. He looked at the workmanship; there was not one false stitch in the whole job; all was so neat and true, that it was quite a masterpiece.

The same day a customer came in, and the shoes suited him so well that he willingly paid a price higher than usual for them; and the poor shoemaker, with the money, bought leather enough to make two pairs more. In the evening he cut out the work, and went to bed early, that he might get up and begin betimes next day; but he was saved all the trouble, for when he got up in the morning the work was done ready to his hand. Soon in came buyers, who paid him handsomely for his goods, so that he bought leather enough for four pair more. He

cut out the work again overnight and found it done in the morning, as before; and so it went on for some time: what was got ready in the evening was always done by daybreak, and the good man soon became thriving and well off again.

One evening, about Christmas-time, as he and his wife were sitting over the fire chatting together, he said to her, "I should like to sit up and watch tonight, that we may see who it is that comes and does my work for me." The wife liked the thought; so they left a light burning, and hid themselves in a corner of the room, behind a curtain that was hung up there, and watched what would happen.

As soon as it was midnight, there came in two little naked dwarfs; and they sat themselves upon the shoemaker's bench, took up all the work that was cut out, and began to ply with their little fingers, stitching and rapping and tapping away at such a rate, that the shoemaker was all wonder, and could not take his eyes off them. And on they went, till the job was quite done, and the shoes stood ready for use upon the

"The Elves and the Cobbler." Illustrator unknown for Edna Henry Lee Turpin, *Grimm's Fairy Tales* (New York: Maynard, Merrill, & Co., 1903). Harvard University.

table. This was long before daybreak; and then they bustled away as quick as lightning.

The next day the wife said to the shoemaker. "These little wights have made us rich, and we ought to be thankful to them, and do them a good turn if we can. I am quite sorry to see them run about as they do; and indeed it is not very decent, for they have nothing upon their backs to keep off the cold. I'll tell you what, I will make each of them a shirt, and a coat and waistcoat, and a pair of pantaloons into the bargain; and do you make each of them a little pair of shoes."

The thought pleased the good cobbler very much; and one evening, when all the things were ready, they laid them on the table, instead of the work that they used to cut out, and then went and hid themselves, to watch what the little elves would do.

About midnight in they came, dancing and skipping, hopped round the room, and then went to sit down to their work as usual; but when they saw the clothes lying for them, they laughed and chuckled, and seemed mightily delighted.

Then they dressed themselves in the twinkling of an eye, and danced and capered and sprang about, as merry as could be; till at last they danced out at the door, and away over the green.

The good couple saw them no more; but everything went well with them from that time forward, as long as they lived.

Illustration by Richard Rhodes from *Poetic Pearls with Notes and Illustrations* (Chicago: Rhodes & McClure, 1885).

Week Thirteen:
"THE CHARGE OF THE LIGHT BRIGADE"

Half a league, half a league,
Half a league onward,
All in the valley of Death
Rode the six hundred.
"Forward, the Light Brigade!
Charge for the guns!" he said:
Into the valley of Death
Rode the six hundred.

"Forward, the Light Brigade!"
Was there a man dismay'd?
Not tho' the soldier knew
Some one had blunder'd:
Theirs not to make reply,
Theirs not to reason why.
Theirs but to do and die:
Into the valley of Death
Rode the six hundred.

Cannon to right of them,
Cannon to left of them,
Cannon in front of them
Volley'd and thunder'd;
Storm'd at with shot and shell
Boldly they rode and well,
Into the jaws of Death,
Into the mouth of Hell
Rode the six hundred.

Flash'd all their sabers bare,
Flash'd as they turn'd in air
Sab'ring the gunners there,
Charging an army, while
All the world wonder'd:
Plunged in the battery-smoke
Right thro' the line they broke;
Cossack and Russian
Reel'd from the saber-stroke
Shatter'd and sunder'd.
Then they rode back, but not
Not the six hundred.

Cannon to right of them,
Cannon to left of them,
Cannon behind them
Volleyed and thundered:
Stormed at with shot and shell,
While horse and hero fell,
They that had fought so well
Came through the jaws of death
Back from the mouth of hell,
All that was left of them—
Left of six hundred.

When can their glory fade?
Oh, the wild charge they made!
All the world wondered.
Honour the charge they made!
Honour the Light Brigade—
Noble six hundred!

ALFRED, LORD TENNYSON
(1809–1892)

Week Fourteen:

LITTLE RED RIDING HOOD

Grimm's Fairy Tale

Once upon a time there was a dear little girl who was loved by everyone who looked at her, but most of all by her grandmother, and there was nothing that she would not have given to the child. Once she gave her a little cap of red velvet, which suited her so well that she would never wear anything else; so she was always called "Little Red-Cap."

One day her mother said to her: "Come, Little Red-Cap, here is a piece of cake and a bottle of wine; take them to your grandmother, she is ill and weak, and they will do her good. Set out before it gets hot, and when you are going, walk nicely and quietly and do not run off the path, or you may fall and break the bottle, and then your grandmother will get nothing; and when you go into her room, don't forget to say, "Good morning", and don't peep into every corner before you do it."

"I will take great care," said Little Red-Cap to her mother, and gave her hand on it.

The grandmother lived out in the wood, half a league from the village, and just as Little Red-Cap entered the wood, a wolf met her. Red-Cap did not know what a wicked creature he was, and was not at all afraid of him.

"Good day, Little Red-Cap," said he.

"Thank you kindly, wolf."

"Whither away so early, Little Red-Cap?"

"To my grandmother's."

"She met a rascally old wolf." Illustration by Honor C. Appleton for Charles Perrault, *Perault's Fairy Tales* (Boston: Dana Estes & Co.; London: Herbert & Daniel, 1911).

"What have you got in your apron?"

"Cake and wine; yesterday was baking-day, so poor sick grandmother is to have something good, to make her stronger."

"Where does your grandmother live, Little Red-Cap?"

"A good quarter of a league farther on in the wood; her house stands under the three large oak-trees, the nut-trees are just below; you surely must know it," replied Little Red-Cap.

The wolf thought to himself: "What a tender young creature! what a nice plump mouthful—she will be better to eat than the old woman. I must act craftily, so as to catch both." So he walked for a short time by the side of Little Red-Cap, and then he said: "See, Little Red-Cap, how pretty the flowers are about here—why do you not look round? I believe, too, that you do not hear how sweetly the little birds are singing; you walk gravely along as if you were going to school, while everything else out here in the wood is merry."

Little Red-Cap raised her eyes, and when she saw the sunbeams dancing here and there through the trees, and pretty flowers growing everywhere, she thought: "Suppose I take grandmother a fresh nosegay; that would please her too. It is so early in the day that I shall still get there in good time'; and so she ran from the path into the wood to look for flowers. And whenever she had picked one, she fancied that she saw a still prettier one farther on, and ran after it, and so got deeper and deeper into the wood.

Meanwhile the wolf ran straight to the grandmother's house and knocked at the door.

"Who is there?"

"Little Red-Cap," replied the wolf. "She is bringing cake and wine; open the door."

"Lift the latch," called out the grandmother, "I am too weak, and cannot get up."

The wolf lifted the latch, the door sprang open, and without saying a word he went straight to the grandmother's bed, and devoured her. Then he put on her clothes, dressed himself in her cap, laid himself in bed and drew the curtains.

Little Red-Cap, however, had been running about picking flowers, and when she had gathered so many that she could carry no more, she remembered her grandmother, and set out on the way to her.

She was surprised to find the cottage-door standing open, and when she went into the room, she had such a strange feeling that she said to herself: "Oh dear! how uneasy I feel today, and at other times I like being with grandmother so much." She called out: "Good morning," but received no answer; so she went to the bed and drew back the curtains. There lay her grandmother with her cap pulled far over her face, and looking very strange.

"Oh! grandmother," she said, "what big ears you have!"

"The better to hear you with, my child," was the reply.

"But, grandmother, what big eyes you have!" she said.

"The better to see you with, my dear."

"But, grandmother, what large hands you have!"

"The better to hug you with."

"Oh! but, grandmother, what a terrible big mouth you have!"

"The better to eat you with!"

And scarcely had the wolf said this, than with one bound he was out of bed and swallowed up Red-Cap.

When the wolf had appeased his appetite, he lay down again in the bed, fell asleep and began to snore very loud. The huntsman was just passing the house, and thought to himself: "How the old woman is snoring! I must just see if she wants anything." So he went into the room, and when he came to the bed, he saw that the wolf was lying in it. "Do I find you here, you old sinner!" said he. "I have long sought you!" Then just as he was going to fire at him, it occurred to him that the wolf might have devoured the grandmother, and that she might still be saved, so he did not fire, but took a pair of scissors, and began to cut open the stomach of the sleeping wolf. When he had made two snips, he saw the little Red-Cap shining, and then he made two snips more, and the little girl sprang out, crying: "Ah, how frightened I have been! How dark it was inside the wolf'; and after that the aged grandmother came out alive also, but scarcely able to breathe. Red-Cap, however, quickly fetched great stones with which they filled the wolf's belly, and when he awoke, he wanted to run away, but the stones were so heavy that he collapsed at once, and fell dead.

Then all three were delighted. The huntsman drew off the wolf's skin and went home with it; the grandmother ate the cake and drank the wine which Red-Cap had brought, and revived, but Red-Cap thought to herself: "As long as I live, I will never by myself leave the path, to run into the wood, when my mother has forbidden me to do so."

It also related that once when Red-Cap was again taking cakes to the old grandmother, another wolf spoke to her, and tried to entice her from the path. Red-Cap, however, was on her guard, and went straight forward on her way, and told her grandmother that she had met the wolf, and that he had said "good morning" to her, but with such a wicked look in his eyes, that if they had not been on the public road she was certain he would have eaten her up. "Well," said the grandmother, "we will shut the door, that he may not come in." Soon afterwards the wolf knocked, and cried: "Open the door, grandmother, I am Little Red-Cap, and am bringing you some cakes." But they did not speak, or open the door, so the grey-beard stole twice or thrice round the house, and at last jumped on the roof, intending to wait until Red-Cap went home in the evening, and then to steal after her and devour her in the darkness. But the grandmother saw what was in his thoughts. In front of the house was a great stone trough, so she said to the child: "Take the pail, Red-Cap; I made some sausages yesterday, so carry the water in which I boiled them to the trough." Red-Cap carried until the great trough was quite full. Then the smell of the sausages reached the wolf, and he sniffed and peeped down, and at last stretched out his neck so far that he could no longer keep his footing and began to slip, and slipped down from the roof straight into the great trough, and was drowned. But Red-Cap went joyously home, and no one ever did anything to harm her again.

"'Yes,' said she, 'now I am emperor.'" Illustration by Rie Cramer for Frances Jenkins Olcott (editor), *Grimm's Fairy Tales* (Philadelphia: The Penn Publishing Company, 1905).

Week Fourteen:
The Fisherman
and His Wife
Grimm's Fairy Tale

There was once a fisherman who lived with his wife in a pigsty, close by the seaside. The fisherman used to go out all day long a-fishing; and one day, as he sat on the shore with his rod, looking at the sparkling waves and watching his line, all of a sudden his float was dragged away deep into the water: and in drawing it up he pulled out a great fish. But the fish said, "Pray let me live! I am not a real fish; I am an enchanted prince: put me in the water again, and let me go!" "Oh, ho!" said the man, "you need not make so many words about the matter; I will have nothing to do with a fish that can talk: so swim away, sir, as soon as you please!" Then he put him back into the water, and the fish darted straight down to the bottom, and left a long streak of blood behind him on the wave.

When the fisherman went home to his wife in the pigsty, he told her how he had caught a great fish, and how it had told him it was an enchanted prince, and how, on hearing it speak, he had let it go again. "Did not you ask it for anything?" said the wife, "we live very wretchedly here, in this nasty dirty pigsty; do go back and tell the fish we want a snug little cottage."

The fisherman did not much like the business: however, he went to the seashore; and when he came back there the water looked all yellow and green. And he stood at the water's edge, and said:

> *"O man of the sea!*
> *Hearken to me!*
> *My wife Ilsabill*
> *Will have her own will,*
> *And hath sent me to beg a boon of thee!"*

Then the fish came swimming to him, and said, "Well, what is her will? What does your wife want?" "Ah!" said the fisherman, "she says that when I had caught you, I ought to have asked you for something before I let you go; she does not like living any longer in the pigsty, and wants a snug little cottage." "Go home, then," said the fish; "she is in the cottage already!" So the man went home, and saw his wife standing at the door of a nice trim little cottage. "Come in, come in!" said she; "is not this much better than the filthy pigsty we had?" And there was a parlour, and a bedchamber, and a kitchen; and behind the cottage there was a little garden, planted with all sorts of flowers and fruits; and there was a courtyard behind, full of ducks and chickens. "Ah!" said the fisherman, "how happily we shall live now!" "We will try to do so, at least," said his wife.

Everything went right for a week or two, and then Dame Ilsabill said, "Husband, there is not near room enough for us in this cottage; the courtyard and the garden are a great deal too small; I should like to have a large stone castle to live in: go to the fish again and tell him to give us a castle." "Wife," said the fisherman, "I don't like to go to him again, for perhaps he will be angry; we ought to be easy with this pretty cottage to live in." "Nonsense!" said the wife; "he will do it very willingly, I know; go along and try!"

The fisherman went, but his heart was very heavy: and when he came to the sea, it looked blue and gloomy, though it was very calm; and he went close to the edge of the waves, and said:

> *"O man of the sea!*
> *Hearken to me!*
> *My wife Ilsabill*

> *Will have her own will,*
> *And hath sent me to beg a boon of thee!"*

"Well, what does she want now?" said the fish. "Ah!" said the man, dolefully, "my wife wants to live in a stone castle." "Go home, then," said the fish; "she is standing at the gate of it already." So away went the fisherman, and found his wife standing before the gate of a great castle. "See," said she, "is not this grand?" With that they went into the castle together, and found a great many servants there, and the rooms all richly furnished, and full of golden chairs and tables; and behind the castle was a garden, and around it was a park half a mile long, full of sheep, and goats, and hares, and deer; and in the courtyard were stables and cow-houses. "Well," said the man, "now we will live cheerful and happy in this beautiful castle for the rest of our lives." "Perhaps we may," said the wife; "but let us sleep upon it, before we make up our minds to that." So they went to bed.

The next morning when Dame Ilsabill awoke it was broad daylight, and she jogged the fisherman with her elbow, and said, "Get up, husband, and bestir yourself, for we must be king of all the land." "Wife, wife," said the man, "why should we wish to be the king? I will not be king." "Then I will," said she. "But, wife," said the fisherman, "how can you be king—the fish cannot make you a king?" "Husband," said she, "say no more about it, but go and try! I will be king." So the man went away quite sorrowful to think that his wife should want to be king. This time the sea looked a dark grey colour, and was overspread with curling waves and the ridges of foam as he cried out:

> *"O man of the sea!*
> *Hearken to me!*
> *My wife Ilsabill*
> *Will have her own will,*
> *And hath sent me to beg a boon of thee!"*

"Well, what would she have now?" said the fish. "Alas!" said the poor man, "my wife wants to be king." "Go home," said the fish; "she is king already."

Then the fisherman went home; and as he came close to the palace he saw a troop of soldiers, and heard the sound of drums and trumpets. And when he went in he saw his wife sitting on a throne of gold and diamonds, with a golden crown upon her head; and on each side of her stood six fair maidens, each a head taller than the other. "Well, wife," said the fisherman, "are you king?" "Yes," said she, "I am king." And when he had looked at her for a long time, he said, "Ah, wife! what a fine thing it is to be king! Now we shall never have anything more to wish for as long as we live." "I don't know how that may be," said she; "never is a long time. I am king, it is true; but I begin to be tired of that, and I think I should like to be emperor." "Alas, wife! why should you wish to be emperor?" said the fisherman. "Husband," said she, "go to the fish! I say I will be emperor." "Ah, wife!" replied the fisherman, "the fish cannot make an emperor, I am sure, and I should not like to ask him for such a thing." "I am king," said Ilsabill, "and you are my slave; so go at once!"

So the fisherman was forced to go; and he muttered as he went along, "This will come to no good, it is too much to ask; the fish will be tired at last, and then we shall be sorry for what we have done." He soon came to the seashore; and the water was quite black and muddy, and a mighty whirlwind blew over the waves and rolled them about, but he went as near as he could to the water's brink, and said:

> "*O man of the sea!*
> *Hearken to me!*
> *My wife Ilsabill*
> *Will have her own will,*
> *And hath sent me to beg a boon of thee!*"

"What would she have now?" said the fish. "Ah!" said the fisherman, "she wants to be emperor." "Go home," said the fish; "she is emperor already."

So he went home again; and as he came near he saw his wife Ilsabill sitting on a very lofty throne made of solid gold, with a great crown on her head full two yards high; and on each side of her stood her guards and attendants in a row, each one smaller than the other, from the tallest giant down to a little dwarf no bigger than my finger. And before her stood princes, and dukes, and earls: and the fisherman went up to her and said, "Wife, are you emperor?" "Yes," said she, "I am emperor." "Ah!" said the man, as he gazed upon her, "what a fine thing it is to be emperor!" "Husband," said she, "why should we stop at being emperor? I will be pope next." "O wife, wife!" said he, "how can you be pope? There is but one pope at a time in Christendom." "Husband," said she, "I will be pope this very day." "But," replied the husband, "the fish cannot make you pope." "What nonsense!" said she; "if he can make an emperor, he can make a pope: go and try him." So the fisherman

"What do you want?" Illustrator unknown for Wilhelm Grimm, *Grimm's Fairy Tales: Retold in One-Syllable Words* (New York: McLoughlin Brothers, 1899). University of North Carolina at Chapel Hill.

went. But when he came to the shore the wind was raging and the sea was tossed up and down in boiling waves, and the ships were in trouble, and rolled fearfully upon the tops of the billows. In the middle of the heavens there was a little piece of blue sky, but towards the south all was red, as if a dreadful storm was rising. At this sight the fisherman was dreadfully frightened, and he trembled so that his knees knocked together: but still he went down near to the shore, and said:

> *"O man of the sea!*
> *Hearken to me!*
> *My wife Ilsabill*
> *Will have her own will,*
> *And hath sent me to beg a boon of thee!"*

"What does she want now?" said the fish. "Ah!" said the fisherman, "my wife wants to be pope." "Go home," said the fish; "she is pope already."

Then the fisherman went home, and found Ilsabill sitting on a throne that was two miles high. And she had three great crowns on her head, and around her stood all the pomp and power of the Church. And on each side of her were two rows of burning lights, of all sizes, the greatest as large as the highest and biggest tower in the world, and the least no larger than a small rushlight. "Wife," said the fisherman, as he looked at all this greatness, "are you pope?" "Yes," said she, "I am pope." "Well, wife," replied he, "it is a grand thing to be pope; and now you must be easy, for you can be nothing greater." "I will think about that," said the wife. Then they went to bed: but Dame Ilsabill could not sleep all night for thinking what she should be next. At last, as she was dropping asleep, morning broke, and the sun rose. "Ha!" thought she, as she woke up and looked at it through the window, "after all I cannot prevent the sun rising." At this thought she was very angry, and wakened her husband, and said, "Husband, go to the fish and tell him I must be lord of the sun and moon." The fisherman was half asleep, but the thought frightened him so much that he started and fell out of bed.

"Alas, wife!" said he, "cannot you be easy with being pope?" "No," said she, "I am very uneasy as long as the sun and moon rise without my leave. Go to the fish at once!"

Then the man went shivering with fear; and as he was going down to the shore a dreadful storm arose, so that the trees and the very rocks shook. And all the heavens became black with stormy clouds, and the lightnings played, and the thunders rolled; and you might have seen in the sea great black waves, swelling up like mountains with crowns of white foam upon their heads. And the fisherman crept towards the sea, and cried out, as well as he could:

> *"O man of the sea!*
> *Hearken to me!*
> *My wife Ilsabill*
> *Will have her own will,*
> *And hath sent me to beg a boon of thee!"*

"What does she want now?" said the fish. "Ah!" said he, "she wants to be lord of the sun and moon." "Go home," said the fish, "to your pigsty again."

And there they live to this very day.

Week Fourteen:
"To a Snowflake"

What heart could have thought you?—
Past our devisal
(O filigree petal!)
Fashioned so purely,
Fragilely, surely,
From what Paradisal
Imagineless metal,
Too costly for cost?
Who hammered you, wrought you,
From argentine vapor?—
God was my shaper.
Passing surmisal,
He hammered, He wrought me,
From curled silver vapor,
To lust of His mind:—
Thou couldst not have thought me!
So purely, so palely,
Tinily, surely,
Mightily, frailly,
Insculped and embossed,
With His hammer of wind,
And His graver of frost."

Francis Thompson
(1859–1907)

"Beauty and the Beast." Illustration by John D. Batten for Joseph Jacobs, *Europa's Fairy Book* (New York and London: The Knickerbocker Press, 1916). Project Gutenberg EBook.

Week Fifteen:
BEAUTY AND THE BEAST
French Fairy Tale

Once upon a time, a long while ago, there was a Beast.

He was a Great Beast, and lived in a Great Castle that stood in the middle of a Great Park, and everybody in the country held the Beast in great fear. In fact everything about the Beast was great; his roar was great and terrific and could be heard for miles around the park, and when he roared the people trembled.

Nobody ever saw the Beast, which was by no means remarkable, for the Beast never came out of his Park, and no one, I can assure you, ever ventured on to his estate.

But matters were not allowed to remain like this for ever, for something very wonderful happened to the Beast and to somebody else, and if that something had not happened this story would never have been written.

About two miles and three quarters from the Castle gates there lived a rich merchant and his three daughters. The two elder girls were ugly disagreeable things, and although they had all they could wish for to make them happy they were always grumbling; but the youngest daughter, whose name was Beauty, was very pretty, and her nature was happy and good, her presence was sunshine, and she was the joy of her father's heart.

Well, one day the two elder sisters had something to grumble about with a vengeance, for a telegram arrived to say that the merchant was no longer a rich merchant, for he had lost all his money.

So the horses and carriages had to be sold, and everything that was of value was got rid of, the servants were sent away, and the merchant and his daughters had to do their own work.

Dear me, it was shocking, the way those two sisters grumbled, but Beauty, oh dear no, she was all smiles, for her heart was as sunny as ever, as she rolled up the sleeves of her print frock, and cooked the dinner, and scrubbed the floors, and made herself useful, here, there, and everywhere.

Things had been going on like this for about three months, when one fine morning another telegram boy came with another telegram to say that somebody who owed the merchant a great deal of money was ready to pay the debt, and all the merchant had to do was to go to the city and get it.

Of course, everybody was delighted at this good news, and the merchant didn't waste any time, but started off to the city at once.

"Mind you bring me something back," said the eldest daughter as he was starting.

"What shall it be?" asked the merchant.

"A white satin dress trimmed with lace and pearls," said his eldest daughter.

"And you must bring me something too, please, father," said the second daughter.

"And what do you want," asked the merchant.

"A purse full of gold so that I can buy what I want myself," said the second daughter.

"I will try and do what you both ask," he said, "and what shall I bring for my Beauty?"

"I will wait a little for my dresses and things," replied the smiling Beauty, as she helped her father on with his cloak, "but I should like you to bring me home a rose, a lovely red rose, if you can."

So her father kissed her, and promised he would bring her the rose, and went on his way full of hopes.

What a pity it is that our hopes cannot be always realized, and that we are so often doomed to disappointment! When the merchant arrived at the city, to his dismay he found that the man who owed him the money was still unable to pay him, the man had been disappointed himself at the last moment.

So the unhappy father had to return home without the white satin dress trimmed with lace and pearls, and without the bag of money, and he dreaded meeting his two daughters, for he knew they would be terribly angry.

Now on his way home from the station to his house he had to pass by part of the wall that surrounded the Great Park where the Great Beast lived in his Great Castle; and as he passed by a corner of the wall what should he see hanging just over the top, and just within his reach if he stood on his toes, but a lovely red rose.

"At any rate I can take my Beauty what she asked for," he said to himself, and, without so much as giving a thought to the wrong he was doing, he stood on his toes and plucked the rose.

He was sorry he did it.

Of a sudden there was a roar, such a roar that the very ground shook, and as to the poor merchant he quivered like a leaf.

Enough to make him quiver indeed, for a gate in the wall suddenly opened, and out rushed the Beast.

Yes, the Beast, if you please, and he seized the merchant by the scruff of his neck, and dragged him into the Park, and shut the gate after him.

"Don't you know it's a sin to steal?" roared the Beast. "How dare you steal my roses? I am going to kill you."

"Oh, mercy, Mr. Beast," cried the unhappy man, flinging himself on his knees before the monster.

"I'm going to kill you," roared the Beast still more loudly. "It's taken years to cultivate this sort of rose, and—and I'm going to kill you. Unless," he added after a pause, "you send me one of your daughters here instead."

"All right," said the merchant and got on his feet again.

"She must be here to-morrow by breakfast time, and I breakfast early," said the Beast, as he let the merchant out of the gate. "If she is not here, I shall come for you, and don't you forget it."

It was by no means likely that he would forget it, in fact he could think of nothing else. He hurried home and told his dreadful news, and received a dreadful scolding from his two elder daughters, who were angry at not getting their presents.

"And it is Beauty's fault that you have got into this trouble," they said. "Beauty and her stupid rose. Beauty had better get you out of the trouble." Beauty said little, but smiled on, with sunshine in her heart, and trust in her loving nature, and cooked the dinner.

Early next morning when the dawn was breaking she left her father's house, leaving a little note behind her begging him not to be anxious but that she had gone to the Beast's castle.

When she came to the gate in the wall she knocked upon it three times and it opened as if by magic, for she could see no one. And she stepped into the garden of red roses, and in the distance across the Park she saw the Castle, and she thought she had never seen anything so beautiful. For it was built of mother-of-pearl, and the red and yellow gleams of the rising sun shone upon its glistening walls, and lit them up with a thousand radiant lights.

Beauty marvelled at the loveliness and walked on. And when she arrived at this beautiful Castle, the huge gates opened as if by magic, and the doors opened as if by magic, for never a soul did she see, nor living thing of any sort.

And in the great hall was the breakfast table laid for two. It was a nice breakfast with steaming hot dishes, and jams, honey, and hot rolls, and brightly polished silver, and sweet flowers.

Then the Beast appeared suddenly from behind a curtain; oh, he was an awful Beast, and Beauty's heart beat fast! But he seemed a polite Beast for all that.

He handed Beauty a chair, and when she had sat down said:

"I bid you welcome; which do you take, tea or coffee?"

"Tea please," answered Beauty.

"Then pour it out," he said, "and I'll take tea too, please. Eggs, do you like eggs hard or soft?"

"I always cook mine three minutes and a half," replied Beauty.

"Half a minute too much, I think. But you shall have just what you like."

And so she had; not only at the breakfast table but in everything. She had only to express a wish and it was immediately gratified. She had ponies to ride, and dogs and cats, and pet birds, and the most beautiful dresses ever worn by real princesses.

And if it had not been that she was away from her father she would really have been happy.

The Beast was most kind and attentive to her, and told her that he loved her, and three times a day he asked her to marry him, but Beauty shook her head and said, oh no, she couldn't.

Well, Beauty had been at the great Castle some time when she began to pine to go home and see her father, and she begged the Beast to let her go.

"Very good," he said with a great sigh, "you may go home to-day, but promise me that you will be back early to-morrow morning. If you do not come back early I am sure I shall die for I love you so dearly."

So Beauty promised and went home, and she took presents for her father and her sisters, and when the sisters heard of all the wonderful things at the great Castle, they were envious and jealous, and made up their minds to do Beauty and the Beast a great injury.

So they mixed something in Beauty's supper that made her sleep nearly all the next day, and so she did not keep her promise. It was evening when she arrived at the gate in the wall, instead of early morning.

But she knocked three times and the gate opened by magic, and she went through the garden and hurried to the Castle, that shone like fire in the light of the setting sun. And the huge gates opened by magic, and the doors opened by magic, and she stood in the great hall, but there was no Beast there. She searched in all the rooms but he was not there; with fear and anxiety in her heart she ran into the gardens, and there she found him at last. Found him lying stretched out on the grass, and she thought he was dead.

"Oh, dear darling Beast," she cried, as she threw herself on her knees beside him, and raised his ugly head, "dear Beast, do not die, for I love you with all my heart, and will marry you to-morrow." And she kissed him. Then of a sudden he sprang to his feet, but no longer the Beast, no longer a hideous monster, but a beautiful prince most beautifully dressed. "Dearest," he said, "a wicked fairy turned me into this brute form until a day should come when a good girl like you should tell me that she loved me. And you will marry me to-morrow."

"Oh, yes," answered Beauty, "but the wicked fairy could not change your nature. I would have married you if you had remained just as you were."

And so they married and lived happy ever afterwards, and they took care of Beauty's father until the end of his days; so he was happy, and they forgave the two sisters and gave them fine dresses and jewels, and the two sisters turned over a new leaf and were less selfish, and they were happy, so this is a very happy ending to the story.

What a pity all stories can't end the same way!

Week Fifteen:
PUSS IN BOOTS
French Fairy Tale

A certain miller had three sons, and when he died the sole worldly goods which he bequeathed to them were his mill, his ass, and his cat. This little legacy was very quickly divided up, and you may be quite sure that neither notary nor attorney were called in to help, for they would speedily have grabbed it all for themselves.

The eldest son took the mill, and the second son took the ass. Consequently all that remained for the youngest son was the cat, and he was not a little disappointed at receiving such a miserable portion.

"My brothers," said he, "will be able to get a decent living by joining forces, but for my part, as soon as I have eaten my cat and made a muff out of his skin, I am bound to die of hunger."

These remarks were overheard by Puss, who pretended not to have been listening, and said very soberly and seriously:

"There is not the least need for you to worry, Master. All you have to do is to give me a pouch, and get a pair of boots made for me so that I can walk in the woods. You will find then that your share is not so bad after all."

Now this cat had often shown himself capable of performing cunning tricks. When catching rats and mice, for example, he would hide himself amongst the meal and hang downwards by the feet as though he were dead. His master, therefore, though he did not build too much on what the cat had said, felt some hope of being assisted in his miserable plight.

"Puss pays respects to the ogre." Illustration by Rie Cramer for Barbara Douglas, *Favorite French Fairy Tales* (New York: Dodd, Mead & Company, c. 1921).

On receiving the boots which he had asked for, Puss gaily pulled them on. Then he hung the pouch round his neck, and holding the cords which tied it in front of him with his paws, he sallied forth to a warren where rabbits abounded. Placing some bran and lettuce in the pouch, he stretched himself out and lay as if dead. His plan was to wait until some young rabbit, unlearned in worldly wisdom, should come and rummage in the pouch for the eatables which he had placed there.

Hardly had he laid himself down when things fell out as he wished. A stupid young rabbit went into the pouch, and Master Puss, pulling the cords tight, killed him on the instant.

Well satisfied with his capture, Puss departed to the king's palace. There he demanded an audience, and was ushered upstairs. He entered the royal apartment, and bowed profoundly to the king.

"I bring you, Sire," said he, "a rabbit from the warren of the marquis of Carabas (such was the title he invented for his master), which I am bidden to present to you on his behalf."

"Tell your master," replied the king, "that I thank him, and am pleased by his attention."

Another time the cat hid himself in a wheatfield, keeping the mouth of his bag wide open. Two partridges ventured in, and by pulling the cords tight he captured both of them. Off he went and presented them to the king, just as he had done with the rabbit from the warren. His Majesty was not less gratified by the brace of partridges, and handed the cat a present for himself.

For two or three months Puss went on in this way, every now and again taking to the king, as a present from his master, some game which he had caught. There came a day when he learned that the king intended to take his daughter, who was the most beautiful princess in the world, for an excursion along the river bank.

"If you will do as I tell you," said Puss to his master, "your fortune is made. You have only to go and bathe in the river at the spot which I shall point out to you. Leave the rest to me."

The marquis of Carabas had no idea what plan was afoot, but did as the cat had directed.

While he was bathing the king drew near, and Puss at once began to cry out at the top of his voice:

"Help! help! the marquis of Carabas is drowning!"

At these shouts the king put his head out of the carriage window. He recognised the cat who had so often brought him game, and bade his escort go speedily to the help of the marquis of Carabas.

While they were pulling the poor marquis out of the river, Puss approached the carriage and explained to the king that while his master was bathing robbers had come and taken away his clothes, though he had cried "Stop, thief!" at the top of his voice. As a matter of fact, the rascal had hidden them under a big stone. The king at once commanded the keepers of his wardrobe to go and select a suit of his finest clothes for the marquis of Carabas.

The king received the marquis with many compliments, and as the fine clothes which the latter had just put on set off his good looks (for he was handsome and comely in appearance), the king's daughter found him very much to her liking. Indeed, the marquis of Carabas had not bestowed more than two or three respectful but sentimental glances upon her when she fell madly in love with him. The king invited him to enter the coach and join the party.

Delighted to see his plan so successfully launched, the cat went on ahead, and presently came upon some peasants who were mowing a field.

"Listen, my good fellows," said he; "if you do not tell the king that the field which you are mowing belongs to the marquis of Carabas, you will all be chopped up into little pieces like mince-meat."

In due course the king asked the mowers to whom the field on which they were at work belonged.

"It is the property of the marquis of Carabas," they all cried with one voice, for the threat from Puss had frightened them.

"You have inherited a fine estate," the king remarked to Carabas.

"As you see for yourself, Sire," replied the marquis; "this is a meadow which never fails to yield an abundant crop each year."

Still travelling ahead, the cat came upon some harvesters.

"Listen, my good fellows," said he; "if you do not declare that every one of these fields belongs to the marquis of Carabas, you will all be chopped up into little bits like mince-meat."

The king came by a moment later, and wished to know who was the owner of the fields in sight.

"It is the marquis of Carabas," cried the harvesters.

At this the king was more pleased than ever with the marquis.

Preceding the coach on its journey, the cat made the same threat to all whom he met, and the king grew astonished at the great wealth of the marquis of Carabas.

Finally Master Puss reached a splendid castle, which belonged to an ogre. He was the richest ogre that had ever been known, for all the lands through which the king had passed were part of the castle domain.

The cat had taken care to find out who this ogre was, and what powers he possessed. He now asked for an interview, declaring that he was unwilling to pass so close to the castle without having the honour of paying his respects to the owner.

The ogre received him as civilly as an ogre can, and bade him sit down.

"I have been told," said Puss, "that you have the power to change yourself into any kind of animal— for example, that you can transform yourself into a lion or an elephant."

"That is perfectly true," said the ogre, curtly; "and just to prove it, you shall see me turn into a lion."

Puss was so frightened on seeing a lion before him that he sprang on to the roof—not without difficulty and danger, for his boots were not meant for walking on the tiles.

"Puss in Boots." Illustration by W. Heath Robinson for Charles Perrault, *Old Time Stories* (New York: Dodd, Mead & Company, 1921). Project Gutenberg EBook.

Perceiving presently that the ogre had abandoned his transformation, Puss descended, and owned to having been thoroughly frightened.

"I have also been told," he added, "but I can scarcely believe it, that you have the further power to take the shape of the smallest animals—for example, that you can change yourself into a rat or a mouse. I confess that to me it seems quite impossible."

"Impossible?" cried the ogre; "you shall see!" And in the same moment he changed himself into a mouse, which began to run about the floor. No sooner did Puss see it than he pounced on it and ate it.

Presently the king came along, and noticing the ogre's beautiful mansion desired to visit it. The cat heard the rumble of the coach as it crossed the castle drawbridge, and running out to the courtyard cried to the king:

"Welcome, your Majesty, to the castle of the marquis of Carabas!"

"What's that?" cried the king. "Is this castle also yours, marquis? Nothing could be finer than this courtyard and the buildings which I see all about. With your permission we will go inside and look round."

The marquis gave his hand to the young princess, and followed the king as he led the way up the staircase. Entering a great hall they found there a magnificent collation. This had been prepared by the ogre for some friends who were to pay him a visit that very day. The latter had not dared to enter when they learned that the king was there.

The king was now quite as charmed with the excellent qualities of the marquis of Carabas as his daughter. The latter was completely captivated by him. Noting the great wealth of which the marquis was evidently possessed, and having quaffed several cups of wine, he turned to his host, saying:

"It rests with you, marquis, whether you will be my son-in-law."

The marquis, bowing very low, accepted the honour which the king bestowed upon him. The very same day he married the princess.

Puss became a personage of great importance, and gave up hunting mice, except for amusement.

Week Fifteen:
"The Owl and the Pussycat"

The Owl and the Pussy-Cat went to sea
In a beautiful pea-green boat;
They took some honey, and plenty of money
Wrapped up in a five-pound note.
The Owl looked up to the moon above,
And sang to a small guitar,
"O lovely Pussy! O Pussy, my love!
What a beautiful Pussy you are,—
        You are,
        You are!
What a beautiful Pussy you are!"

Pussy said to the Owl, "You elegant fowl!
How wonderful sweet you sing!
Oh, let us be married,—too long we have tarried,—
But what shall we do for a ring?"
They sailed away for a year and a day
To the land where the Bong-tree grows,
And there in a wood a piggy-wig stood
With a ring in the end of his nose,—
        His nose,
        His nose,
With a ring in the end of his nose.

"Dear Pig, are you willing to sell for one shilling
Your ring?" Said the piggy, "I will."
So they took it away, and were married next day
By the turkey who lives on the hill.
They dined upon mince and slices of quince,
Which they ate with a runcible spoon,
And hand in hand on the edge of the sand
They danced by the light of the moon,—
    The moon,
    The moon,
They danced by the light of the moon.

EDWARD LEAR
(1812–1888)

"The Owl and the Pussycat." Illustration by Leslie Brooke for Edward Lear, *Nonsense Songs* (London: Warne, 1910).

Week Sixteen:

CINDERELLA
French Fairy Tale

Once there was a gentleman who married, for his second wife, the proudest and most haughty woman that was ever seen. She had, by a former husband, two daughters of her own humor, who were, indeed, exactly like her in all things. He had likewise, by another wife, a young daughter, but of unparalleled goodness and sweetness of temper, which she took from her mother, who was the best creature in the world.

No sooner were the ceremonies of the wedding over but the mother-in-law began to show herself in her true colors. She could not bear the good qualities of this pretty girl, and the less because they made her own daughters appear the more odious. She employed her in the meanest work of the house: she scoured the dishes, tables, etc., and scrubbed madam's chamber, and those of misses, her daughters; she lay up in a sorry garret, upon a wretched straw bed, while her sisters lay in fine rooms, with floors all inlaid, upon beds of the very newest fashion, and where they had looking-glasses so large that they might see themselves at their full length from head to foot.

The poor girl bore all patiently, and dared not tell her father, who would have rattled her off; for his wife governed him entirely. When she had done her work, she used to go into the chimney-corner, and sit down among cinders and ashes, which made her commonly be called Cinderwench; but the youngest, who was not so rude and uncivil as the eldest, called her Cinderella. However, Cinderella, notwithstanding

"Aschenputtel [Cinderella]." Illustrator unknown for Jacob and Wilhelm Grimm, *Children's and Household Fairy Tales [Kinder-und Hausmärchen Gesammelt Durch die Brüder Jacob und Wilhelm Grimm]* (Gütersloh, Bertelsmann, 1889).

her mean apparel, was a hundred times handsomer than her sisters, though they were always dressed very richly.

It happened that the King's son gave a ball, and invited all persons of fashion to it. Our young misses were also invited, for they cut a very grand figure among the quality. They were mightily delighted at this invitation, and wonderfully busy in choosing out such gowns, petticoats, and head-clothes as might become them. This was a new trouble to Cinderella; for it was she who ironed her sisters' linen, and plaited their ruffles; they talked all day long of nothing but how they should be dressed.

"For my part," said the eldest, "I will wear my red velvet suit with French trimming."

"And I," said the youngest, "shall have my usual petticoat; but then, to make amends for that, I will put on my gold-flowered manteau, and my diamond stomacher, which is far from being the most ordinary one in the world."

They sent for the best tire-woman they could get to make up their head-dresses and adjust their double pinners, and they had their red brushes and patches from Mademoiselle de la Poche.

Cinderella was likewise called up to them to be consulted in all these matters, for she had excellent notions, and advised them always for the best, nay, and offered her services to dress their heads, which they were very willing she should do. As she was doing this, they said to her:

"Cinderella, would you not be glad to go to the ball?"

"Alas!" said she, "you only jeer me; it is not for such as I am to go thither."

"Thou art in the right of it," replied they; "it would make the people laugh to see a Cinderwench at a ball."

Anyone but Cinderella would have dressed their heads awry, but she was very good, and dressed them perfectly well They were almost two days without eating, so much were they transported with joy. They broke above a dozen laces in trying to be laced up close, that they might have a fine slender shape, and they were continually at their looking-glass. At last the happy day came; they went to Court, and Cinderella followed them with her eyes as long as she could, and when she had lost sight of them, she fell a-crying.

Her godmother, who saw her all in tears, asked her what was the matter.

"I wish I could—I wish I could—"; she was not able to speak the rest, being interrupted by her tears and sobbing.

This godmother of hers, who was a fairy, said to her, "Thou wishest thou couldst go to the ball; is it not so?"

"Y—es," cried Cinderella, with a great sigh.

"Well," said her godmother, "be but a good girl, and I will contrive that thou shalt go." Then she took her into her chamber, and said to her, "Run into the garden, and bring me a pumpkin."

Cinderella went immediately to gather the finest she could get, and brought it to her godmother, not being able to imagine how this pumpkin could make her go to the ball. Her godmother scooped out all the inside of it, having left nothing but the rind; which done, she struck it with her wand, and the pumpkin was instantly turned into a fine coach, gilded all over with gold.

She then went to look into her mouse-trap, where she found six mice, all alive, and ordered Cinderella to lift up a little the trapdoor, when, giving each mouse, as it went out, a little tap with her wand, the mouse was that moment turned into a fine horse, which altogether made a very fine set of six horses of a beautiful mouse-colored dapple-gray. Being at a loss for a coachman,

"I will go and see," says Cinderella, "if there is never a rat in the rat-trap—we may make a coachman of him."

"Thou art in the right," replied her godmother; "go and look."

Cinderella brought the trap to her, and in it there were three huge rats. The fairy made choice of one of the three which had the largest beard, and, having touched him with her wand, he was turned into a fat, jolly coachman, who had the smartest whiskers eyes ever beheld. After that, she said to her:

"Go again into the garden, and you will find six lizards behind the watering-pot, bring them to me."

She had no sooner done so but her godmother turned them into six footmen, who skipped up immediately behind the coach, with their liveries all bedaubed with gold and silver, and clung as close behind each other as if they had done nothing else their whole lives. The Fairy then said to Cinderella:

"Well, you see here an equipage fit to go to the ball with; are you not pleased with it?"

"Oh! yes," cried she; "but must I go thither as I am, in these nasty rags?"

Her godmother only just touched her with her wand, and, at the same instant, her clothes were turned into cloth of gold and silver, all beset with jewels. This done, she gave her a pair of glass slippers, the prettiest in the whole world. Being thus decked out, she got up into her coach; but her godmother, above all things, commanded her not to stay till after midnight, telling her, at the same time, that if she stayed one moment longer, the coach would be a pumpkin again, her horses mice, her coachman a rat, her footmen lizards, and her clothes become just as they were before.

She promised her godmother she would not fail of leaving the ball before midnight; and then away she drives, scarce able to contain herself for joy. The King's son who was told that a great princess, whom nobody knew, was come, ran out to receive her; he gave her his hand as she alighted out of the coach, and led her into the ball, among all the company. There was immediately a profound silence, they left off dancing, and the violins ceased to play, so attentive was everyone to contemplate the singular beauties of the unknown new-comer. Nothing was then heard but a confused noise of:

"Ha! how handsome she is! Ha! how handsome she is!"

The King himself, old as he was, could not help watching her, and telling the Queen softly that it was a long time since he had seen so beautiful and lovely a creature.

All the ladies were busied in considering her clothes and headdress, that they might have some made next day after the same pattern, provided they could meet with such fine material and as able hands to make them.

The King's son conducted her to the most honorable seat, and afterward took her out to dance with him; she danced so very gracefully that they all more and more admired her. A fine collation was served up, whereof the young prince ate not a morsel, so intently was he busied in gazing on her.

She went and sat down by her sisters, showing them a thousand civilities, giving them part of the oranges and citrons which the Prince had presented her with, which very much surprised them, for they did not know her. While Cinderella was thus amusing her sisters, she heard the clock strike eleven and three-quarters, whereupon she immediately made a courtesy to the company and hasted away as fast as she could.

When she got home she ran to seek out her godmother, and, after having thanked her, she said she could not but heartily wish she might go next day to the ball, because the King's son had desired her.

As she was eagerly telling her godmother whatever had passed at the ball, her two sisters knocked at the door, which Cinderella ran and opened.

"How long you have stayed!" cried she, gaping, rubbing her eyes and stretching herself as if she had been just waked out of her sleep; she had not, however, any manner of inclination to sleep since they went from home.

"If thou hadst been at the ball," said one of her sisters, "thou wouldst not have been tired with it. There came thither the finest princess, the most beautiful ever was seen with mortal eyes; she showed us a thousand civilities, and gave us oranges and citrons."

Cinderella seemed very indifferent in the matter; indeed, she asked them the name of that princess; but they told her they did not know it, and that the King's son was very uneasy on her account and would give all the world to know who she was. At this Cinderella, smiling, replied:

"She must, then, be very beautiful indeed; how happy you have been! Could not I see her? Ah! dear Miss Charlotte, do lend me your yellow suit of clothes which you wear every day."

"Ay, to be sure!" cried Miss Charlotte; "lend my clothes to such a dirty Cinderwench as thou art! I should be a fool."

Cinderella, indeed, expected well such answer, and was very glad of the refusal; for she would have been sadly put to it if her sister had lent her what she asked for jestingly.

The next day the two sisters were at the ball, and so was Cinderella, but dressed more magnificently than before. The King's son was always by her, and never ceased his compliments and kind speeches to her; to whom all this was so far from being tiresome that she quite forgot what her godmother had recommended to her; so that she, at last, counted the clock striking twelve when she took it to be no more than eleven; she then rose up and fled, as nimble as a deer. The Prince followed, but could not overtake her. She left behind one of her glass slippers, which the Prince took up most carefully. She got home but quite out of breath, and in her nasty old clothes, having nothing left her of all her finery but one of the little slippers, fellow to that she dropped. The guards at the palace gate were asked:

If they had not seen a princess go out.

Who said: They had seen nobody go out but a young girl, very meanly dressed, and who had more the air of a poor country wench than a gentlewoman.

When the two sisters returned from the ball Cinderella asked them: If they had been well diverted, and if the fine lady had been there.

They told her: Yes, but that she hurried away immediately when it struck twelve, and with so much haste that she dropped one of her little glass slippers, the prettiest in the world, which the King's son had taken up; that he had done nothing but look at her all the time at the ball, and that most certainly he was very much in love with the beautiful person who owned the glass slipper.

What they said was very true; for a few days after the King's son caused it to be proclaimed, by sound of trumpet, that he would marry her whose foot the slipper would just fit. They whom he employed began to try it upon the princesses, then the duchesses and all the Court, but in vain; it was brought to the two sisters, who did all they possibly could to thrust their foot into the slipper, but they could not

"It went on very easily." Illustration by D. J. Munro for Charles Perrault, *The Tales of Mother Goose* (Boston, New York, Chicago: D. C. Heath & Co., Publishers, 1901).

effect it. Cinderella, who saw all this, and knew her slipper, said to them, laughing:

"Let me see if it will not fit me."

Her sisters burst out a-laughing, and began to banter her. The gentleman who was sent to try the slipper looked earnestly at Cinderella, and, finding her very handsome, said:

It was but just that she should try, and that he had orders to let everyone make trial.

He obliged Cinderella to sit down, and, putting the slipper to her foot, he found it went on very easily, and fitted her as if it had been made of wax. The astonishment her two sisters were in was excessively great, but still abundantly greater when Cinderella pulled out of her pocket the other slipper, and put it on her foot. Thereupon, in came her godmother, who, having touched with her wand Cinderella's clothes, made them richer and more magnificent than any of those she had before.

And now her two sisters found her to be that fine, beautiful lady whom they had seen at the ball. They threw themselves at her feet to beg pardon for all the ill-treatment they had made her undergo. Cinderella took them up, and, as she embraced them, cried:

That she forgave them with all her heart, and desired them always to love her.

She was conducted to the young prince, dressed as she was; he thought her more charming than ever, and, a few days after, married her. Cinderella, who was no less good than beautiful, gave her two sisters lodgings in the palace, and that very same day matched them with two great lords of the Court.

"She drew some water from the best part of the fountain." Illustration by Honor C. Appleton for Charles Perrault, *Perault's Fairy Tales*. (Boston: Dana Estes & Co.; London: Herbert & Daniel, 1911).

Week Sixteen:

THE FAIRY

French Fairy Tale

Once upon a time there was a widow who had two daughters. The elder was so much like her, both in looks and character, that whoever saw the daughter saw the mother. They were both so disagreeable and so proud that there was no living with them. The younger, who was the very picture of her father for sweetness of temper and virtue, was withal one of the most beautiful girls ever seen. As people naturally love their own likeness, this mother doted on her elder daughter, and at the same time had a great aversion for the younger. She made her eat in the kitchen and work continually.

Among other things, this unfortunate child had to go twice a day to draw water more than a mile and a half from the house, and bring home a pitcherful of it. One day, as she was at this fountain, there came to her a poor woman, who begged of her to let her drink.

"Oh, yes, with all my heart, Goody," said this pretty little girl. Rinsing the pitcher at once, she took some of the clearest water from the fountain, and gave it to her, holding up the pitcher all the while, that she might drink the easier.

The good woman having drunk, said to her:—

"You are so pretty, so good and courteous, that I cannot help giving you a gift." For this was a fairy, who had taken the form of a poor country-woman, to see how far the civility and good manners of this pretty girl would go. "I will give you for gift," continued the Fairy,

"With all my heart, Goody." Illustration by D. J. Munro for Charles Perrault, *The Tales of Mother Goose* (Boston, New York, Chicago: D. C. Heath & Co., Publishers, 1901).

"that, at every word you speak, there shall come out of your mouth either a flower or a jewel."

When this pretty girl returned, her mother scolded at her for staying so long at the fountain.

"I beg your pardon, mamma," said the poor girl, "for not making more haste."

And in speaking these words there came out of her mouth two roses, two pearls, and two large diamonds.

"What is it I see there?" said her mother, quite astonished. "I think pearls and diamonds come out of the girl's mouth! How happens this, my child?"

This was the first time she had ever called her "my child."

The girl told her frankly all the matter, not without dropping out great numbers of diamonds.

"Truly," cried the mother, "I must send my own dear child thither. Fanny, look at what comes out of your sister's mouth when she speaks. Would you not be glad, my dear, to have the same gift? You have only to go and draw water out of the fountain, and when a poor woman asks you to let her drink, to give it to her very civilly."

"I should like to see myself going to the fountain to draw water," said this ill-bred minx.

"I insist you shall go," said the mother, "and that instantly."

She went, but grumbled all the way, taking with her the best silver tankard in the house.

She no sooner reached the fountain than she saw coming out of the wood, a magnificently dressed lady, who came up to her, and asked to drink. This was the same fairy who had appeared to her sister, but she had now taken the air and dress of a princess, to see how far this girl's rudeness would go.

"Am I come hither," said the proud, ill-bred girl, "to serve you with water, pray? I suppose this silver tankard was brought purely for your ladyship, was it? However, you may drink out of it, if you have a fancy."

"You are scarcely polite," answered the fairy, without anger. "Well, then, since you are so disobliging, I give you for gift that at every word you speak there shall come out of your mouth a snake or a toad."

So soon as her mother saw her coming, she cried out:—

"Well, daughter?"

"Well, mother?" answered the unhappy girl, throwing out of her mouth a viper and a toad.

"Oh, mercy!" cried the mother, "what is it I see? It is her sister who has caused all this, but she shall pay for it," and immediately she ran to beat her. The poor child fled away from her, and went to hide herself in the forest nearby.

The King's son, who was returning from the chase, met her, and seeing her so beautiful, asked her what she did there alone and why she cried.

"Alas! sir, my mother has turned me out of doors."

The King's son, who saw five or six pearls and as many diamonds come out of her mouth, desired her to tell him how that happened. She told him the whole story. The King's son fell in love with her, and, considering that such a gift was worth more than any marriage portion another bride could bring, conducted her to the palace of the King, his father, and there married her.

As for her sister, she made herself so much hated that her own mother turned her out of doors. The miserable girl, after wandering about and finding no one to take her in, went to a corner of the wood, and there died.

Week Sixteen:

"THE SWING"

How do you like to go up in a swing,
　　Up in the air so blue?
Oh, I do think it the pleasantest thing
　　Ever a child can do!

Up in the air and over the wall,
　　Till I can see so wide,
Rivers and trees and cattle and all
　　Over the countryside—

Till I look down on the garden green,
　　Down on the roof so brown—
Up in the air I go flying again,
　　Up in the air and down!
　　　　ROBERT LOUIS STEVENSON
　　　　　(1850–1894)

"The Swing." Illustration by Jessie Willcox Smith for Robert Louis Stevenson, *A Child's Garden of Verses,* Verse 142 (New York: Charles Scribner's Sons, 1905).

Week Seventeen:
Sunshine Stories
Hans Christian Andersen, Danish

I am going to tell a story," said the Wind.

"I beg your pardon," said the Rain, "but now it is my turn. Have you not been howling round the corner this long time, as hard as ever you could?"

"Is this the gratitude you owe me?" said the Wind; "I, who in honor of you turn inside out—yes, even break—all the umbrellas, when the people won't have anything to do with you."

"I will speak myself," said the Sunshine. "Silence!" and the Sunshine said it with such glory and majesty that the weary Wind fell prostrate, and the Rain, beating against him, shook him, as she said:

"We won't stand it! She is always breaking through—is Madame Sunshine. Let us not listen to her; what she has to say is not worth hearing." And still the Sunshine began to talk, and this is what she said:

"A beautiful swan flew over the rolling, tossing waves of the ocean. Every one of its feathers shone like gold; and one feather drifted down to the great merchant vessel that, with sails all set, was sailing away.

"The feather fell upon the light curly hair of a young man, whose business it was to care for the goods in the ship—the supercargo he was called. The feather of the bird of fortune touched his forehead, became a pen in his hand, and brought him such luck that he soon became a wealthy merchant, rich enough to have bought for himself spurs of gold—rich enough to change a golden plate into a nobleman's shield,

The egg cracked and opened . . .

on which," said the Sunshine, "I shone."

"The swan flew farther, away and away, over the sunny green meadow, where the little shepherd boy, only seven years old, had lain down in the shade of the old tree, the only one there was in sight.

"In its flight the swan kissed one of the leaves of the tree, and falling into the boy's hand, it was changed to three leaves—to ten—to a whole book; yes, and in the book he read about all the wonders of nature, about his native language, about faith and knowledge. At night he laid the book under his pillow, that he might not forget what he had been reading.

"The wonderful book led him also to the schoolroom, and thence everywhere, in search of knowledge. I have read his name among the names of learned men," said the Sunshine.

"The swan flew into the quiet, lonely forest, and rested awhile on the deep, dark lake where the lilies grow, where the wild apples are to be found on the shore, where the cuckoo and the wild pigeon have their homes.

"In the wood was a poor woman gathering firewood—branches and dry sticks that had fallen. She bore them on her back in a bundle, and in her arms she held her little child. She too saw the golden swan, the bird of fortune, as it rose from among the reeds on the shore. What was it that glittered so? A golden egg that was still quite warm. She laid it in her bosom, and the warmth remained. Surely there was life in the

"The Sunshine Stories." Illustration by Edna F. Hart for Hans Christian Andersen, *Hans Andersen's Fairy Tales First Series* (Boston: Finn and Company, 1866).

egg! She heard the gentle pecking inside the shell, but she thought it was her own heart that was beating.

"At home in her poor cottage she took out the egg. "Tick! tick!" it said, as if it had been a gold watch, but it was not; it was an egg—a real, living egg.

"The egg cracked and opened, and a dear little baby swan, all feathered as with the purest gold, pushed out its tiny head. Around its neck were four rings, and as this woman had four boys—three at home, and this little one that was with her in the lonely wood—she understood at once that there was one for each boy. Just as she had taken them the little gold bird took flight.

"She kissed each ring, then made each of the children kiss one of the rings, laid it next the child's heart awhile, then put it on his finger. I saw it all," said the Sunshine, "and I saw what happened afterward.

"One of the boys, while playing by a ditch, took a lump of clay in his hand, then turned and twisted it till it took shape and was like Jason, who went in search of the Golden Fleece and found it.

"The second boy ran out upon the meadow, where stood the flowers—flowers of all imaginable colors. He gathered a handful and squeezed them so tightly that the juice flew into his eyes, and some of it wet the ring upon his hand. It cribbled and crawled in his brain and in his hands, and after many a day and many a year, people in the great city talked of the famous painter that he was.

"The third child held the ring in his teeth, and so tightly that it gave forth sound—the echo of a song in the depth of his heart. Then thoughts and feelings rose in beautiful sounds,—rose like singing swans,—plunged, too, like swans, into the deep, deep sea. He became a great musical composer, a master, of whom every country has the right to say, "He was mine, for he was the world's."

"And the fourth little one—yes, he was the "ugly duck" of the family. They said he had the pip and must eat pepper and butter like a sick chicken, and that was what was given him; but of me he got a warm, sunny kiss," said the Sunshine. "He had ten kisses for one. He was a poet and was first kissed, then buffeted all his life through.

"But he held what no one could take from him—the ring of fortune from Dame Fortune's golden swan. His thoughts took wing and flew up and away like singing butterflies—emblems of an immortal life."

"That was a dreadfully long story," said the Wind.

"And so stupid and tiresome," said the Rain. "Blow upon me, please, that I may revive a little."

And while the Wind blew, the Sunshine said: "The swan of fortune flew over the lovely bay where the fishermen had set their nets. The very poorest one among them was wishing to marry—and marry he did.

"To him the swan brought a piece of amber. Amber draws things toward itself, and this piece drew hearts to the house where the fisherman lived with his bride. Amber is the most wonderful of incense, and there came a soft perfume, as from a holy place, a sweet breath from beautiful nature, that God has made. And the fisherman and his wife were happy and grateful in their peaceful home, content even in their poverty. And so their life became a real Sunshine Story."

"I think we had better stop now," said the Wind. "I am dreadfully bored. The Sunshine has talked long enough."

"I think so, too," said the Rain.

And what do we others who have heard the story say?

We say, "Now the story's done."

Week Seventeen:

THE EMPEROR'S NEW CLOTHES

Hans Christian Andersen, Danish

Many years ago there was an Emperor, who was so excessively fond of new clothes that he spent all his money on them. He cared nothing about his soldiers, nor for the theatre, nor for driving in the woods except for the sake of showing off his new clothes. He had a costume for every hour in the day, and instead of saying, as one does about any other king or emperor, "He is in his council chamber," here one always said, "The Emperor is in his dressing-room."

Life was very gay in the great town where he lived; hosts of strangers came to visit it every day, and among them one day two swindlers. They gave themselves out as weavers, and said that they knew how to weave the most beautiful stuffs imaginable. Not only were the colours and patterns unusually fine, but the clothes that were made of the stuffs had the peculiar quality of becoming invisible to every person who was not fit for the office he held, or if he was impossibly dull.

"Those must be splendid clothes," thought the Emperor. "By wearing them I should be able to discover which men in my kingdom are unfitted for their posts. I shall distinguish the wise men from the fools. Yes, I certainly must order some of that stuff to be woven for me."

He paid the two swindlers a lot of money in advance so that they might begin their work at once.

They did put up two looms and pretended to weave, but they had nothing whatever upon their shuttles. At the outset they asked for a quantity of the finest silk and the purest gold thread, all of which they put into their own bags, while they worked away at the empty looms far into the night.

"I should like to know how those weavers are getting on with the stuff," thought the Emperor; but he felt a little queer when he reflected

"The poor old minister stared as hard as he could, but he could not see anything." Illustration by Edmund Dulac for Hans Christian Andersen, *Stories from Hans Andersen* (London and New York: Hodder & Stoughton, 1911).

that any one who was stupid or unfit for his post would not be able to see it. He certainly thought that he need have no fears for himself, but still he thought he would send somebody else first to see how it was getting on. Everybody in the town knew what wonderful power the stuff possessed, and every one was anxious to see how stupid his neighbour was.

"I will send my faithful old minister to the weavers," thought the Emperor. "He will be best able to see how the stuff looks, for he is a clever man, and no one fulfils his duties better than he does!"

So the good old minister went into the room where the two swindlers sat working at the empty loom.

"Heaven preserve us!" thought the old minister, opening his eyes very wide. "Why, I can't see a thing!" But he took care not to say so.

Both the swindlers begged him to be good enough to step a little nearer, and asked if he did not think it a good pattern and beautiful colouring. They pointed to the empty loom, and the poor old minister stared as hard as he could, but he could not see anything, for of course there was nothing to see.

"Good heavens!" thought he, "is it possible that I am a fool. I have never thought so, and nobody must know it. Am I not fit for my post? It will never do to say that I cannot see the stuffs."

"Well, sir, you don't say anything about the stuff," said the one who was pretending to weave.

"Oh, it is beautiful! quite charming!" said the old minister, looking through his spectacles; "this pattern and these colours! I will certainly tell the Emperor that the stuff pleases me very much."

"We are delighted to hear you say so," said the swindlers, and then they named all the colours and described the peculiar pattern. The old minister paid great attention to what they said, so as to be able to repeat it when he got home to the Emperor. Then the swindlers went on to demand more money, more silk, and more gold, to be able to proceed with the weaving; but they put it all into their own pockets—not a single strand was ever put into the loom, but they went on as before weaving at the empty loom.

The Emperor soon sent another faithful official to see how the stuff was getting on, and if it would soon be ready. The same thing happened to him as to the minister; he looked and looked, but as there was only the empty loom, he could see nothing at all.

"Is not this a beautiful piece of stuff?" said both the swindlers, showing and explaining the beautiful pattern and colours which were not there to be seen.

"I know I am not a fool!" thought the man, "so it must be that I am unfit for my good post! It is very strange, though! However, one must not let it appear!" So he praised the stuff he did not see, and assured them of his delight in the beautiful colours and the originality of the design. "It is absolutely charming!" he said to the Emperor. Everybody in the town was talking about this splendid stuff.

Now the Emperor thought he would like to see it while it was still on the loom. So, accompanied by a number of selected courtiers, among whom were the two faithful officials who had already seen the imaginary stuff, he went to visit the crafty impostors, who were working away as hard as ever they could at the empty loom.

"It is magnificent!" said both the honest officials. "Only see, your Majesty, what a design! What colours!" And they pointed to the empty loom, for they thought no doubt the others could see the stuff.

"What!" thought the Emperor; "I see nothing at all! This is terrible! Am I a fool? Am I not fit to be Emperor? Why, nothing worse could happen to me!"

"Oh, it is beautiful!" said the Emperor. "It has my highest approval!" and he nodded his satisfaction as he gazed at the empty loom. Nothing would induce him to say that he could not see anything.

The whole suite gazed and gazed, but saw nothing more than all the others. However, they all exclaimed with his Majesty, "It is very beautiful!" and they advised him to wear a suit made of this wonderful cloth on the occasion of a great procession which was just about to take place. "It is magnificent! gorgeous! excellent!" went from mouth to mouth; they were all equally delighted with it. The Emperor gave each of the rogues an order of knighthood to be worn in their buttonholes and the title of "Gentlemen weavers."

The swindlers sat up the whole night, before the day on which the procession was to take place, burning sixteen candles; so that people might see how anxious they were to get the Emperor's new clothes ready. They pretended to take the stuff off the loom. They cut it out in the air with a huge pair of scissors, and they stitched away with needles without any thread in them. At last they said: "Now the Emperor's new clothes are ready!"

The Emperor, with his grandest courtiers, went to them himself, and both the swindlers raised one arm in the air, as if they were holding something, and said: "See, these are the trousers, this is the coat, here is the mantle!" and so on. "It is as light as a spider's web. One might think one had nothing on, but that is the very beauty of it!"

"Yes!" said all the courtiers, but they could not see anything, for there was nothing to see.

"Will your imperial majesty be graciously pleased to take off your clothes," said, the impostors, "so that we may put on the new ones, along here before the great mirror?"

The Emperor took off all his clothes, and the impostors pretended to give him one article of dress after the other of the new ones which they had pretended to make. They pretended to fasten something round his waist and to tie on something; this was the train, and the Emperor turned round and round in front of the mirror.

"How well his majesty looks in the new clothes! How becoming they are!" cried all the people round. "What a design, and what colours! They are most gorgeous robes!"

"The canopy is waiting outside which is to be carried over your majesty in the procession," said the master of the ceremonies.

"Well, I am quite ready," said the Emperor. "Don't the clothes fit well?" and then he turned round again in front of the mirror, so that he should seem to be looking at his grand things.

The chamberlains who were to carry the train stooped and pretended to lift it from the ground with both hands, and they walked along with their hands in the air. They dared not let it appear that they could not see anything.

Then the Emperor walked along in the procession under the gorgeous canopy, and everybody in the streets and at the windows exclaimed, "How beautiful the Emperor's new clothes are! What a splendid train! And they fit to perfection!" Nobody would let it appear that he could see nothing, for then he would not be fit for his post, or else he was a fool.

None of the Emperor's clothes had been so successful before.

"But he has got nothing on," said a little child.

"Oh, listen to the innocent," said its father; and one person whispered to the other what the child had said. "He has nothing on; a child says he has nothing on!"

"But he has nothing on!" at last cried all the people.

The Emperor writhed, for he knew it was true, but he thought "the

procession must go on now," so held himself stiffer than ever, and the chamberlains held up the invisible train.

"But he has got nothing on!" Illustration by Helen Stratton for Hans Christian Andersen, *The Fairy Tales of Hans Christian Andersen* (Philadelphia: Lippincott, c. 1899).

Week Seventeen:
"THE DUEL"

The gingham dog and the calico cat
Side by side on the table sat;
'T was half-past twelve, and (what do you
    think!)
Nor one nor t' other had slept a wink!
    The old Dutch clock and the Chinese
        plate
    Appeared to know as sure as fate
There was going to be a terrible spat.
    (I wasn't there; I simply state
    What was told to me by the Chinese
        plate!)

The gingham dog went
    "bow-wow-wow!"
And the calico cat replied "mee-ow!"
The air was littered, an hour or so,
With bits of gingham and calico,
    While the old Dutch clock in the
        chimney place
    Up with its hands before its
        face,
For it always dreaded a family row!
    (Now mind: I'm only telling you
    What the old Dutch clock declares is true!)

(THIS PAGE AND NEXT) Illustrations by Charles Robinson for Eugene Field, *Lullaby-Land: Songs of Childhood* (Toronto: George N. Morang & Company, Ltd., 1900).

The Chinese plate looked very blue,
And wailed, "Oh, dear! what shall we do!"
But the gingham dog and the calico cat
Wallowed this way and tumbled that,
　　Employing every tooth and claw
　　In the awfullest way you ever saw—
And, oh! how the gingham and calico flew!
　　(Don't fancy I exaggerate—
　　I got my news from the Chinese plate!)

Next morning, where the two had sat
They found no trace of dog or cat;
And some folks think unto this day
That burglars stole that pair away!
　　But the truth about the cat and pup
　　Is this: they ate each other up!
Now what do you really think of that!
　　('The old Dutch clock it told me so,
　　And that is how I came to know.)
　　　　　　　　Eugene Field
　　　　　　　（1850–1895）

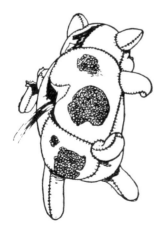

Week Eighteen:
THE TSAREVNA FROG
Russian Fairy Tale

In an old, old Russian tsarstvo, I do not know when, there lived a sovereign prince with the princess his wife. They had three sons, all of them young, and such brave fellows that no pen could describe them. The youngest had the name of Ivan Tsarevitch. One day their father said to his sons:

"My dear boys, take each of you an arrow, draw your strong bow and let your arrow fly; in whatever court it falls, in that court there will be a wife for you."

The arrow of the oldest Tsarevitch fell on a boyar-house just in front of the terem where women live; the arrow of the second Tsarevitch flew to the red porch of a rich merchant, and on the porch there stood a sweet girl, the merchant's daughter. The youngest, the brave Tsarevitch Ivan, had the ill luck to send his arrow into the midst of a swamp, where it was caught by a croaking frog.

Ivan Tsarevitch came to his father: "How can I marry the frog?" complained the son. "Is she my equal? Certainly she is not."

"Never mind," replied his father, "you have to marry the frog, for such is evidently your destiny."

Thus the brothers were married: the oldest to a young boyarishnia, a nobleman's child; the second to the merchant's beautiful daughter, and the youngest, Tsarevitch Ivan, to a croaking frog.

After a while the sovereign prince called his three sons and said to them:

"Have each of your wives bake a loaf of bread by to-morrow morning."

Ivan returned home. There was no smile on his face, and his brow was clouded.

"C-R-O-A-K! C-R-O-A-K! Dear husband of mine, Tsarevitch Ivan, why so sad?" gently asked the frog. "Was there anything disagreeable in the palace?"

"Disagreeable indeed," answered Ivan Tsarevitch; "the Tsar, my father, wants you to bake a loaf of white bread by to-morrow."

"Do not worry, Tsarevitch. Go to bed; the morning hour is a better adviser than the dark evening."

The Tsarevitch, taking his wife's advice, went to sleep. Then the frog threw off her frogskin and turned into a beautiful, sweet girl, Vassilissa by name. She now stepped out on the porch and called aloud:

"Nurses and waitresses, come to me at once and prepare a loaf of white bread for to-morrow morning, a loaf exactly like those I used to eat in my royal father's palace."

In the morning Tsarevitch Ivan awoke with the crowing cocks, and you know the cocks and chickens are never late. Yet the loaf was already made, and so fine it was that nobody could even describe it, for only in fairyland one finds such marvelous loaves. It was adorned all about with pretty figures, with towns and fortresses on each side, and within it was white as snow and light as a feather.

The Tsar father was pleased and the Tsarevitch received his special thanks.

"Now there is another task," said the Tsar smilingly. "Have each of your wives weave a rug by to-morrow."

Tsarevitch Ivan came back to his home. There was no smile on his face and his brow was clouded.

"C-R-O-A-K! C-R-O-A-K! Dear Tsarevitch Ivan, my husband and master, why so troubled again? Was not father pleased?"

"How can I be otherwise? The Tsar, my father, has ordered a rug by to-morrow."

"Do not worry, Tsarevitch. Go to bed; go to sleep. The morning hour will bring help."

Again the frog turned into Vassilissa, the wise maiden, and again she called aloud:

"Dear nurses and faithful waitresses, come to me for new work. Weave a silk rug like the one I used to sit upon in the palace of the king, my father."

Once said, quickly done. When the cocks began their early "cock-a-doodle-doo," Tsarevitch Ivan awoke, and lo! there lay the most beautiful silk rug before him, a rug that no one could begin to describe. Threads of silver and gold were interwoven among bright-colored silken ones, and the rug was too beautiful for anything but to admire.

The Tsar father was pleased, thanked his son Ivan, and issued a new order. He now wished to see the three wives of his handsome sons, and they were to present their brides on the next day.

The Tsarevitch Ivan returned home. Cloudy was his brow, more cloudy than before.

"C-R-O-A-K! C-R-O-A-K! Tsarevitch, my dear husband and master, why so sad? Hast thou heard anything unpleasant at the palace?"

"Unpleasant enough, indeed! My father, the Tsar, ordered all of us to present our wives to him. Now tell me, how could I dare go with thee?"

"It is not so bad after all, and might be much worse," answered the frog, gently croaking. "Thou shalt go alone and I will follow thee. When thou hearest a noise, a great noise, do not be afraid; simply say: 'There is my miserable froggy coming in her miserable box.'"

The two elder brothers arrived first with their wives, beautiful, bright, and cheerful, and dressed in rich garments. Both the happy bridegrooms made fun of the Tsarevitch Ivan.

"Why alone, brother?" they laughingly said to him. "Why didst thou not bring thy wife along with thee? Was there no rag to cover her?

"The Tsarevna Frog." Illustration by Lucy Fitch Perkins for Verra X. K. de Blumenthal, *Folk Tales from the Russian* (Great Neck, New York: Core Collection Books, Inc, 1903). Library of Congress.

Where couldst thou have gotten such a beauty? We are ready to wager that in all the swamps in the dominion of our father it would be hard to find another one like her." And they laughed and laughed.

Lo! what a noise! The palace trembled, the guests were all frightened. Tsarevitch Ivan alone remained quiet and said:

"No danger; it is my froggy coming in her box."

To the red porch came flying a golden carriage drawn by six splendid white horses, and Vassilissa, beautiful beyond all description, gently reached her hand to her husband. He led her with him to the heavy oak tables, which were covered with snow-white linen and loaded with many wonderful dishes such as are known and eaten only in the land of fairies and never anywhere else. The guests were eating and chatting gayly.

Vassilissa drank some wine, and what was left in the tumbler she poured into her left sleeve. She ate some of the fried swan, and the bones she threw into her right sleeve. The wives of the two elder brothers watched her and did exactly the same.

When the long, hearty dinner was over, the guests began dancing and singing. The beautiful Vassilissa came forward, as bright as a star, bowed to her sovereign, bowed to the honorable guests and danced with her husband, the happy Tsarevitch Ivan.

While dancing, Vassilissa waved her left sleeve and a pretty lake appeared in the midst of the hall and cooled the air. She waved her right sleeve and white swans swam on the water. The Tsar, the guests, the servants, even the gray cat sitting in the corner, all were amazed and wondered at the beautiful Vassilissa. Her two sisters-in-law alone envied her. When their turn came to dance, they also waved their left sleeves as Vassilissa had done, and, oh, wonder! they sprinkled wine all around. They waved their right sleeves, and instead of swans the bones flew in the face of the Tsar father. The Tsar grew very angry and bade them leave the palace. In the meantime Ivan Tsarevitch watched a moment to slip away unseen. He ran home, found the frogskin, and burned it in the fire.

Vassilissa, when she came back, searched for the skin, and when she could not find it her beautiful face grew sad and her bright eyes filled with tears. She said to Tsarevitch Ivan, her husband:

"Oh, dear Tsarevitch, what hast thou done? There was but a short time left for me to wear the ugly frogskin. The moment was near when we could have been happy together forever. Now I must bid thee good-by. Look for me in a far-away country to which no one knows the roads, at the palace of Kostshei the Deathless;" and Vassilissa turned into a white swan and flew away through the window.

Tsarevitch Ivan wept bitterly. Then he prayed to the almighty God, and making the sign of the cross northward, southward, eastward, and westward, he went on a mysterious journey.

No one knows how long his journey was, but one day he met an old, old man. He bowed to the old man, who said:

"Good-day, brave fellow. What art thou searching for, and whither art thou going?"

Tsarevitch Ivan answered sincerely, telling all about his misfortune without hiding anything.

"And why didst thou burn the frogskin? It was wrong to do so. Listen now to me. Vassilissa was born wiser than her own father, and as he envied his daughter's wisdom he condemned her to be a frog for three long years. But I pity thee and want to help thee. Here is a magic ball. In whatever direction this ball rolls, follow without fear."

Ivan Tsarevitch thanked the good old man, and followed his new guide, the ball. Long, very long, was his road. One day in a wide, flowery field he met a bear, a big Russian bear. Ivan Tsarevitch took his bow and was ready to shoot the bear.

"Do not kill me, kind Tsarevitch," said the bear. "Who knows but that I may be useful to thee?" And Ivan did not shoot the bear.

Above in the sunny air there flew a duck, a lovely white duck. Again the Tsarevitch drew his bow to shoot it. But the duck said to him:

"Do not kill me, good Tsarevitch. I certainly shall be useful to thee some day."

And this time he obeyed the command of the duck and passed by. Continuing his way he saw a blinking hare. The Tsarevitch prepared an arrow to shoot it, but the gray, blinking hare said:

"Do not kill me, brave Tsarevitch. I shall prove myself grateful to thee in a very short time."

The Tsarevitch did not shoot the hare, but passed by. He walked farther and farther after the rolling ball, and came to the deep blue sea. On the sand there lay a fish. I do not remember the name of the fish, but it was a big fish, almost dying on the dry sand.

"O Tsarevitch Ivan!" prayed the fish, "have mercy upon me and push me back into the cool sea."

The Tsarevitch did so, and walked along the shore. The ball, rolling all the time, brought Ivan to a hut, a queer, tiny hut standing on tiny hen's feet.

"Izboushka! Izboushka!"—for so in Russia do they name small huts—"Izboushka, I want thee to turn thy front to me," cried Ivan, and lo! the tiny hut turned its front at once. Ivan stepped in and saw a witch, one of the ugliest witches he could imagine.

"Ho! Ivan Tsarevitch! What brings thee here?" was his greeting from the witch.

"O, thou old mischief!" shouted Ivan with anger. "Is it the way in holy Russia to ask questions before the tired guest gets something to eat, something to drink, and some hot water to wash the dust off?"

Baba Yaga, the witch, gave the Tsarevitch plenty to eat and drink, besides hot water to wash the dust off. Tsarevitch Ivan felt refreshed. Soon he became talkative, and related the wonderful story of his marriage. He told how he had lost his dear wife, and that his only desire was to find her.

"I know all about it," answered the witch. "She is now at the palace of Kostshei the Deathless, and thou must understand that Kostshei is terrible. He watches her day and night and no one can ever conquer him. His death depends on a magic needle. That needle is within a hare; that hare is within a large trunk; that trunk is hidden in the branches of an old oak tree; and that oak tree is watched by Kostshei as closely as Vassilissa herself, which means closer than any treasure he has."

Then the witch told Ivan Tsarevitch how and where to find the oak tree. Ivan hastily went to the place. But when he perceived the oak tree he was much discouraged, not knowing what to do or how to begin the work. Lo and behold! that old acquaintance of his, the Russian bear, came running along, approached the tree, uprooted it, and the trunk fell and broke. A hare jumped out of the trunk and began to run fast; but another hare, Ivan's friend, came running after, caught it and tore it to pieces. Out of the hare there flew a duck, a gray one which flew very high and was almost invisible, but the beautiful white duck followed the bird and struck its gray enemy, which lost an egg. That egg fell into the deep sea. Ivan meanwhile was anxiously watching his faithful friends helping him. But when the egg disappeared in the blue waters he could not help weeping. All of a sudden a big fish came swimming up, the same fish he had saved, and brought the egg in his mouth. How happy Ivan was when he took it! He broke it and found the needle inside, the magic needle upon which everything depended.

At the same moment Kostshei lost his strength and power forever. Ivan Tsarevitch entered his vast dominions, killed him with the magic needle, and in one of the palaces found his own dear wife, his beautiful Vassilissa. He took her home and they were very happy ever after.

Week Eighteen:
Baba Yaga
Russian Fairy Tale

Somewhere, I cannot tell you exactly where, but certainly in vast Russia, there lived a peasant with his wife and they had twins—son and daughter. One day the wife died and the husband mourned over her very sincerely for a long time. One year passed, and two years, and even longer. But there is no order in a house without a woman, and a day came when the man thought, "If I marry again possibly it would turn out all right." And so he did, and had children by his second wife.

The stepmother was envious of the stepson and daughter and began to use them hardly. She scolded them without any reason, sent them away from home as often as she wished, and gave them scarcely enough to eat. Finally she wanted to get rid of them altogether. Do you know what it means to allow a wicked thought to enter one's heart?

The wicked thought grows all the time like a poisonous plant and slowly kills the good thoughts. A wicked feeling was growing in the stepmother's heart, and she determined to send the children to the witch, thinking sure enough that they would never return.

"Dear children," she said to the orphans, "go to my grandmother who lives in the forest in a hut on hen's feet. You will do everything she wants you to, and she will give you sweet things to eat and you will be happy."

The orphans started out. But instead of going to the witch, the sister, a bright little girl, took her brother by the hand and ran to their own old, old grandmother and told her all about their going to the forest.

"Oh, my poor darlings!" said the good old grandmother, pitying the children, "my heart aches for you, but it is not in my power to help

"Like a whirlwind she rushed away with him." Written and illustrated by Katharine Pyle in *Wonder Tales Retold* (Boston: Little, Brown, c. 1905).

you. You have to go not to a loving grandmother, but to a wicked witch. Now listen to me, my darlings," she continued; "I will give you a hint: Be kind and good to everyone; do not speak ill words to any one; do not despise helping the weakest, and always hope that for you, too, there will be the needed help."

The good old grandmother gave the children some delicious fresh milk to drink and to each a big slice of ham. She also gave them some cookies—there are cookies everywhere—and when the children departed she stood looking after them a long, long time.

The obedient children arrived at the forest and, oh, wonder! there stood a hut, and what a curious one! It stood on tiny hen's feet, and at the top was a rooster's head. With their shrill, childish voices they called out loud:

"Izboushka, Izboushka! turn thy back to the forest and thy front to us!"

The hut did as they commanded. The two orphans looked inside and saw the witch resting there, her head near the threshold, one foot in one corner, the other foot in another corner, and her knees quite close to the ridge pole.

"Fou, Fou, Fou!" exclaimed the witch; "I feel the Russian spirit."

The children were afraid, and stood close, very close together, but in spite of their fear they said very politely:

"Ho, grandmother, our stepmother sent us to thee to serve thee."

"All right; I am not opposed to keeping you, children. If you satisfy all my wishes I shall reward you; if not, I shall eat you up."

Without any delay the witch ordered the girl to spin the thread, and the boy, her brother, to carry water in a sieve to fill a big tub. The poor orphan girl wept at her spinning-wheel and wiped away her bitter tears. At once all around her appeared small mice squeaking and saying:

"Sweet girl, do not cry. Give us cookies and we will help thee."

The little girl willingly did so.

"Now," gratefully squeaked the mice, "go and find the black cat. He is very hungry; give him a slice of ham and he will help thee."

The girl speedily went in search of the cat and saw her brother in great distress about the tub, so many times he had filled the sieve, yet the tub was still dry. The little birds passed, flying near by, and chirped to the children:

"Kind-hearted little children, give us some crumbs and we will advise you."

The orphans gave the birds some crumbs and the grateful birds chirped again:

"Some clay and water, children dear!"

Then away they flew through the air.

The children understood the hint, spat in the sieve, plastered it up with clay and filled the tub in a very short time. Then they both returned to the hut and on the threshold met the black cat. They generously gave him some of the good ham which their good grandmother had given them, petted him and asked:

"Dear Kitty-cat, black and pretty, tell us what to do in order to get away from thy mistress, the witch?"

"Well," very seriously answered the cat, "I will give you a towel and a comb and then you must run away. When you hear the witch running after you, drop the towel behind your back and a large river will appear in place of the towel. If you hear her once more, throw down the comb and in place of the comb there will appear a dark wood. This wood will protect you from the wicked witch, my mistress."

Baba Yaga came home just then.

"Is it not wonderful?" she thought; "everything is exactly right."

"Well," she said to the children, "today you were brave and smart; let us see to-morrow. Your work will be more difficult and I hope I shall eat you up."

The poor orphans went to bed, not to a warm bed prepared by loving hands, but on the straw in a cold corner. Nearly scared to death from fear, they lay there, afraid to talk, afraid even to breathe. The next morning the witch ordered all the linen to be woven and a large supply of firewood to be brought from the forest.

The children took the towel and comb and ran away as fast as their feet could possibly carry them. The dogs were after them, but they threw them the cookies that were left; the gates did not open themselves, but the children smoothed them with oil; the birch tree near the path almost scratched their eyes out, but the gentle girl fastened a pretty ribbon to it. So they went farther and farther and ran out of the dark forest into the wide, sunny fields.

The cat sat down by the loom and tore the thread to pieces, doing it with delight. Baba Yaga returned.

"Where are the children?" she shouted, and began to beat the cat. "Why hast thou let them go, thou treacherous cat? Why hast thou not scratched their faces?"

"The children ran away as fast as their feet could possibly carry them." Illustration by Lucy Fitch Perkins for Verra X. K. de Blumenthal, *Folk Tales from the Russian* (Great Neck, New York: Core Collection Books, Inc., 1903). Library of Congress.

The cat answered: "Well, it was because I have served thee so many years and thou hast never given me a bite, while the dear children gave me some good ham."

The witch scolded the dogs, the gates, and the birch tree near the path.

"Well," barked the dogs, "thou certainly art our mistress, but thou hast never done us a favor, and the orphans were kind to us."

The gates replied:

"We were always ready to obey thee, but thou didst neglect us, and the dear children smoothed us with oil."

The birch tree lisped with its leaves, "Thou hast never put a simple thread over my branches and the little darlings adorned them with a pretty ribbon."

Baba Yaga understood that there was no help and started to follow the children herself. In her great hurry she forgot to look for the towel and the comb, but jumped astride a broom and was off. The children heard her coming and threw the towel behind them. At once a river, wide and blue, appeared and watered the field. Baba Yaga hopped along the shore until she finally found a shallow place and crossed it.

Again the children heard her hurry after them and so they threw down the comb. This time a forest appeared, a dark and dusky forest in which the roots were interwoven, the branches matted together, and the tree-tops touching each other. The witch tried very hard to pass through, but in vain, and so, very, very angry, she returned home.

The orphans rushed to their father, told him all about their great distress, and thus concluded their pitiful story:

"Ah, father dear, why dost thou love us less than our brothers and sisters?"

The father was touched and became angry. He sent the wicked stepmother away and lived a new life with his good children. From that time he watched over their happiness and never neglected them any more.

How do I know this story is true? Why, one was there who told me about it.

Week Eighteen:
"THE YEAR'S AT THE SPRING"

The year's at the spring,
The day's at the morn;
Morning's at seven;
The hillside's dew pearled;
The lark's on the wing;
The snail's on the thorn;
God's in His heaven—
All's right with the world!
                    ROBERT BROWNING
                      (1812–1889)

"He took the Lamp from the niche." Illustration by Walter Crane and Edmund Evans from *Aladdin, and the Wonderful Lamp* (London and New York: J. Lane, c. 1890).

Week Nineteen:

ALADDIN, AND THE WONDERFUL LAMP

Middle Eastern Folk Tale

Aladdin was the son of a poor tailor in an Eastern city. He was a spoiled boy, and loved play better than work; so that when Mustapha, his father, died, he was not able to earn his living; and his poor mother had to spin cotton all day long to procure food for their support. But she dearly loved her son, knowing that he had a good heart, and she believed that as he grew older he would do better, and become at last a worthy and prosperous man. One day, when Aladdin was walking outside the town, an old man came up to him, and looking very hard in his face, said he was his father's brother, and had long been away in a distant country, but that now he wished to help his nephew to get on. He then put a ring on the boy's finger, telling him that no harm could happen to him so long as he wore it. Now, this strange man was no uncle of Aladdin, nor was he related at all to him; but he was a wicked magician, who wanted to make use of the lad's services, as we shall see presently.

The old man led Aladdin a good way into the country, until they came to a very lonely spot between two lofty black mountains. Here he lighted a fire, and threw into it some gum, all the time repeating many strange words. The ground then opened just before them, and a stone trap-door appeared. After lifting this up, the Magician told Aladdin to go below, down some broken steps, and at the foot of these he would find three halls, in the last of which was a door leading to a garden full

of beautiful trees; this he was to cross, and after mounting some more steps, he would come to a terrace, when he would see a niche, in which there was a lighted Lamp. He was then to take the Lamp, put out the light, empty the oil, and bring it away with him.

Aladdin found all the Magician had told him to be true; he passed quickly but cautiously through the three halls, so as not even to touch the walls with his clothes, as the Magician had directed. He took the Lamp from the niche, threw out the oil, and put it in his bosom. As he came back through the garden, his eyes were dazzled with the bright-coloured fruits on the trees, shining like glass. Many of these he plucked and put in his pockets, and then returned with the Lamp, and called upon his uncle to help him up the broken steps. "Give me the Lamp," said the old man, angrily. "Not till I get out safe," cried the boy. The Magician, in a passion, then slammed down the trap-door, and Aladdin was shut up fast enough. While crying bitterly, he by chance rubbed the ring, and a figure appeared before him, saying, "I am your slave, the [Genie] of the Ring; what do you desire?"

Aladdin told the [Genie] of the Ring that he only wanted to be set free, and to be taken back to his mother. In an instant he found himself at home, very hungry, and his poor mother was much pleased to see him again. He told her all that had happened; she then felt curious to look at the Lamp he had brought, and began rubbing it, to make it shine brighter. Both were quite amazed at seeing rise before them a strange figure; this proved to be the [Genie] of the Lamp, who asked for their commands. On hearing that food was what they most wanted, a

"Aladdin, or the Wonderful Lamp." Illustrator unknown for *Aladdin* (London: Yorkshire J. S. Publishing and Stationery Co. Limited, 1854). McGill University Library.

black slave instantly entered with the choicest fare upon a dainty dish of silver, and with silver plates for them to eat from.

Aladdin and his mother feasted upon the rich fare brought to them, and sold the silver dish and plates, on the produce of which they lived happily for some weeks. Aladdin was now able to dress well, and in taking his usual walk, he one day chanced to see the Sultan's daughter coming with her attendants from the baths. He was so much struck with her beauty, that he fell in love with her at once, and told his mother that she must go to the Sultan, and ask him to give the Princess to be his wife. The poor woman said he must be crazy; but her son not only knew what a treasure he had got in the Magic Lamp, but he had also found how valuable were the shining fruits he had gathered, which he thought at the time to be only coloured glass. At first he sent a bowlful of these jewels—for so they were—to the Sultan, who was amazed at their richness, and said to Aladdin's mother: "Your son shall have his wish, if he can send me, in a week, forty bowls like this, carried by twenty white and twenty black slaves, handsomely dressed."

He thought by this to keep what he had got, and to hear no more of Aladdin. But the [Genie] of the Lamp soon brought the bowls of jewels and the slaves, and Aladdin's mother went with them to the Sultan.

The Sultan was overjoyed at receiving these rich gifts, and at once agreed that the Princess Bulbul should be the wife of Aladdin. The happy youth then summoned the

"He one day chanced to see the Sultan's daughter." Illustration by Felix O. C. Darley in *Aladdin, or the Wonderful Lamp* (Philadelphia: Porter & Coates, 1872).

[Genie] of the Lamp to assist him; and shortly set out for the Palace. He was dressed in a handsome suit of clothes, and rode a beautiful horse; by his side marched a number of attendants, scattering handfuls of gold among the people. As soon as they were married, Aladdin ordered the [Genie] of the Lamp to build, in the course of a night, a most superb Palace, and there the young couple lived quite happily for some time. One day, when Aladdin was out hunting with the Sultan, the wicked Magician, who had heard of his good luck, and wished to get hold of the Magic Lamp, cried out in the streets, "New lamps for old ones!" A silly maid in the Palace, hearing this, got leave of the Princess to change Aladdin's old Lamp, which she had seen on a cornice where he always left it, for a new one, and so the Magician got possession of it.

As soon as the Magician had safely got the Lamp, he caused the [Genie] to remove the Palace, and Bulbul within it, to Africa. Aladdin's grief was very great, and so was the rage of the Sultan at the loss of the Princess, and poor Aladdin's life was in some danger, for the Sultan threatened to kill him if he did not restore his daughter in three days. Aladdin first called upon the [Genie] of the Ring to help him, but all he could do was to take him to Africa. The Princess was rejoiced to see him again, but was very sorry to find that she had been the cause of all their trouble by parting with the wonderful Lamp. Aladdin, however, consoled her, and told her that he had thought of a plan for getting it back. He then left her, but soon returned with a powerful sleeping-draught, and advised her to receive the Magician with pretended kindness, and pour it into his wine at dinner that day, so as to make him fall sound asleep, when they could take the Lamp from him. Everything happened as they expected; the Magician drank the wine, and when Aladdin came in, he found that he had fallen back lifeless on the couch. Aladdin took the Lamp from his bosom, and called upon the [Genie] to transport the Palace, the Princess, and himself, back to their native city. The Sultan was as much astonished and pleased at their return, as he had been provoked at the loss of his daughter; and Aladdin, with his Bulbul, lived long afterwards to enjoy his good fortune.

Week Nineteen:

THE KING AND THE FISHERMAN

Persian Fairy Tale

he countries washed by the great rivers Tigris and Euphrates were once ruled by a certain King who was passionately fond of fish.

He was seated one day with Sherem, his wife, in the royal gardens that stretch down to the banks of the Tigris, at the point where it is spanned by the wonderful bridge of boats; and looking up spied a boat gliding by, in which was seated a fisherman having a large fish.

Noticing that the King was looking closely at him, and knowing how much the King liked this particular kind of fish, the fisherman made his obeisance, and skilfully bringing his boat to the shore, came before the King and begged that he would accept the fish as a present. The King was

"The King and the Fisherman." Illustration by John R. Neill for Hartwell James, *A Book of Persian Fairy Tales* (Philadelphia, Pennsylvania: Henry Altemus Company, 1906). Project Gutenberg EBook.

greatly pleased at this, and ordered that a large sum of money be given to the fisherman.

But before the fisherman had left the royal presence, the Queen turned towards the King and said: "You have done a foolish thing." The King was astonished to hear her speak in this way, and asked how that could be. The Queen replied:

"The news of your having given so large a reward for so small a gift will spread through the city and it will be known as the fisherman's gift. Every fisherman who catches a big fish will bring it to the palace, and should he not be paid in like manner, he will go away discontented, and secretly speak evil of you among his fellows."

"Thou speakest the truth, light of my eyes," said the King, "but can not you see how mean it would be for a King, if for that reason he were to take back his gift?" Then perceiving that the Queen was ready to argue the matter, he turned away angrily, saying: "The matter is closed."

However, later in the day, when he was in a more amiable frame of mind, the Queen again approached him, and said that if that was his only reason for not taking back his gift, she would arrange it. "You must summon the fisherman," she said, "and then ask him, "Is this fish male or female?" If he says male, then you will tell him that you wanted a female fish; but if he should say female, your reply will be that you wanted a male fish. In this way the matter will be properly adjusted."

The King thought this an easy way out of the difficulty, and commanded the fisherman to be brought before him. When the fisherman, who by the way, was a most intelligent man, stood before the King, the King said to him: "O fisherman, tell me, is this fish male or female?"

The fisherman replied, "The fish is neither male nor female." Whereupon the King smiled at the clever answer, and to add to the Queen's annoyance, directed the keeper of the royal purse to give the fisherman a further sum of money.

Then the fisherman placed the money in his leather bag, thanked the King, and swinging the bag over his shoulder, hurried away, but not so quickly that he did not notice that he had dropped one small coin.

Placing the bag on the ground, he stooped and picked up the coin, and again went on his way, with the King and Queen carefully watching his every action.

"Look! what a miser he is!" said Sherem, triumphantly. "He actually put down his bag to pick up one small coin because it grieved him to think that it might reach the hands of one of the King's servants, or some poor person, who, needing it, would buy bread and pray for the long life of the King."

"Again thou speakest the truth," replied the King, feeling the justice of this remark; and once more was the fisherman brought into the royal presence. "Are you a human being or a beast?" the King asked him. "Although I made it possible for you to become rich without toil, yet the miser within you could not allow you to leave even one small piece of money for others." Then the King bade him to go forth and show his face no more within the city.

At this the fisherman fell on his knees and cried: "Hear me, O King, protector of the poor! May God grant the King a long life. Not for its value did thy servant pick up the coin, but because on one side it bore the name of God, and on the other the likeness of the King. Thy servant feared that someone, not seeing the coin, would tread it into the dirt, and thus defile both the name of God and the face of the King. Let the King judge if by so doing I have merited reproach."

This answer pleased the King beyond all measure, and he gave the fisherman another large sum of money. And the Queen's wrath was turned away, and she looked kindly upon the fisherman as he departed with his bag laden with money.

"Small Daffodils" by Charles Demuth. Watercolor and graphite on paper. Metropolitan Museum of Art, Afred Stieglitz Collection, 1949. c. 1914. Creative Commons Universal Public Domain 1.0.

Week Nineteen:
"DAFFODILS"

I wandered lonely as a cloud
That floats on high o'er vales and hills,
When all at once I saw a crowd,
A host, of golden daffodils;
Beside the lake, beneath the trees,
Fluttering and dancing in the breeze.

Continuous as the stars that shine
And twinkle on the milky way,
They stretched in never-ending line
Along the margin of a bay:
Ten thousand saw I at a glance,
Tossing their heads in sprightly dance.

The waves beside them danced; but they
Out-did the sparkling waves in glee:
A poet could not but be gay,
In such a jocund company:
I gazed—and gazed—but little thought
What wealth the show to me had brought:

For oft, when on my couch I lie
In vacant or in pensive mood,
They flash upon that inward eye
Which is the bliss of solitude;
And then my heart with pleasure fills,
And dances with the daffodils.

WILLIAM WORDSWORTH
(1770–1850)

(This page) "The Queen is entrapped." (Opposite) "The crow begged him to set him free." Illustrations by Willy Pogany for Ignacz Kunos from *Forty-Four Turkish Fairy Tales* (London: G. Harrap & Co., 1913). New York Public Library.

Week Twenty:
THE CROW-PERI
Turkish Fairy Tale

There was once a youth named Hassan, who was so poor that he had scarcely rags to cover him, and he was often obliged to go hungry to bed.

One day Hassan went out to the forest beyond the city and set a snare, hoping to catch a bird or some small animal that would serve him for a meal. After setting it, he hid himself in the bushes near by to wait. He had not been there long when he heard a loud flapping, and running out he saw that a large black crow was caught in the snare.

Hassan was greatly disappointed. He had hoped for something more worth eating than a crow. However, even that was better than nothing. He took the bird from the snare, and was about to wring its neck when it spoke to him in a human voice.

"Hassan, Hassan, do not kill me! Spare my life and I will make your fortune for you."

Hassan was greatly surprised to hear the crow speak, but after a moment he swallowed his surprise and answered it.

"Make my fortune!" cried he. "How can you make my fortune?—you, a crow? No, no, I am hungry, and the best fortune that can happen to me now is to have a full stomach!"

Again he was about to wring the bird's neck, but it called to him so piteously that he could not but pause.

"Hassan! Hassan! You do not know what you are doing. I am no common crow. Let me go now, and do you return to-morrow to this same spot and you will find something in the snare that will be worth more to you than I can possibly be."

"Very well," said Hassan. "I will let you go, but I do this through pity, and not because I believe in the least that you can better my fortunes."

"That is well," said the crow. "You will see, however, that I will keep my promise. But before you let me go, pluck three feathers from my wings. If you are ever in trouble, blow one of these feathers into the air and call to me, and I will come and give you aid."

Hassan did as the crow bade him. He plucked three feathers from its wings, but as he did so he could not keep from laughing.

"You may laugh," said the crow, "but you will soon find that my promises are not vain. To-morrow return to your snare, and you will find in it something that will be of value to you."

It then spread its wings and flew away over the tree-tops, flapping heavily.

Hassan returned home, but the next day he came to the forest again. As he approached the spot where the snare was, he gave a cry of joy and wonder. Caught in it was the most beautiful bird he had ever seen or dreamed of. Its feathers were of pure silver, and over them played the most gorgeous colours, like the colours of a rainbow. Its eyes shone like diamonds, and its crest was tipped with jewels of seven different kinds.

"Such a bird as this is not to be eaten," said Hassan to himself. "It is a gift that is fit for the King. I will take it to the palace and present it to him, and he will be sure to reward me handsomely." At the same time he could not help marvelling to think how truly the crow had spoken.

The youth hastened back to the city and borrowed a cage from a neighbour. Then he returned to the tree, and put the wonderful bird in the cage, and set out for the palace. He had thrown a piece of cloth over the cage, so as to hide the bird, but the light from it was so bright that it shone through, and set every one to wondering what it could be that the ragged youth was carrying so carefully.

At the palace Hassan found that it was a difficult matter to see the King. At last, however, he was allowed to come before his presence, and at once he uncovered the cage so that the bird could be seen.

The King was filled with wonder at the sight. He had never seen such a bird before. He questioned Hassan and made him repeat again and again the story of how he had caught the bird, and exactly what it was that the crow had said to him.

"There is some magic in this," said the King. "I will keep the bird, and never before have I received a gift that pleased me so much. I will also prove to you that the crow spoke the truth, for, from now on, your fortune is made."

The King then caused the youth to be clothed in magnificent garments, and he also gave him for his own a handsome house near to the palace, and slaves to serve him, and gold to spend. Every day he sent for Hassan to come to him, and because the youth was clever and handsome and adroit, he soon became the King's favourite above all others.

But success is sure to make enemies. The King's former favourite became very jealous of Hassan, and he began to scheme to destroy the youth, and win back the King's favour to himself. One day he went to the King and said, "What a pity it is that such a wonderful bird as Hassan has brought you should be kept in a cage! What it should have is an ivory palace, in which you could visit it and sit at ease to watch it."

"That is true," answered the King, "but I do not know how I could obtain such a palace. There is not enough ivory in all my kingdom to build such a thing."

"It is plain enough," answered Hassan's enemy, "that Hassan is the favourite of some magic power. Ask him to build the palace, and if he refuses, threaten him with death. Then I am sure that in some way he will be able to provide it for you."

This the enemy said, not because he at all believed it, but because he wished to destroy Hassan.

After spending a short time in thought, the King agreed to this plan. He sent for Hassan and said to him, "I am, as you know, greatly delighted with the bird that you have given me, but now I wish for still another thing. I wish you to build an ivory palace in which the bird can live, and in which I can go to visit it."

"Alas, your Majesty, how can I build such a place as that?" cried Hassan. "I have nothing of my own, as you know, but only what you yourself have given me, and in all your kingdom there is not enough ivory to build a whole palace of it."

"Nevertheless, you must provide it," answered the King, "and if you do not do so, your life shall answer for it."

When Hassan heard these words, he was greatly troubled. He went out from the King's presence and returned home, and there he prepared to die, for he knew not where to find enough ivory to build one room, to say nothing of a whole palace.

Suddenly, in the midst of his despair, he remembered the three feathers that he had plucked from the crow's wing. He feared they were lost, but after some search he found them laid away in a corner with the rags he had once worn. He took them up, and blowing one of them into the air he called upon the crow to come and help him.

Almost at once he heard outside a heavy flapping of wings, and a large crow flew in through the window and lighted beside him.

"What do you wish?" asked the crow, "and why have you called upon me? Are you in trouble?"

"Trouble enough," answered Hassan, "and trouble that may end in my losing my life." He then told the crow what it was that the King had demanded of him, and that he did not see how it would be possible for him to carry it out.

"Do not despair over this," answered the crow. "It is not such a difficult matter as you seem to think. Ask the King to give you forty cartloads of wine, with bullocks to pull them, and forty slaves to drive the carts, and do you come away with me into the forest, and I may be able to get the ivory for you."

The youth had little hope of this. Still, he asked the King for the things, as the crow had bade him,—forty cartloads of wine, the bullocks, and the forty slaves, and the King was not slow to give them to him. Then Hassan went away with them into the forest, and the crow flew before to show him in which direction to go. After they had journeyed a long distance, they came to a pool, and all round this pool were marks that showed that it was the drinking-place for a great herd of elephants. There had been a drought, however, and the water had almost dried up.

The crow bade Hassan fill the pool with the wine he had brought with him, and this he did. Then, by the crow's directions, Hassan hid himself and the carts and bullocks and slaves some little distance away.

Toward evening there was a great noise of trampling and trumpeting in the forest, and a huge herd of elephants came down to the pool to drink. They were very thirsty, for the supply of water had been low for some days. When they found the pool full to the brim, they trumpeted with joy and rushed to it to drink. They drank and drank, and presently they were all overcome with the wine and fell down and lay as though dead.

Then Hassan called to the forty slaves, and they came and cut off all the elephants' tusks and loaded them upon the carts, and there were forty cartloads.

Hassan and his slaves and carts left the forest before the elephants awoke, and by the next day they were back in the city again.

When the King saw the loads of ivory that Hassan had brought with him, he could not wonder enough.

Hassan's enemy was filled with rage and envy, but he dissembled. "Did I not know it?" said he to the King. "I tell you there is nothing in the world that Hassan cannot do if only he wishes to."

The ivory palace was built, and every day the King went there to sit and watch the bird, and Hassan was more of a favourite with him than ever.

But one day Hassan's enemy thought of a new plot to destroy him. He went to the King and said, "What a pity it is that such a beautiful bird as this should never make a sound. No doubt it could make the most ravishing music if it would but sing."

"Yes, it is a pity," answered the King, and at once he became dissatisfied.

"It must be that the bird misses its former owner," said the enemy. "If Hassan really wished to please you, he would find the former owner and bring him here, so that the bird might sing again."

"Yes, that is true," said the King, "and I would greatly like to hear it sing."

He then sent for Hassan and told him what he wished.

"But, your Majesty," cried Hassan in despair, "I do not know who was the owner of the bird, nor have I any means for finding out. As you know, I caught it in a snare far away from the city, and where there is no house within sight."

Nevertheless the King was determined that Hassan must find the former owner of the bird and bring him to the palace. If he did not, his life should answer for it.

Hassan went out from the King's presence very sad. Then he bethought himself of the crow's feathers. He took one of the two that still remained, and blew it into the air, and called to the crow to come.

Almost at once the crow appeared and settled on the ground beside him.

"What is it that you wish now?" it asked. "Are you again in trouble?"

"Yes, I am in trouble, and my trouble is very grievous." Hassan then told the crow what it was that the King demanded of him.

"This is a more difficult matter than the former one," answered the crow. "Nevertheless, it may be managed. Do you ask the King to give you a vessel fitted out in the most complete and magnificent way. The sails must be of silk and the figurehead of gold. It must be painted and gilded within and without. There must be a dining-hall hung about with velvet curtains, and the dishes must be of solid gold. There must also be a bathroom with a marble bath-tub, and there must be damsels on the ship, dressed in shining colours, and with bracelets and anklets of gold set with precious stones. Do this, and then, when the vessel is ready, I will instruct you further."

Hassan did as the crow bade him. He went to the King and asked him for a vessel fitted out in exactly the manner the crow had described to him. This the King gave him.

When the vessel was finished, Hassan went on board, taking the crow with him. They sailed away and sailed away, and always the crow told Hassan in which direction to steer. After seven days and seven nights, they came within sight of an island. The island was very pleasant to look upon, for there were flowers and trees loaded with fruit, and shining domes and palaces.

"Look, Hassan," said the crow. "That is the place whither we are bound. Now listen attentively to what I tell you, for I can guide you no farther; I must leave you, but if you will follow out exactly all my directions, everything will go well with you. That island belongs to the Queen of the Peris. She is a very powerful fairy, and very beautiful. She is very curious as well. When she sees your vessel, she will be anxious to find out about it, whence it comes, and who is the owner. She will send her messengers to inquire about it. But you must answer no questions, and you must let no one but the Queen herself come on board. She will wish to go all over the vessel, and when she sees the bathroom she will admire it so much that she will wish to take a bath there. This you must agree to. Then, while she is bathing, you must sail away with her, for she is the owner of the Wonder Bird, and for her and her alone will it sing."

Hassan promised to do exactly as the crow bade him in all things, and then it spread its wings and flew away and out of sight. Hassan ordered the captain to sail the vessel up close to the shore of the island, and there they dropped anchor.

Presently he could see that they had been observed from the island. People gathered on the shore, many of them magnificently dressed, and presently several boats put out and were rowed over to the ship's side. In them were messengers from the Queen.

These messengers questioned Hassan as to whence the vessel came and whose it was. But Hassan would answer none of these questions. Neither would he allow them to come on board to examine the vessel, though they greatly wished it, and it had been, indeed, their Queen's commands that they should do so.

"If the Queen wishes to know about the vessel, she must come herself," said Hassan.

The messengers returned to shore very much dissatisfied. But presently another boat put forth from the shore, and in it was the Queen herself. She was rowed over to the ship's side, and she said to the youth that she would now come on board herself and bring her maidens with her.

She was so beautiful and so magnificent that Hassan scarcely knew how to refuse her. However, he remembered the crow's words, and was determined to obey them.

"Your majesty, if you will do me the honour to enter my ship, it and all that are in it are yours," he said; "but as to anyone's coming on board with you, that I cannot allow, for I was expressly forbidden to permit anyone but yourself to visit the ship."

The Queen was very much offended by Hassan's words. Still, she was so very curious that she could not resist coming on board to see whether the ship was really as magnificent within as it seemed from the outside.

The youth showed her all over it, and she was filled with admiration at the beauty and completeness of its furnishing. When she entered the room where the marble bath was, she was particularly delighted, and after examining all the arrangements she signified to Hassan that she would like to bathe in the marble tub.

Hassan at once retired and sent the damsels he had brought with him to attend the Queen.

While she was bathing, the sails were set, and the ship sailed away from the island and back across the sea toward Hassan's own country.

When the Queen had finished bathing, and had returned to the deck, she was amazed to find the ship under way and the island already lost to view. She commanded Hassan to carry her back at once to her island, but this the youth would in nowise consent to do. He explained to the Queen why it was that he had carried her off—that it was to save his own life. He said that later on, if she wished, she might return to her own country, but first she must see whether the bird belonged to her, and whether it would sing for her. He also told her so many pleasant things about the King, his master, that the Queen became quite curious to see him.

"I make no doubt from what you tell me," said she, "that the bird is one that I lost some time ago. If it is, I shall be glad to make it sing for your master, but after that I must of course return home, and I shall take the bird with me."

The youth doubted whether the King would agree to this, but he kept his thoughts to himself, and at last brought the Queen to the city and into the King's palace.

When the King saw the lady Hassan had brought with him, he was amazed at her beauty. He could think of nothing else. Even the bird was forgotten. He caused her to sit at his right hand and did all he could to entertain her.

The Queen was no less pleased with him, and some time was spent in talking pleasantly together.

"And now, your Majesty," said the Queen at last, "let us visit the ivory palace where the Wonder Bird is kept, and see whether it is mine, and if it is, I can promise you that it will immediately begin to sing, and that its voice is as beautiful as its plumage."

The King at once arose, and together they went to the ivory palace. No sooner had the Queen crossed the threshold than the bird burst into song, and its song was so beautiful that all who heard it stood as though enchanted. They could not stir, nor scarcely breathe until the song was ended.

After the first day at the King's palace, the Queen spoke no more of returning to her own island. She had fallen deeply in love with the King, and he with her.

Before long they were married, and then Hassan became more of a favourite with them than ever. Wealth and honours were heaped upon him, and there was nothing that the King and Queen were not ready to do for him.

The former favourite was more filled with rage and envy than ever. He could scarcely eat or sleep, he was so envious.

Now after the King and Queen had been married for little more than a year the Queen fell ill, and her illness was so grievous that all the doctors in the kingdom could do nothing for her. At last it seemed as though she must surely die.

When this became known, Hassan's enemy went to the King and said, "Your Majesty, I am but an ignorant man. I know you think nothing of me or my words, but is it not possible that there is some drug in the Queen's own country that might cure her? And if so, why should not Hassan be sent to fetch it for her? For he and he alone knows where her island lies."

This the enemy said because he hoped that if Hassan returned to the island the people there would either kill him or make a prisoner of him because he had carried off their Queen.

The King, however, never thought of that. He thought only of what might save the Queen's life. The advice he received seemed to him very wise. He at once sent for Hassan and told him what he wished him to do—that he was to return to the Queen's own country, and demand of her court physician some drug that would make her well.

Hassan thoroughly understood how dangerous this errand might prove. He knew, too, why his enemy had suggested it; that it was not through any love of the Queen, but from hatred of him.

However, he said nothing of this to the King. He only agreed to what his master wished and at once made ready to set out. First, however, he took out the third feather that the crow had given him, blew it into the air, and called the crow to come to him.

At once the crow appeared.

"What would you have of me now?" it asked of the youth. "Has some new trouble come upon you?"

"That I do not know," answered Hassan, "but the King is sending me upon a mission that may, it seems to me, prove very dangerous."

He then told the crow what it was that the King required of him.

The crow seemed greatly disturbed when it heard of the Queen's illness. "You must go," it said, "and go at once. There is indeed a drug in the Queen's palace that will save her life if you can but fetch it in time. You will suffer no harm from the people in the palace. They will, indeed, give you the drug at once when they learn that the Queen is in need of it. But at the gateway of the palace there are two fierce lions. These would certainly tear you to pieces before ever you could enter, unless you had my help to depend on."

The crow then bade the youth look carefully at its right wing. "You will find there a single silver feather," it said. "Pluck it out and carry it with you. When the lions spring at you, you must at once touch them with that feather, and then they will become gentle, and you can pass them by unharmed."

"He stroked their maws with the feather."

"He stroked their maws with the feather." Illustration by Willy Pogany for Ignacz Kunos from *Forty-Four Turkish Fairy Tales* (London: G. Harrap & Co., 1913). New York Public Library.

The crow stooped before Hassan and spread wide its wings, and Hassan saw that the third feather from the tip of the right wing was of pure silver. He plucked it out, and having hidden it in a safe place in his clothing, he started out on his journey. For seven days and seven nights he sailed across the seas in the same direction as he had gone before, and on the morning of the eighth day he came within sight of the island. He landed and made his way toward the palace, and he saw no one on his way. No sooner did he approach the gateway than two fierce lions sprang out and rushed at him as though to tear him to pieces.

Hassan was terrified at their appearance. It seemed as though he must surely lose his life, but he stood firm until they were almost upon him, and then he touched them with the feather. At once they became perfectly gentle, and even fawned at his feet as though he were their master. So Hassan passed by them unharmed and entered the palace.

Those who were there were very much surprised to see a stranger enter. They could not understand how it was he had been able to pass by the lions without being torn to pieces.

The youth explained the matter to them, however, and showed them the silver feather. He also told them the sore need of their Queen, and begged them, if they had any drug that could save her, to bring it to him at once and let him go.

The people of the palace looked at him strangely when he showed them the feather. But when he made known the illness of the Queen they hastened to fetch a drug she always used, and gave it to him.

"This will save her," they told him, "for she has often used it to bring back life when it was almost gone."

They then escorted him to the seashore, showing him the greatest honour, and many of them wished to return with him to the King's country, but this he dared not allow.

It was again seven days and seven nights before Hassan came to the end of the journey, and by that time the King was in despair. He had no longer any hope. However, when he heard that the ship had arrived, he sent his swiftest horses and riders to meet Hassan and bring him to the palace.

The youth was at once taken into the room where the Queen was lying stretched upon a couch, seemingly lifeless. The King, the court physician, and her attendants were with her.

"Have you brought it? The drug?" cried the King.

Hassan drew it forth from his bosom, where he carried it, and placed it in the hands of the Queen's physician. He did not notice that the crow had followed him into the room.

The physician poured a few drops of the drug into a goblet and held it to the Queen's lips. No sooner had she swallowed it than a wonderful change came over her. The colour returned to her cheeks and the life to her limbs. She opened her eyes and sat up and looked about her.

At once her eyes fell upon the crow, and it was to it that she addressed her first words.

"Oh, thou careless and disobedient one!" she cried, "into what danger didst thou not throw thy mistress."

"Alas!" answered the crow, "thou hast indeed been near to death. But all that is over now. There is only happiness before thee. But for me, is my misery never to end?"

"Yes, and that right soon," cried the Queen. "If I owe my danger to thee, so also do I owe to thee my happiness. Draw near to me."

All in the room had listened in wonder to this talk between the Queen and the crow. But a still stranger thing was to happen.

As the crow hopped close to the couch, the Queen took a few drops of water from a vial near by and sprinkled it over the bird, at the same time pronouncing some magic words.

At once, instead of the crow, a tall and graceful maiden stood there before the Queen, a maiden of such great beauty that she was even the equal of the Queen herself.

The King and Hassan were filled with wonder at this sight.

The Queen then turned to the King with a gentle smile.

"This maiden," said she, "was my favourite of all the Peris that once attended me. But she grew proud and haughty because of my favour, and at last presumed to disobey even me. To punish her, I changed her into a crow and sent her to fly about the world, despised by all. But I will now forgive her because she brought me to you, and will take her back into favour if she can assure me of her repentance."

The Peri sank on her knees before the Queen and kissed her hand, weeping. She assured her mistress that her pride was indeed broken, and that from now on she would be her faithful and obedient servant.

The Queen then raised her from her knees and made her sit beside her, and all was joy and happiness.

As for Hassan, he found the maiden so beautiful that he could not keep his eyes from her. Already he loved her with his whole heart, and longed for nothing so much as to have her for a wife. The Peri returned his love, and with the consent of the King and Queen they were married, and from that time on they lived in the greatest joy and contentment.

As for the former favourite, he was so miserable over the sight of Hassan's happiness that at length he could bear it no longer. He sold his house and goods and sailed away, no one knew whither, and if anyone regretted him, it was not Hassan.

Week Twenty:
"Ozymandias of Egypt"

I met a traveller from an antique land
Who said: "Two vast and trunkless legs of stone
Stand in the desert. Near them on the sand,
Half sunk, a shattered visage lies, whose frown
And wrinkled lip and sneer of cold command
Tell that its sculptor well those passions read
Which yet survive, stamped on these lifeless things,
The hand that mock'd them and the heart that fed;
And on the pedestal these words appear:
"My name is Ozymandias, king of kings:
Look on my works, ye mighty, and despair!"
Nothing beside remains: round the decay
Of that colossal wreck, boundless and bare,
The lone and level sands stretch far away."
                    PERCY BYSSHE SHELLEY
                      (1792–1822)

Week Twenty-One:

RABBIT'S EYES

Korean Fairy Tale

Once upon a time the king of the fishes fell ill, and no one knew what was the matter with him. All the doctors in the sea were called in, one after another, and not one of them could cure him.

Once when the fishes were talking about it, a turtle stuck its head out of a crack in a rock. "It is a pity," said the turtle, "that no one has ever thought of asking my advice. I could cure the king in a twinkling. All he has to do is to swallow the eye of a live rabbit, and he will become perfectly well again."

This the turtle said, not because he knew anything at all about the matter, but because he wished to appear wise before the fishes.

Now it so chanced that one of the fishes that heard him was the son of the king's councillor, and he swam straight home and told his father what he had heard the turtle say. The councillor told the king, and the king, who was feeling very ill that day, bade them bring the turtle to him immediately.

When the messengers told the turtle that the king wished to speak to him, the turtle was very much frightened. He drew his head and his tail into his shell and pretended that he was asleep, but in the end he was obliged to go with the messengers.

They soon reached the palace, and the turtle was taken immediately to where the king was. He was lying on a bed of seaweed and looking very ill indeed, and all his doctors were gathered round him.

The king turned his eyes toward the turtle, and spoke in a weak voice. "Tell me, friend, is it true that you said you could cure me?"

Yes, it was true.

"And that all I have to do is to swallow the eye of a live rabbit, and I will be well again?"

Yes, that was true too.

"Then go get a live rabbit and bring it here immediately, that I may be well."

When the turtle heard these words he was in despair. It did not seem at all likely that he could catch a rabbit and bring it down into the sea, but he was so much afraid of the king that he did not dare to explain this to him. He said nothing, but crawled away as soon as he could, wishing he could find some crack where he could hide himself and never be found again.

Suddenly he remembered he had once seen a rabbit frisking about on a hill not far from the seashore, and he determined to set out to find it.

He crawled out of the sea and started up the hill. He climbed and he climbed, and after a while he came to the top, and there he sat down to rest.

Presently along came the rabbit, and it stopped to speak to him.

"Good day," said the rabbit.

"Good day," said the turtle.

"And what are you doing so far away from the sea?" asked the rabbit.

"Oh, I only came up here to look about and see what the green world was like," answered the turtle.

"And what do you think of it, now you are here?"

"Oh, it's not so bad; but you ought to see the beautiful palaces and gardens we have down under the sea." The turtle began telling the rabbit about them, and he talked so long and said so many fine things about them, that the rabbit began to wish to see them for himself.

"Would it be very hard for me to live down under the water?" he asked.

"Oh, no," said the turtle. "It might be a little inconvenient at first, but that would not last long. If you like, I will take you on my back and carry you down to the bottom of the sea, and then you can see whether it is not all just as grand and beautiful as I have been telling you."

Well, the rabbit could not resist his curiosity, and he agreed to go with the turtle.

They went to the edge of the sea, and then the rabbit got on the turtle's back, and down they went through the water to the very bottom of the sea. The rabbit did not like it at first, but he soon grew used to it, and when he saw all the fine palaces and gardens that were there, he was filled with wonder.

The turtle took him directly to the palace of the king. There he bade the rabbit get down and wait awhile, and he promised that presently he would show him the king of all this magnificence.

The rabbit was delighted and willingly agreed to wait there while the turtle went to announce him.

But while the turtle was away the rabbit heard two fishes talking in the room next to where he was. He was very inquisitive, so he cocked his ears forward and listened to what they were saying. What was his horror to find that they were talking about taking out his eyes and giving them to the king. The rabbit did not know what to do, nor how he was to escape from the dangerous position he was in.

Presently the turtle came back, and the chief councillor came with him, and immediately the rabbit began to talk. "Well," said he, "it all seems very fine here, and I am glad I came, but I wish now I had brought my own eyes with me so that I could see it better. You see, the eyes I have in my head now are only glass eyes. I am so afraid of getting my own eyes hurt or dusty that I generally keep them in a safe place, and wear these glass eyes instead. But if I had only known how much there would be to look at, I would certainly have brought my own eyes."

When the turtle and the councillor heard this, they were very much disappointed, for they believed the rabbit was speaking the truth, and that the eyes he had in his head at the time were only glass eyes.

"I will take you back to the shore," said the turtle, "and then you can go and get your real eyes and come back again, for there are many more things for you to see here—things more wonderful and beautiful than anything I have yet shown you."

Well, the rabbit was willing to do that, so he got upon the turtle's back, and the turtle swam up and up with him through the sea.

As soon as they reached the shore the rabbit leaped from the turtle's back, and away he went up the hill as fast as he could scamper, and he was glad enough to be out of that scrape, I can tell you. But the turtle waited, and he waited, and he waited, but the rabbit never did come back, and at last the turtle was obliged to go home without him.

As for the king of the fishes, if he ever got well, it was not the eye of a live rabbit that cured him; of that you may be sure.

Week Twenty-One:

THE MAGIC RICE KETTLE

Korean Fairy Tale

There was once an old man who was so poor he was scarcely able to buy food enough to keep him alive.

He had never married, and so he had no children, but he had a little dog and cat that lived with him, and these two he loved as though they were his own son and daughter. What little he had was shared with them, and if they were sometimes hungry, it was because he had nothing in the house to eat.

One day the old man found that all he had was one scant handful of rice.

"Alas, my little dog and cat, what will become of us now?" he cried. "This handful of rice is all that is left to keep us alive. After it is gone, you must seek another master who can feed you better than I. Even if I must starve, that is no reason why you should too."

The little cat mewed, and the dog looked up into his master's face, as though they had understood all he said to them.

The old man put the rice over the fire to cook, and just as it was done, and he was about to feed the animals, the light in the hut was darkened; looking round, he saw a tall stranger standing in the open doorway.

"Good day," said the stranger.

"Good day," answered the old man.

"I have come a long way," said the stranger, "and I am footsore and weary. May I come in and rest?"

Yes, he might do that and welcome.

The stranger came in and sat down in the most comfortable place. "I am hungry as well as weary."

"Alas," cried the old man, "this is a poor house in which to seek for food."

The stranger looked all about him. "Is not that rice that I see?" he asked, pointing to the kettle.

"Yes, it is rice, but my little dog and cat are hungry also, and not another morsel have we in the house beside that."

"Nevertheless, it is right that a man should be fed before dumb brutes," said the stranger. "Give me at least a taste of the rice before you feed them."

The old man did not know how to refuse him.

"Take some of it, then," he said, "but leave a little for them, I beg of you."

At once the stranger dipped into the kettle and began to eat, and he ate so fast that before the old man could stop him, all the rice was gone from the kettle, to the very last grain.

The old man was cut to the heart to think that his guest could have done this. Now his little dog and cat would have to go to bed hungry. All the same, he said nothing. He took up the empty kettle and was about to put it back on the shelf when the stranger said to him, "Fill the kettle with water and hang it over the fire again."

"Why should I do that?" asked the old man. "Water will not fill our stomachs or satisfy our hunger."

"Nevertheless, do as I bid you," said the stranger.

He spoke in such a way that the old man did not dare to disobey him. Muttering to himself, he filled the kettle with water and hung it over the fire.

The stranger drew out a piece of something that looked like amber and threw it in the pot. At once the water began to boil, and as it did so it became filled with rice. And such rice! The grains were twice as big as usual, and from them arose a smell more delicious than anything the old man had ever smelled before in all his life.

Filled with wonder and fear, he turned toward where the stranger had been sitting, but the guest was gone. He had disappeared, and only the little cat and dog were left in the room, waiting hungrily for their dinner.

The old man lifted the kettle from the fire and began to serve out the rice. And now a still more wonderful thing happened. No matter how much was dipped out from the kettle, still it was always full. He could hardly believe his eyes. He dipped and dipped. Soon all the pots and kettles and bowls in the house were full of rice, and still the more he took out the more there was.

"It is magic," cried the old man. "It must be that the amber the stranger threw in the pot was a charm. If so, puss and my dog and I need never suffer hunger again."

And so it turned out to be. As long as the amber was in the kettle, it was always full of rice to the brim. The rice was always fresh, and delicious too, so that not only the neighbours but the people from the village across the river came to buy it; and they paid well for it.

The little cat and dog grew fat and sleek. As for the man, he not only had enough to eat, but he was able to buy for himself all the clothes he needed and to make presents to those who were poorer than himself.

One evening the old man felt very tired. So many people had come through the day to buy rice that his arm quite ached with serving it out.

He took a bowl and filled it for the cat and dog, and was about to set it on the floor when he noticed to his surprise that the kettle was not as full as it had been. He took another bowl and dipped out some more of the rice. The kettle failed to fill itself.

Again he dipped, and the more he took out, the emptier the kettle grew. The old man was very much frightened. He plunged his hands into the rice that was left in the kettle and began to feel about for the charm, but it was not there. Somehow, that day, while he was dipping out the rice for his customers, he must have dipped out the charm, and some one had carried it off home with his bowl of rice.

The old man was ready to tear his hair with despair. At once he ran out and began to go about the neighbourhood, knocking at all the doors and begging to know whether a piece of amber had been found in the rice the people there had bought that day. But every one told him no. They had found nothing in their bowls but rice.

Worn out with sorrow, he went back to his hut at last and threw himself on the floor to sleep. It was a long time, however, before he could close his eyes. Soon all the money that had been paid him for the rice would be spent, and he was too old to work. Then there would be nothing for him but the same poverty and hunger he had endured for so many years. And his little dog and cat would have to suffer with him unless they were wise enough to run away and seek another master. At last, toward morning, the old man fell asleep, and then the dog and cat began to talk together in low tones.

"This is a bad business," said the dog.

"Bad enough," answered puss. "Our master has been very careless. He deserves to suffer. As for me, I have no notion of being half-starved again the way I used to be. I shall go away and try to find another home where there will be more to eat than here."

"You are very ungrateful," answered the dog. "Instead of planning to run away, you ought to set your wits to work to think how we can help our master."

"But how could we do that? I know of no way."

"Let us go out and hunt for the charm. Perhaps we can find it. Our sense of smell is so keen that if we came anywhere near where it is I am sure we could find it, however well it was hidden. We will go from house to house—all through the village, if need be. I will nose about in the gardens and out-buildings, and you must manage to creep into the houses and hunt about through the rooms."

"Very well," answered the cat. "I am sure I would be glad enough to help our master, and to stay with him too, if only he could give us enough to eat."

So, early the next day, before the old man was awake, the dog and the cat started out together on their search. The people of the village were still asleep, but the cat managed to find a way to creep into several of the houses, and the dog searched about outside, as he had promised to do.

But with all their searchings, they found nothing except some scraps of food here and there. These they ate, and so satisfied their hunger somewhat. Then, when night came, they returned home, footsore and weary.

The old man was very glad to see them. All day he had missed them and had wondered where they were. He had saved some supper for them and was surprised that they did not seem more hungry for it. He was still very sad. All day people had been coming to the hut to buy rice from him, and when they found he had none to sell, they had been very much disappointed. Some of them had even been angry and had scolded him.

The following day the dog and cat continued their search, but night found them still unsuccessful. So it went on, day after day and week after week. At last they had visited every house in the village, but they had seen and heard nothing of the charm.

"Now you see how it is. We are only wasting our time," said the cat. "I knew we could not find it, and I, for one, shall begin to look for another home."

"Nay, but wait a bit," answered the dog. "Have you forgotten that many of our master's customers came from the village across the river? We have not searched there yet."

"No, nor will we as far as I am concerned," answered the cat. "I am no swimmer. I have no idea of getting drowned. If you want to search there, you will have to go by yourself."

The dog began to beg and plead with her. "Very soon," said he, "the river will be frozen, and then we can cross on the ice without your wetting even the smallest toe of your paw. Only come!"

"Very well," said the cat at last. "I will do it; but mind you, we must wait until the river is well frozen, and there is no chance of our breaking through."

The dog agreed to this, and so, one cold day, when the river was as hard as stone, the two friends crossed to the farther side, and at once began to search the houses there.

At the first house they found nothing. At the second it was the same thing; but no sooner had the cat entered the third house than she smelled something that reminded her of the rice that had bubbled up in the magic kettle. She made her way from one room to the other, and at last she came to a small upper chamber that seemed to be unused. And now she could smell the charm more strongly than ever, and the smell seemed to come from the top of a high chest of drawers.

With a bound puss leaped to the top of it and looked about her. There, pushed well back against the wall, was a heavy wooden box, and the moment the cat put her nose to the keyhole she knew that the charm was inside of it.

She had found the charm, and that was one thing, but how to get it out of the box was quite a different matter. The box was locked, and puss soon found it was impossible to raise the lid. She tried to push it off the chest of drawers, hoping that if it fell on the floor it might burst open, but the box was so heavy that she could not budge it a hair's breadth. It seemed a hopeless matter. If the dog were only there, no doubt he could have pushed the box off; but then he had no way of getting into the house; and even if he did, he could not climb to the top of the chest of drawers.

But when puss went down to tell him about it, he did not seem to think it was such a hopeless matter after all. He was overjoyed that she had found the charm, and was sure that they could get it out of the box some way or other.

"What we need," said he, "is to get a good big rat to come and gnaw a hole in the box for us."

"Yes, but that is not so easy to do," said the cat. "The rats have no love for me, as you very well know. I have caught and eaten too many of them. I believe they would be glad to starve me to death if they only could."

"You might make a bargain with them," said the dog. "They would be glad enough to help you, if you, in return, would promise not to catch any of them for ten years to come."

Well, the cat did not want to make that bargain at all. She was too fond of catching the rats whenever she could. She and the dog argued about it for a long time, but at last she agreed to do as he wished.

The next thing was to get a message to the king of the rats, and puss knew of a way to manage that. She had seen a mouse-hole near one of the out-buildings, and now she set herself very patiently to wait beside it until the mouse should come out. She had to wait for a long time too. Perhaps the mouse had heard the two friends prowling about. At any rate, it lay so still in its hole that no one would have guessed it was there at all except a cat. At length, toward evening, the mouse thought it might be safe to venture out. But scarcely had it poked its nose out of its hole when the cat pounced upon it and held it in her claws.

The mouse began to beg and plead for mercy. "Oh, good Mrs. Cat—oh, dear Mrs. Cat, spare me, I pray of you! I have a wife and five little mouselings at home, and they would surely die of grief if any harm came to me."

"I am not going to hurt you," answered the cat, though her mouth watered to eat it. "Instead, I am going to let you go, if you will promise to carry a message for me to the king of the rats."

When the mouse heard that the cat would let it go, it could hardly believe in its good fortune. It promised that it would do anything the cat wished it to, and at once the cat took her paws off it and set it free. Then she told it what the message was that she wished it to carry for her: she wished the king to send a rat to gnaw a hole in a box so that she could get a charm that was locked away in it; if the king would do this, she, in return, would promise not to hurt or harm any mouse or rat for ten long years.

The mouse listened attentively, and as soon as he was sure he quite understood the message he hurried away to carry it to the king of the rats. He was only gone for a short time, and when he came back he brought a stout, strong young rat with him. This rat had been sent by the king, who was ready to agree to the bargain the cat had proposed, and had sent the strongest, sharpest-toothed rat he had to gnaw the hole in the box.

As soon as the cat heard this, she made her way back into the house, while the rat and the mouse followed close after her, leaving the dog to wait for them outside. The cat led the way to the upper room and showed the rat the box on the chest of drawers. At once he set to work on it. He gnawed and gnawed and gnawed, but the wood was as hard as stone, as well as very thick.

At last he gnawed through it, but the hole was too small for him to crawl through, and he was too exhausted to make it any larger. The cat, indeed, could reach her paw through, and could even feel the charm, but she could not hook it out, though she tried again and again. But here the mouse made itself of use. It slipped through the hole into the box and quickly brought the charm out in its mouth.

When the cat saw the charm she purred with joy. Once again she promised the rat and mouse that she would not even try to catch them or any of their kind for ten years. Then she took the charm in her mouth and ran down to where the dog was.

The dog was even more delighted than she when he saw the charm.

"Oh, my dear master!" he cried. "How happy he will be."

"Yes," said the cat; "but now make haste. If the people in the house discover the charm is gone, they might suspect us, and follow us, and try to get it back."

"Come, then," said the dog. "But, oh, my dear master! I can hardly wait to show him the charm."

The cat and dog hurried on down to the river, but when they reached the bank they met with a new difficulty. The weather had suddenly turned very warm and the ice had begun to melt. In many places it was gone altogether, and where it was left it was too thin even to bear such small animals as themselves.

"And now what are we to do?" cried the cat. "We will never be able to get back to our village."

"Oh, yes, we can," replied the dog. "Do you mount upon my back. Dig your claws deep into my long hair and hold on tight, and I will carry you across."

The cat was terribly frightened at the thought of such a thing, but still she saw no other way to cross the river. She climbed upon the dog's back, fastened her claws well in his hair, and then he plunged into the water and began to swim across.

All went well until they neared the other bank. A crowd of children had gathered there to see the ice break up. When they saw the dog swimming across with the cat on his back, it seemed to them the funniest thing they had ever seen in all their lives.

The dog was so busy swimming that he did not even notice them, but the cat, upon his back, saw everything that was going on. She herself suddenly began to think what a funny thing it was that she should be riding at ease on the dog's back, while he was swimming so hard.

She tried not to laugh, but she was so amused that at last she could refrain no longer. She burst into a loud cat-laugh, and at once the charm slipped from her mouth plump into the river, and sank to the bottom.

"The charm! The charm!" the cat cried. "I have dropped it in the river, and it has sunk to the bottom."

As soon as the dog heard that, he dived down into the river to regain it. He was in such a hurry that he never thought of telling the cat of what he meant to do.

The cat's claws were fastened so firmly in his hair that she could not have let go if she had wished. Also her mouth was open, so that when they went down into the river she swallowed a great deal of water. By the time the dog came to the top again, panting and snorting, the cat was almost drowned.

But the dog was too angry to think anything of that. "Wait till we get to the shore," he growled. "Just wait until we get to the shore, and see what I will do to you for dropping the charm."

But the cat had no idea of waiting for this. As they came near the shore, she bounded from the dog's back to the dry land, and then she raced away and up a tall tree.

The dog chased after her, but he could not catch her. For some time he stood at the foot of the tree, barking and growling, but at last he trotted on home with drooping head and ears and a sad heart.

The old man was very glad to welcome the dog home again. He had feared it was lost. He looked out from the door in all directions, hoping to see the cat also, but the cat, which had now climbed down from the tree, had gone to look for another home. It feared the dog's anger too much to venture back to the hut. Moreover, it had no liking for poverty and hunger, and it hoped to find some place where it would be better fed than with the old man.

And now indeed there were hard times in the hut. The old man grew poorer and poorer, and thinner and thinner, and it was just as bad with the faithful dog. The dog spent much of his time down at the river looking sadly at the place where the charm had been lost and wishing there were some way for him to find it.

Now there was a great deal of fishing done in that river, and sometimes one of the fishermen, more kind-hearted than the rest, would throw a fish to the hungry dog. This the dog always carried home to his master, and the two faithful friends would share it together. It was always a feast day when this happened.

One day one of the fishermen, who had been very lucky, called to the dog and threw him a particularly large fish.

The dog caught it in his mouth and started home with it. Suddenly he smelled something: it was like the magic rice that had bubbled up in the pot; it must be the charm; it could be nothing but that; and the smell came from the fish he was carrying in his mouth.

As soon as the dog was sure of this, he began to run. He could not get home fast enough. He reached the hut and bounded in and laid the fish upon the table.

"Good dog! Good dog!" cried his master. "Have you brought us a fine dinner to-day?"

He took his knife and began to prepare the fish, but scarcely had he cut into it before the blade struck against something hard. The old man looked to see what it was, and what was his joy and amazement to find that it was the charm, which the fish must have swallowed.

The old man was so delighted that he hardly knew how to contain himself.

"Oh, my precious charm!" he cried. "Oh, what good fortune! Oh, how happy I am! Wait until I fill the kettle, my dear little dog, and then what a feast we will have."

He took out the pot and filled it with water, and hung it over the fire. Then he threw the charm into it. At once the rice began to boil and bubble up. The whole house was filled with the delicious smell of it.

It did not take long for the neighbours to find out that the old man had his wonderful rice again. They hastened to buy of him, and soon he had made even more money than before.

One day the cat, which had grown very lean and thin, came sneaking into the house with one of the customers. As soon as the dog saw her he gave a snarl and was about to fly at her, but the old man caught the cat up in his arms. "Oh, my dear little cat," he cried, "how glad I am to see you. But how thin you have grown! Never mind; there is plenty in the house now, and soon you will grow fat again."

So the cat came back to her master again, but for as long as she lived the dog never forgave her, and they never became friends again. The old man did not know that however. He loved them both; he was quite happy to have them as companions, and lived very prosperous and contented until the end of his days.

"Little lamb, who made thee?" Illustration by Charles Robinson for William Blake in *Songs of Innocence* (London: J. M. Dent & Sons; New York: E. P. Dutton & Co. 1912).

Week Twenty-One:
"THE LAMB"

ittle Lamb, who made thee?
  Dost thou know who made thee?
Gave thee life & bid thee feed
By the stream & o'er the mead;
Gave thee clothing of delight,
Softest clothing, wooly, bright;
Gave thee such a tender voice,
Making all the vales rejoice?
  Little Lamb, who made thee?
  Dost thou know who made thee?

  Little Lamb, I'll tell thee,
  Little Lamb, I'll tell thee:
He is called by thy name,
For he calls himself a Lamb.
He is meek, & he is mild;
He became a little child.
I a child, & thou a lamb,
We are called by his name.
  Little Lamb, God bless thee!
  Little Lamb, God bless thee!

WILLIAM BLAKE
(1757–1827)

"Putting aside all fear, he went forward dauntlessly." Illustrator unknown for Yei Theodora Ozaki (translator) from *The Japanese Fairy Book* (New York: E. P. Dutton & Company, 1903). University of Carolina at Chapel Hill.

Week Twenty-Two:

MY LORD BAG OF RICE

Japanese Fairy Tale

Long, long ago there lived, in Japan a brave warrior known to all as Tawara Toda, or "My Lord Bag of Rice." His true name was Fujiwara Hidesato, and there is a very interesting story of how he came to change his name.

One day he sallied forth in search of adventures, for he had the nature of a warrior and could not bear to be idle. So he buckled on his two swords, took his huge bow, much taller than himself, in his hand, and slinging his quiver on his back started out. He had not gone far when he came to the bridge of Seta-no-Karashi spanning one end of the beautiful Lake Biwa. No sooner had he set foot on the bridge than he saw lying right across his path a huge serpent-dragon. Its body was so big that it looked like the trunk of a large pine tree and it took up the whole width of the bridge. One of its huge claws rested on the parapet of one side of the bridge, while its tail lay right against the other. The monster seemed to be asleep, and as it breathed, fire and smoke came out of its nostrils.

At first Hidesato could not help feeling alarmed at the sight of this horrible reptile lying in his path, for he must either turn back or walk right over its body. He was a brave man, however, and putting aside all fear went forward dauntlessly. Crunch, crunch! he stepped now on the dragon's body, now between its coils, and without even one glance backward he went on his way.

He had only gone a few steps when he heard some one calling him from behind. On turning back he was much surprised to see that the monster dragon had entirely disappeared and in its place was a strange-looking man, who was bowing most ceremoniously to the ground. His red hair streamed over his shoulders and was surmounted by a crown in the shape of a dragon's head, and his sea-green dress was patterned with shells. Hidesato knew at once that this was no ordinary mortal and he wondered much at the strange occurrence. Where had the dragon gone in such a short space of time? Or had it transformed itself into this man, and what did the whole thing mean? While these thoughts passed through his mind he had come up to the man on the bridge and now addressed him:

"Was it you that called me just now?"

"Yes, it was I," answered the man: "I have an earnest request to make to you. Do you think you can grant it to me?"

"If it is in my power to do so I will," answered Hidesato, "but first tell me who you are?"

"I am the Dragon King of the Lake, and my home is in these waters just under this bridge."

"And what is it you have to ask of me?" said Hidesato.

"I want you to kill my mortal enemy the centipede, who lives on the mountain beyond," and the Dragon King pointed to a high peak on the opposite shore of the lake.

"I have lived now for many years in this lake and I have a large family of children and grand-children. For some time past we have lived in terror, for a monster centipede has discovered our home, and night after night it comes and carries off one of my family. I am power-less to save them. If it goes on much longer like this, not only shall I lose all my children, but I myself must fall a victim to the monster. I am, therefore, very unhappy, and in my extremity I determined to ask the help of a human being. For many days with this intention I have waited on the bridge in the shape of the horrible serpent-dragon that you saw, in the hope that some strong brave man would come along. But all who came this way, as soon as they saw me were terrified and ran away as fast as they could. You are the first man I have found able to look at me without fear, so I knew at once that you were a man of great courage. I beg you to have pity upon me. Will you not help me and kill my enemy the centipede?"

Hidesato felt very sorry for the Dragon King on hearing his story, and readily promised to do what he could to help him. The warrior asked where the centipede lived, so that he might attack the creature at once. The Dragon King replied that its home was on the mountain Mikami, but that as it came every night at a certain hour to the palace of the lake, it would be better to wait till then. So Hidesato was conducted to the palace of the Dragon King, under the bridge. Strange to say, as he followed his host downwards the waters parted to let them pass, and his clothes did not even feel damp as he passed through the flood. Never had Hidesato seen anything so beautiful as this palace built of white marble beneath the lake. He had often heard of the Sea King's palace at the bottom of the sea, where all the servants and retainers were salt-water fishes, but here was a magnificent building in the heart of Lake Biwa. The dainty goldfishes, red carp, and silvery trout, waited upon the Dragon King and his guest.

Hidesato was astonished at the feast that was spread for him. The dishes were crystallized lotus leaves and flowers, and the chopsticks were of the rarest ebony. As soon as they sat down, the sliding doors opened and ten lovely goldfish dancers came out, and behind them followed ten red-carp musicians with the koto and the samisen. Thus the hours flew by till midnight, and the beautiful music and dancing had banished all thoughts of the centipede. The Dragon King was about to pledge the warrior in a fresh cup of wine when the palace was suddenly shaken by a tramp, tramp! as if a mighty army had begun to march not far away.

Hidesato and his host both rose to their feet and rushed to the balcony, and the warrior saw on the opposite mountain two great balls of glowing fire coming nearer and nearer. The Dragon King stood by the warrior's side trembling with fear.

"The centipede! The centipede! Those two balls of fire are its eyes. It is coming for its prey! Now is the time to kill it."

Hidesato looked where his host pointed, and, in the dim light of the starlit evening, behind the two balls of fire he saw the long body of an enormous centipede winding round the mountains, and the light in its hundred feet glowed like so many distant lanterns moving slowly towards the shore.

Hidesato showed not the least sign of fear. He tried to calm the Dragon King.

"Don't be afraid. I shall surely kill the centipede. Just bring me my bow and arrows."

The Dragon King did as he was bid, and the warrior noticed that he had only three arrows left in his quiver. He took the bow, and fitting an arrow to the notch, took careful aim and let fly.

The arrow hit the centipede right in the middle of its head, but instead of penetrating, it glanced off harmless and fell to the ground.

Nothing daunted, Hidesato took another arrow, fitted it to the notch of the bow and let fly. Again the arrow hit the mark, it struck the centipede right in the middle of its head, only to glance off and fall to the ground. The centipede was invulnerable to weapons! When the Dragon King saw that even this brave warrior's arrows were powerless to kill the centipede, he lost heart and began to tremble with fear.

The warrior saw that he had now only one arrow left in his quiver, and if this one failed he could not kill the centipede. He looked across the waters. The huge reptile had wound its horrid body seven times round the mountain and would soon come down to the lake. Nearer and nearer gleamed fireballs of eyes, and the light of its hundred feet began to throw reflections in the still waters of the lake.

Then suddenly the warrior remembered that he had heard that human saliva was deadly to centipedes. But this was no ordinary centipede. This was so monstrous that even to think of such a creature made one creep with horror. Hidesato determined to try his last chance. So taking his last arrow and first putting the end of it in his mouth, he fitted the notch to his bow, took careful aim once more and let fly.

This time the arrow again hit the centipede right in the middle of its head, but instead of glancing off harmlessly as before, it struck home to the creature's brain. Then with a convulsive shudder the serpentine body stopped moving, and the fiery light of its great eyes and hundred feet darkened to a dull glare like the sunset of a stormy day, and then went out in blackness. A great darkness now overspread the heavens, the thunder rolled and the lightning flashed, and the wind roared in fury, and it seemed as if the world were coming to an end. The Dragon King and his children and retainers all crouched in different parts of the palace, frightened to death, for the building was shaken to its foundation. At last the dreadful night was over. Day dawned beautiful and clear. The centipede was gone from the mountain.

Then Hidesato called to the Dragon King to come out with him on the balcony, for the centipede was dead and he had nothing more to fear.

Then all the inhabitants of the palace came out with joy, and Hidesato pointed to the lake. There lay the body of the dead centipede floating on the water, which was dyed red with its blood.

The gratitude of the Dragon King knew no bounds. The whole family came and bowed down before the warrior, calling him their preserver and the bravest warrior in all Japan.

Another feast was prepared, more sumptuous than the first. All kinds of fish, prepared in every imaginable way, raw, stewed, boiled and roasted, served on coral trays and crystal dishes, were put before him, and the wine was the best that Hidesato had ever tasted in his life. To add to the beauty of everything the sun shone brightly, the lake glittered like a liquid diamond, and the palace was a thousand times more beautiful by day than by night.

His host tried to persuade the warrior to stay a few days, but Hidesato insisted on going home, saying that he had now finished what he had come to do, and must return. The Dragon King and his family were all very sorry to have him leave so soon, but since he would go they begged him to accept a few small presents (so they said) in token of their gratitude to him for delivering them forever from their horrible enemy the centipede.

As the warrior stood in the porch taking leave, a train of fish was suddenly transformed into a retinue of men, all wearing ceremonial robes and dragon's crowns on their heads to show that they were servants of the great Dragon King. The presents that they carried were as follows:

First, a large bronze bell.
Second, a bag of rice.
Third, a roll of silk.
Fourth, a cooking pot.
Fifth, a bell.

Hidesato did not want to accept all these presents, but as the Dragon King insisted, he could not well refuse.

The Dragon King himself accompanied the warrior as far as the bridge, and then took leave of him with many bows and good wishes, leaving the procession of servants to accompany Hidesato to his house with the presents.

The warrior's household and servants had been very much concerned when they found that he did not return the night before, but they finally concluded that he had been kept by the violent storm and had taken shelter somewhere. When the servants on the watch for his return caught sight of him they called to every one that he was approaching, and the whole household turned out to meet him, wondering much what the retinue of men, bearing presents and banners, that followed him, could mean.

As soon as the Dragon King's retainers had put down the presents they vanished, and Hidesato told all that had happened to him.

The presents which he had received from the grateful Dragon King were found to be of magic power. The bell only was ordinary, and as Hidesato had no use for it he presented it to the temple near by, where it was hung up, to boom out the hour of day over the surrounding neighborhood.

The single bag of rice, however much was taken from it day after day for the meals of the knight and his whole family, never grew less—the supply in the bag was inexhaustible.

The roll of silk, too, never grew shorter, though time after time long pieces were cut off to make the warrior a new suit of clothes to go to Court in at the New Year.

The cooking pot was wonderful, too. No matter what was put into it, it cooked deliciously whatever was wanted without any firing—truly a very economical saucepan.

The fame of Hidesato's fortune spread far and wide, and as there was no need for him to spend money on rice or silk or firing, he became very rich and prosperous, and was henceforth known as My Lord Bag of Rice.

"The Tongue-Cut Sparrow." Illustration by Eitaku Kobayashi for David Thompson (translator) from *The Tongue-Cut Sparrow* (Tokyo: T. Hasegawa, 1885). Library of Congress.

Week Twenty-Two:
THE TONGUE-CUT SPARROW
Japanese Fairy Tale

Long, long ago in Japan there lived an old man and his wife. The old man was a good, kind-hearted, hard-working old fellow, but his wife was a regular cross-patch, who spoiled the happiness of her home by her scolding tongue. She was always grumbling about something from morning to night. The old man had for a long time ceased to take any notice of her crossness. He was out most of the day at work in the fields, and as he had no child, for his amusement when he came home, he kept a tame sparrow. He loved the little bird just as much as if she had been his child.

When he came back at night after his hard day's work in the open air it was his only pleasure to pet the sparrow, to talk to her and to teach her little tricks, which she learned very quickly. The old man would open her cage and let her fly about the room, and they would play together. Then when supper-time came, he always saved some tit-bits from his meal with which to feed his little bird.

Now one day the old man went out to chop wood in the forest, and the old woman stopped at home to wash clothes. The day before, she had made some starch, and now when she came to look for it, it was all gone; the bowl which she had filled full yesterday was quite empty.

While she was wondering who could have used or stolen the starch, down flew the pet sparrow, and bowing her little feathered head—a trick which she had been taught by her master—the pretty bird chirped and said:

"It is I who have taken the starch. I thought it was some food put out for me in that basin, and I ate it all. If I have made a mistake I beg you to forgive me! Tweet, tweet, tweet!"

You see from this that the sparrow was a truthful bird, and the old woman ought to have been willing to forgive her at once when she asked her pardon so nicely. But not so.

The old woman had never loved the sparrow, and had often quarreled with her husband for keeping what she called a dirty bird about the house, saying that it only made extra work for her. Now she was only too delighted to have some cause of complaint against the pet. She scolded and even cursed the poor little bird for her bad behavior, and not content with using these harsh, unfeeling words, in a fit of rage she seized the sparrow—who all this time had spread out her wings and bowed her head before the old woman, to show how sorry she was—and fetched the scissors and cut off the poor little bird's tongue.

"I suppose you took my starch with that tongue! Now you may see what it is like to go without it!" And with these dreadful words she drove the bird away, not caring in the least what might happen to it and without the smallest pity for its suffering, so unkind was she!

The old woman, after she had driven the sparrow away, made some more rice-paste, grumbling all the time at the trouble, and after starching all her clothes, spread the things on boards to dry in the sun, instead of ironing them as they do in England.

In the evening the old man came home. As usual, on the way back he looked forward to the time when he should reach his gate and see his pet come flying and chirping to meet him, ruffling out her feathers to show her joy, and at last coming to rest on his shoulder. But to-night the old man was very disappointed, for not even the shadow of his dear sparrow was to be seen.

He quickened his steps, hastily drew off his straw sandals, and stepped on to the veranda. Still no sparrow was to be seen. He now felt sure that his wife, in one of her cross tempers, had shut the sparrow up in its cage. So he called her and said anxiously:

"Where is Suzume San (Miss Sparrow) today?"

The old woman pretended not to know at first, and answered:

"Your sparrow? I am sure I don't know. Now I come to think of it, I haven't seen her all the afternoon. I shouldn't wonder if the ungrateful bird had flown away and left you after all your petting!"

But at last, when the old man gave her no peace, but asked her again and again, insisting that she must know what had happened to his pet, she confessed all. She told him crossly how the sparrow had eaten the rice-paste she had specially made for starching her clothes, and how when the sparrow had confessed to what she had done, in great anger she had taken her scissors and cut out her tongue, and how finally she had driven the bird away and forbidden her to return to the house again.

Then the old woman showed her husband the sparrow's tongue, saying:

"Here is the tongue I cut off! Horrid little bird, why did it eat all my starch?"

"How could you be so cruel? Oh! how could you so cruel?" was all that the old man could answer. He was too kind-hearted to punish his shrew of a wife, but he was terribly distressed at what had happened to his poor little sparrow.

"What a dreadful misfortune for my poor Suzume San to lose her tongue!" he said to himself. "She won't be able to chirp any more, and surely the pain of the cutting of it out in that rough way must have made her ill! Is there nothing to be done?"

The old man shed many tears after his cross wife had gone to sleep. While he wiped away the tears with the sleeve of his cotton robe, a bright thought comforted him: he would go and look for the sparrow on the morrow. Having decided this he was able to go to sleep at last.

The next morning he rose early, as soon as ever the day broke, and snatching a hasty breakfast, started out over the hills and through the woods, stopping at every clump of bamboos to cry:

"Where, oh where does my tongue-cut sparrow stay? Where, oh where, does my tongue-cut sparrow stay!"

He never stopped to rest for his noonday meal, and it was far on in the afternoon when he found himself near a large bamboo wood. Bamboo groves are the favorite haunts of sparrows, and there sure enough at the edge of the wood he saw his own dear sparrow waiting to welcome him. He could hardly believe his eyes for joy, and ran forward quickly to greet her. She bowed her little head and went through a number of the tricks her master had taught her, to show her pleasure at seeing her old friend again, and, wonderful to relate, she could talk as of old. The old man told her how sorry he was for all that had happened, and inquired after her tongue, wondering how she could speak so well without it. Then the sparrow opened her beak and showed him that a new tongue had grown in place of the old one, and begged him not to think any more about the past, for she was quite well now. Then the old man knew that his sparrow was a fairy, and no common bird. It would be difficult to exaggerate the old man's rejoicing now. He forgot all his troubles, he forgot even how tired he was, for he had found his lost sparrow, and instead of being ill and without a tongue as he had feared and expected to find her, she was well and happy and with a new tongue, and without a sign of the ill-treatment she had received from his wife. And above all she was a fairy.

The sparrow asked him to follow her, and flying before him she led him to a beautiful house in the heart of the bamboo grove. The old man was utterly astonished when he entered the house to find what a beautiful place it was. It was built of the whitest wood, the soft cream-colored mats which took the place of carpets were the finest he had ever seen, and the cushions that the sparrow brought out for him to sit on were made of the finest silk and crape. Beautiful vases and lacquer boxes adorned the tokonoma [an alcove where precious objects are displayed] of every room.

The sparrow led the old man to the place of honor, and then, taking her place at a humble distance, she thanked him with many polite bows for all the kindness he had shown her for many long years.

Then the Lady Sparrow, as we will now call her, introduced all her family to the old man. This done, her daughters, robed in dainty crape gowns, brought in on beautiful old-fashioned trays a feast of all kinds of delicious foods, till the old man began to think he must be dreaming. In the middle of the dinner some of the sparrow's daughters performed a wonderful dance, called the "suzume-odori" or the "Sparrow's dance," to amuse the guest.

Never had the old man enjoyed himself so much. The hours flew by too quickly in this lovely spot, with all these fairy sparrows to wait upon him and to feast him and to dance before him.

But the night came on and the darkness reminded him that he had a long way to go and must think about taking his leave and return home. He thanked his kind hostess for her splendid entertainment, and begged her for his sake to forget all she had suffered at the hands of his cross old wife. He told the Lady Sparrow that it was a great comfort and happiness to him to find her in such a beautiful home and to know that she wanted for nothing. It was his anxiety to know how she fared and what had really happened to her that had led him to seek her. Now he knew that all was well he could return home with a light heart. If ever she wanted him for anything she had only to send for him and he would come at once.

The Lady Sparrow begged him to stay and rest several days and enjoy the change, but the old man said he must return to his old wife—who would probably be cross at his not coming home at the usual time—and to his work, and there-fore, much as he wished to do so, he could not accept her kind invitation. But now that he knew where the Lady Sparrow lived he would come to see her whenever he had the time.

When the Lady Sparrow saw that she could not persuade the old man to stay longer, she gave an order to some of her servants, and they at once brought in two boxes, one large and the other small. These were placed before the old man, and the Lady Sparrow asked him to choose whichever he liked for a present, which she wished to give him.

The old man could not refuse this kind proposal, and he chose the smaller box, saying:

"I am now too old and feeble to carry the big and heavy box. As you are so kind as to say that I may take whichever I like, I will choose the small one, which will be easier for me to carry."

Then the sparrows all helped him put it on his back and went to the gate to see him off, bidding him good-by with many bows and entreating him to come again whenever he had the time. Thus the old man and his pet sparrow separated quite happily, the sparrow showing not the least ill-will for all the unkindness she had suffered at the hands of the old wife. Indeed, she only felt sorrow for the old man who had to put up with it all his life.

When the old man reached home he found his wife even crosser than usual, for it was late on in the night and she had been waiting up for him for a long time.

"Where have you been all this time?" she asked in a big voice. "Why do you come back so late?"

The old man tried to pacify her by showing her the box of presents he had brought back with him, and then he told her of all that had happened to him, and how wonderfully he had been entertained at the sparrow's house.

"Now let us see what is in the box," said the old man, not giving her time to grumble again. "You must help me open it." And they both sat down before the box and opened it.

To their utter astonishment they found the box filled to the brim with gold and silver coins and many

"The Tongue-Cut Sparrow." Illustration by Eitaku Kobayashi for David Thompson (translator) from *The Tongue-Cut Sparrow* (Tokyo: T. Hasegawa, 1885). Library of Congress.

other precious things. The mats of their little cottage fairly glittered as they took out the things one by one and put them down and handled them over and over again. The old man was overjoyed at the sight of the riches that were now his. Beyond his brightest expectations was the sparrow's gift, which would enable him to give up work and live in ease and comfort the rest of his days.

He said: "Thanks to my good little sparrow! Thanks to my good little sparrow!" many times.

But the old woman, after the first moments of surprise and satisfaction at the sight of the gold and silver were over, could not suppress the greed of her wicked nature. She now began to reproach the old man for not having brought home the big box of presents, for in the innocence of his heart he had told her how he had refused the large box of presents which the sparrows had offered him, preferring the smaller one because it was light and easy to carry home.

"You silly old man," said she, "Why did you not bring the large box? Just think what we have lost. We might have had twice as much silver and gold as this. You are certainly an old fool!" she screamed, and then went to bed as angry as she could be.

The old man now wished that he had said nothing about the big box, but it was too late; the greedy old woman, not contented with the good luck which had so unexpectedly befallen them and which she so little deserved, made up her mind, if possible, to get more.

Early the next morning she got up and made the old man describe the way to the sparrow's house. When he saw what was in her mind he tried to keep her from going, but it was useless. She would not listen to one word he said. It is strange that the old woman did not feel ashamed of going to see the sparrow after the cruel way she had treated her in cutting off her tongue in a fit of rage. But her greed to get the big box made her forget everything else. It did not even enter her thoughts that the sparrows might be angry with her—as, indeed, they were—and might punish her for what she had done.

Ever since the Lady Sparrow had returned home in the sad plight in which they had first found her, weeping and bleeding from the mouth, her whole family and relations had done little else but speak of the cruelty of the old woman. "How could she," they asked each other, "inflict such a heavy punishment for such a trifling offense as that of eating some rice-paste by mistake?" They all loved the old man who was so kind and good and patient under all his troubles, but the old woman they hated, and they determined, if ever they had the chance, to punish her as she deserved. They had not long to wait.

After walking for some hours the old woman had at last found the bamboo grove which she had made her husband carefully describe, and now she stood before it crying out:

"Where is the tongue-cut sparrow's house? Where is the tongue-cut sparrow's house?"

At last she saw the eaves of the house peeping out from amongst the bamboo foliage. She hastened to the door and knocked loudly.

When the servants told the Lady Sparrow that her old mistress was at the door asking to see her, she was somewhat surprised at the unexpected visit, after all that had taken place, and she wondered not a little at the boldness of the old woman in venturing to come to the house. The Lady Sparrow, however, was a polite bird, and so she went out to greet the old woman, remembering that she had once been her mistress.

The old woman intended, however, to waste no time in words, she went right to the point, without the least shame, and said:

"You need not trouble to entertain me as you did my old man. I have come myself to get the box which he so stupidly left behind. I shall soon take my leave if you will give me the big box—that is all I want!"

The Lady Sparrow at once consented, and told her servants to bring out the big box. The old woman eagerly seized it and hoisted it on her back, and without even stopping to thank the Lady Sparrow began to hurry homewards.

The box was so heavy that she could not walk fast, much less run, as she would have liked to do, so anxious was she to get home and see what was inside the box, but she had often to sit down and rest herself by the way.

While she was staggering along under the heavy load, her desire to open the box became too great to be resisted. She could wait no longer, for she supposed this big box to be full of gold and silver and precious jewels like the small one her husband had received.

At last this greedy and selfish old woman put down the box by the wayside and opened it carefully, expecting to gloat her eyes on a mine of wealth. What she saw, however, so terrified her that she nearly lost her senses. As soon as she lifted the lid, a number of horrible and frightful looking demons bounced out of the box and surrounded her as if they intended to kill her. Not even in nightmares had she ever seen such horrible creatures as her much-coveted box contained. A demon with one huge eye right in the middle of its forehead came and glared at her, monsters with gaping mouths looked as if they would devour her, a huge snake coiled and hissed about her, and a big frog hopped and croaked towards her.

The old woman had never been so frightened in her life, and ran from the spot as fast as her quaking legs would carry her, glad to escape alive. When she reached home she fell to the floor and told her husband with tears all that had happened to her, and how she had been nearly killed by the demons in the box.

Then she began to blame the sparrow, but the old man stopped her at once, saying:

"Don't blame the sparrow, it is your wickedness which has at last met with its reward. I only hope this may be a lesson to you in the future!"

The old woman said nothing more, and from that day she repented of her cross, unkind ways, and by degrees became a good old woman, so that her husband hardly knew her to be the same person, and they spent their last days together happily, free from want or care, spending carefully the treasure the old man had received from his pet, the tongue-cut sparrow.

"Wynken, Blynken, and Nod." Illustration by Alice L. Harris for Eugene Field, *Eugene Field Reader* (New York: Charles Scribner's Sons, 1905).

Week Twenty-Two:
"Wynken, Blynken, and Nod"

Wynken, Blynken, and Nod one night
Sailed off in a wooden shoe,—
Sailed on a river of crystal light
Into a sea of dew.
"Where are you going, and what do you wish?"
The old moon asked the three.
"We have come to fish for the herring-fish
That live in this beautiful sea;
Nets of silver and gold have we,"
            Said Wynken,
            Blynken,
            And Nod.

The old moon laughed and sang a song,
As they rocked in the wooden shoe;
And the wind that sped them all night long
Ruffled the waves of dew;
The little stars were the herring-fish
That lived in the beautiful sea.
"Now cast your nets wherever you wish,—
Never afeard are we!"
So cried the stars to the fishermen three,
            Wynken,
            Blynken,
            And Nod.

All night long their nets they threw
To the stars in the twinkling foam,—
Then down from the skies came the wooden shoe,
Bringing the fishermen home:
"Twas all so pretty a sail, it seemed
As if it could not be;
And some folk thought "twas a dream they'd dreamed
Of sailing that beautiful sea;
But I shall name you the fishermen three:
        Wynken,
        Blynken,
        And Nod.

Wynken and Blynken are two little eyes,
And Nod is a little head,
And the wooden shoe that sailed the skies
Is a wee one's trundle-bed;
So shut your eyes while Mother sings
Of wonderful sights that be,
And you shall see the beautiful things
As you rock on the misty sea
Where the old shoe rocked the fishermen three,
        Wynken,
        Blynken,
        And Nod.
                EUGENE FIELD
                (1850–1895)

Illustration by Charles Robinson for Eugene Field, *Lullaby-Land: Songs of Childhood*
(Toronto: George N. Morang & Company, Ltd., 1900).

Week Twenty-Three:
HOW THE WHALE
GOT HIS THROAT
Rudyard Kipling, English

In the sea, once upon a time, O my Best Beloved, there was a Whale, and he ate fishes. He ate the starfish and the garfish, and the crab and the dab, and the plaice and the dace, and the skate and his mate, and the mackereel and the pickereel, and the really truly twirly-whirly eel. All the fishes he could find in all the sea he ate with his mouth—so! Till at last there was only one small fish left in all the sea, and he was a small "Stute Fish, and he swam a little behind the Whale's right ear, so as to be out of harm's way. Then the Whale stood up on his tail and said, "I'm hungry." And the small "Stute Fish said in a small "stute voice, "Noble and generous Cetacean, have you ever tasted Man?"

"No," said the Whale. "What is it like?"

"Nice," said the small "Stute Fish. "Nice but nubbly."

"Then fetch me some," said the Whale, and he made the sea froth up with his tail.

"One at a time is enough," said the "Stute Fish. "If you swim to latitude Fifty North, longitude Forty West (that is magic), you will find, sitting on a raft, in the middle of the sea, with nothing on but a pair of blue canvas breeches, a pair of suspenders (you must not forget the suspenders, Best Beloved), and a jack-knife, one shipwrecked Mariner, who, it is only fair to tell you, is a man of infinite-resource-and-sagacity."

So the Whale swam and swam to latitude Fifty North, longitude Forty West, as fast as he could swim, and on a raft, in the middle of the sea, with nothing to wear except a pair of blue canvas breeches, a pair of suspenders (you must particularly remember the suspenders, Best Beloved), and a jack-knife, he found one single, solitary shipwrecked Mariner, trailing his toes in the water. (He had his mummy's leave to paddle, or else he would never have done it, because he was a man of infinite-resource-and-sagacity.)

Then the Whale opened his mouth back and back and back till it nearly touched his tail, and he swallowed the shipwrecked Mariner, and the raft he was sitting on, and his blue canvas breeches, and the suspenders (which you must not forget), and the jack-knife—He swallowed them all down into his warm, dark, inside cupboards, and then he smacked his lips—so, and turned round three times on his tail.

But as soon as the Mariner, who was a man of infinite-resource-and-sagacity, found himself truly inside the Whale's warm, dark, inside cupboards, he stumped and he jumped and he thumped and he bumped, and he pranced and he danced, and he banged and he clanged, and he hit and he bit, and he leaped and he creeped, and he

"How the Whale Got His Throat." Written and illustrated by Rudyard Kipling, *Just So Stories* (Garden City, New York: The Country Life Press, 1897).

prowled and he howled, and he hopped and he dropped, and he cried and he sighed, and he crawled and he bawled, and he stepped and he lepped, and he danced hornpipes where he shouldn't, and the Whale felt most unhappy indeed. (Have you forgotten the suspenders?)

So he said to the "Stute Fish, "This man is very nubbly, and besides he is making me hiccough. What shall I do?"

"Tell him to come out," said the "Stute Fish.

So the Whale called down his own throat to the shipwrecked Mariner, "Come out and behave yourself. I've got the hiccoughs."

"Nay, nay!" said the Mariner. "Not so, but far otherwise. Take me to my natal-shore and the white-cliffs-of-Albion, and I'll think about it." And he began to dance more than ever.

"You had better take him home," said the "Stute Fish to the Whale. "I ought to have warned you that he is a man of infinite-resource-and-sagacity."

So the Whale swam and swam and swam, with both flippers and his tail, as hard as he could for the hiccoughs; and at last he saw the Mariner's natal-shore and the white-cliffs-of-Albion, and he rushed half-way up the beach, and opened his mouth wide and wide and wide, and said, "Change here for Winchester, Ashuelot, Nashua, Keene, and stations on the Fitchburg Road;" and just as he said "Fitch" the Mariner walked out of his mouth. But while the Whale had been swimming, the Mariner, who was indeed a person of infinite-resource-and-sagacity, had taken his jack-knife and cut up the raft into a little square grating all running criss-cross, and he had tied it firm with his suspenders (now you know why you were not to forget the suspenders!), and he dragged that grating good and tight into the Whale's throat, and there it stuck! Then he recited the following Sloka, which, as you have not heard it, I will now proceed to relate—

By means of a grating
I have stopped your ating.

For the Mariner he was also an Hi-ber-ni-an. And he stepped out on the shingle, and went home to his mother, who had given him leave to trail his toes in the water; and he married and lived happily ever afterward. So did the Whale. But from that day on, the grating in his throat, which he could neither cough up nor swallow down, prevented him eating anything except very, very small fish; and that is the reason why whales nowadays never eat men or boys or little girls.

The small "Stute Fish went and hid himself in the mud under the Door-sills of the Equator. He was afraid that the Whale might be angry with him.

The Sailor took the jack-knife home. He was wearing the blue canvas breeches when he walked out on the shingle. The suspenders were left behind, you see, to tie the grating with; and that is the end of that tale.

> *When the cabin port-holes are dark and green*
> *Because of the seas outside;*
> *When the ship goes wop (with a wiggle between)*
> *And the steward falls into the soup-tureen,*
> *And the trunks begin to slide;*
> *When Nursey lies on the floor in a heap,*
>   *And Mummy tells you to let her sleep,*
>   *And you aren't waked or washed or dressed,*
>   *Why, then you will know (if you haven't guessed)*
>   *You're "Fifty North and Forty West!"*

Week Twenty-Three:
How the Camel
Got His Hump
Rudyard Kipling, English

Now this is the next tale, and it tells how the Camel got his big hump.

In the beginning of years, when the world was so new and all, and the Animals were just beginning to work for Man, there was a Camel, and he lived in the middle of a Howling Desert because he did not want to work; and besides, he was a Howler himself. So he ate sticks and thorns and tamarisks and milkweed and prickles, most "scruci-ating idle; and when anybody spoke to him he said "Humph!" Just "Humph!" and no more.

Presently the Horse came to him on Monday morning, with a saddle on his back and a bit in his mouth, and said, "Camel, O Camel, come out and trot like the rest of us."

"Humph!" said the Camel; and the Horse went away and told the Man.

Presently the Dog came to him, with a stick in his mouth, and said, "Camel, O Camel, come and fetch and carry like the rest of us."

"Humph!" said the Camel; and the Dog went away and told the Man.

Presently the Ox came to him, with the yoke on his neck and said, "Camel, O Camel, come and plough like the rest of us."

"Humph!" said the Camel; and the Ox went away and told the Man.

"How the Camel Got His Hump." Illustration by Joseph M. Gleeson for Rudyard Kipling, *Just So Stories* (Doubleday Page & Company, 1912).

At the end of the day the Man called the Horse and the Dog and the Ox together, and said, "Three, O Three, I'm very sorry for you (with the world so new-and-all); but that Humph-thing in the Desert can't work, or he would have been here by now, so I am going to leave him alone, and you must work double-time to make up for it."

That made the Three very angry (with the world so new-and-all), and they held a palaver, and an indaba, and a punchayet, and a pow-wow on the edge of the Desert; and the Camel came chewing milkweed most "scruciating idle, and laughed at them. Then he said "Humph!" and went away again.

Presently there came along the Djinn in charge of All Deserts, rolling in a cloud of dust (Djinns always travel that way because it is Magic), and he stopped to palaver and pow-pow with the Three.

"Djinn of All Deserts," said the Horse, "is it right for any one to be idle, with the world so new-and-all?"

"Certainly not," said the Djinn.

"Well," said the Horse, "there's a thing in the middle of your Howling Desert (and he's a Howler himself) with a long neck and long legs, and he hasn't done a stroke of work since Monday morning. He won't trot."

"Whew!" said the Djinn, whistling, "that's my Camel, for all the gold in Arabia! What does he say about it?"

"He says "Humph!" said the Dog; "and he won't fetch and carry."

"Does he say anything else?"

"Only "Humph!"; and he won't plough," said the Ox.

"Very good," said the Djinn. "I'll humph him if you will kindly wait a minute."

The Djinn rolled himself up in his dust-cloak, and took a bearing across the desert, and found the Camel most 'scruciatingly idle, looking at his own reflection in a pool of water.

"My long and bubbling friend," said the Djinn, "what's this I hear of your doing no work, with the world so new-and-all?"

"Humph!" said the Camel.

The Djinn sat down, with his chin in his hand, and began to think a Great Magic, while the Camel looked at his own reflection in the pool of water.

"You've given the Three extra work ever since Monday morning, all on account of your "scruciating idleness," said the Djinn; and he went on thinking Magics, with his chin in his hand.

"Humph!" said the Camel.

"I shouldn't say that again if I were you," said the Djinn; "you might say it once too often. Bubbles, I want you to work."

And the Camel said "Humph!" again; but no sooner had he said it than he saw his back, that he was so proud of, puffing up and puffing up into a great big lolloping humph.

"Do you see that?" said the Djinn. "That's your very own humph that you've brought upon your very own self by not working. To-day is Thursday, and you've done no work since Monday, when the work began. Now you are going to work."

"How can I," said the Camel, "with this humph on my back?"

"That's made a-purpose," said the Djinn, "all because you missed those three days. You will be able to work now for three days without eating, because you can live on your humph; and don't you ever say I never did anything for you. Come out of the Desert and go to the Three, and behave. Humph yourself!"

And the Camel humphed himself, humph and all, and went away to join the Three. And from that day to this the Camel always wears a humph (we call it "hump" now, not to hurt his feelings); but he has never yet caught up with the three days that he missed at the beginning of the world, and he has never yet learned how to behave.

> The Camel's hump is an ugly lump
>   Which well you may see at the Zoo;
> But uglier yet is the hump we get
>   From having too little to do.
>
> Kiddies and grown-ups too-oo-oo,
> If we haven't enough to do-oo-oo,

We get the hump—
Cameelious hump—
The hump that is black and blue!

We climb out of bed with a frouzly head
 And a snarly-yarly voice.
We shiver and scowl and we grunt and we growl
 At our bath and our boots and our toys;

And there ought to be a corner for me
(And I know there is one for you)
 When we get the hump—
 Cameelious hump—
The hump that is black and blue!

The cure for this ill is not to sit still,
 Or frowst with a book by the fire;
But to take a large hoe and a shovel also,
 And dig till you gently perspire;

And then you will find that the sun and the wind,
And the Djinn of the Garden too,
 Have lifted the hump—
 The horrible hump—
The hump that is black and blue!

I get it as well as you-oo-oo—
If I haven't enough to do-oo-oo—
 We all get hump—
 Cameelious hump—
Kiddies and grown-ups too!

"How the Camel Got His Hump." Written and illustrated
by Rudyard Kipling, *Just So Stories* (Garden City, New
York: The Country Life Press, 1897).

(THIS PAGE)"The General Sherman Bigtree in the Sequoia National Park, California."
(OPPOSITE) "A juniper centuries old." Illustrator unknown for the United States
Department of Agriculture in *Trees: The Yearbook of Agriculture* (Washington, DC: United
States Government Printing Office, 1949).

Week Twenty-Three:
"TREES"
(FOR MRS. HENRY MILLS ALDEN)

I think that I shall never see
A poem lovely as a tree.

A tree whose hungry mouth is prest
Against the earth's sweet flowing breast;

A tree that looks at God all day,
And lifts her leafy arms to pray;

A tree that may in Summer
    wear
A nest of robins in her hair;

Upon whose bosom snow
    has lain;
Who intimately lives
    with rain.

Poems are made by
    fools like me,
But only God can make
    a tree.

JOYCE KILMER
(1886–1918)

"Why the Fish Laughed." Illustration by John D. Batten and Gloria Cardew for Joseph Jacobs, *Indian Fairy Tales* (London, England: David Nutt, 270, 271 Strand, 1882).

Week Twenty-Four:
WHY THE FISH LAUGHED
Indian Fairy Tale

As a certain fisherwoman passed by a palace crying her fish, the queen appeared at one of the windows and beckoned her to come near and show what she had. At that moment a very big fish jumped about in the bottom of the basket.

"Is it a he or a she?" inquired the queen. "I wish to purchase a she fish."

On hearing this the fish laughed aloud.

"It's a he," replied the fisherwoman, and proceeded on her rounds.

The queen returned to her room in a great rage; and on coming to see her in the evening, the king noticed that something had disturbed her.

"Are you indisposed?" he said.

"No; but I am very much annoyed at the strange behaviour of a fish. A woman brought me one to-day, and on my inquiring whether it was a male or female, the fish laughed most rudely."

"A fish laugh! Impossible! You must be dreaming."

"I am not a fool. I speak of what I have seen with my own eyes and have heard with my own ears."

"Passing strange! Be it so. I will inquire concerning it."

On the morrow the king repeated to his vizier what his wife had told him, and bade him investigate the matter, and be ready with a satisfactory answer within six months, on pain of death. The vizier promised to do his best, though he felt almost certain of failure. For five months he laboured indefatigably to find a reason for the laughter of the fish. He sought everywhere and from every one. The wise and learned, and they who were skilled in magic and in all manner of trickery, were consulted. Nobody, however, could explain the matter; and so he returned broken-hearted to his house, and began to arrange his affairs in prospect of certain death, for he had had sufficient experience of the king to know that His Majesty would not go back from his threat. Amongst other things, he advised his son to travel for a time, until the king's anger should have somewhat cooled.

The young fellow, who was both clever and handsome, started off whithersoever Kismat might lead him. He had been gone some days, when he fell in with an old farmer, who also was on a journey to a certain village. Finding the old man very pleasant, he asked him if he might accompany him, professing to be on a visit to the same place.

"Why the Fish Laughed." Illustration by John D. Batten and Gloria Cardew for Joseph Jacobs, *Indian Fairy Tales* (London, England: David Nutt, 270, 271 Strand, 1882).

The old farmer agreed, and they walked along together. The day was hot, and the way was long and weary.

"Don't you think it would be pleasanter if you and I sometimes gave one another a lift?" said the youth.

"What a fool the man is!" thought the old farmer.

Presently they passed through a field of corn ready for the sickle, and looking like a sea of gold as it waved to and fro in the breeze.

"Is this eaten or not?" said the young man.

Not understanding his meaning, the old man replied, "I don't know."

After a little while the two travellers arrived at a big village, where the young man gave his companion a clasp-knife, and said, "Take this, friend, and get two horses with it; but mind and bring it back, for it is very precious."

The old man, looking half amused and half angry, pushed back the knife, muttering something to the effect that his friend was either a fool himself or else trying to play the fool with him. The young man pretended not to notice his reply, and remained almost silent till they reached the city, a short distance outside which was the old farmer's house. They walked about the bazaar and went to the mosque, but nobody saluted them or invited them to come in and rest.

"What a large cemetery!" exclaimed the young man.

"What does the man mean," thought the old farmer, "calling this largely populated city a cemetery?"

On leaving the city their way led through a cemetery where a few people were praying beside a grave and distributing chapatis and kulchas to passers-by, in the name of their beloved dead. They beckoned to the two travellers and gave them as much as they would.

"What a splendid city this is!" said the young man.

"Now, the man must surely be demented!" thought the old farmer. "I wonder what he will do next? He will be calling the land water, and the water land; and be speaking of light where there is darkness, and of darkness when it is light." However, he kept his thoughts to himself.

Presently they had to wade through a stream that ran along the edge of the cemetery. The water was rather deep, so the old farmer took off his shoes and paijamas and crossed over; but the young man waded through it with his shoes and paijamas on.

"Well! I never did see such a perfect fool, both in word and in deed," said the old man to himself.

However, he liked the fellow; and thinking that he would amuse his wife and daughter, he invited him to come and stay at his house as long as he had occasion to remain in the village.

"Thank you very much," the young man replied; "but let me first inquire, if you please, whether the beam of your house is strong."

The old farmer left him in despair, and entered his house laughing.

"There is a man in yonder field," he said, after returning their greetings. "He has come the greater part of the way with me, and I wanted him to put up here as long as he had to stay in this village. But the fellow is such a fool that I cannot make anything out of him. He wants to know if the beam of this house is all right. The man must be mad!" and saying this, he burst into a fit of laughter.

"Father," said the farmer's daughter, who was a very sharp and wise girl, "this man, whosoever he is, is no fool, as you deem him. He only wishes to know if you can afford to entertain him."

"Oh! of course," replied the farmer. "I see. Well perhaps you can help me to solve some of his other mysteries. While we were walking together he asked whether he should carry me or I should carry him, as he thought that would be a pleasanter mode of proceeding."

"Most assuredly," said the girl. "He meant that one of you should tell a story to beguile the time."

"Oh yes. Well, we were passing through a corn-field, when he asked me whether it was eaten or not."

"And didn't you know the meaning of this, father? He simply wished to know if the man was in debt or not; because, if the owner of the field was in debt, then the produce of the field was as good as eaten to him; that is, it would have to go to his creditors."

"Yes, yes, yes; of course! Then, on entering a certain village, he bade me take his clasp knife and get two horses with it, and bring back the knife again to him."

"Are not two stout sticks as good as two horses for helping one along on the road? He only asked you to cut a couple of sticks and be careful not to lose his knife."

"I see," said the farmer. "While we were walking over the city we did not see anybody that we knew, and not a soul gave us a scrap of anything to eat, till we were passing the cemetery; but there some people called to us and put into our hands some chapatis and kulchas; so my companion called the city a cemetery, and the cemetery a city."

"This also is to be understood, father, if one thinks of the city as the place where everything is to be obtained, and of inhospitable people as worse than the dead. The city, though crowded with people, was as if dead, as far as you were concerned; while, in the cemetery, which is crowded with the dead, you were saluted by kind friends and provided with bread."

"True, true!" said the astonished farmer. "Then, just now, when we were crossing the stream, he waded through it without taking off his shoes and paijamas."

"I admire his wisdom," replied the girl. "I have often thought how stupid people were to venture into that swiftly flowing stream and over those sharp stones with bare feet. The slightest stumble and they would fall, and be wetted from head to foot. This friend of yours is a most wise man. I should like to see him and speak to him."

"Very well," said the farmer; "I will go and find him, and bring him in."

"Tell him, father, that our beams are strong enough, and then he will come in. I'll send on ahead a present to the man, to show him that we can afford to have him for our guest."

Accordingly she called a servant and sent him to the young man with a present of a basin of ghee, twelve chapatis, and a jar of milk, and the following message:—"O friend, the moon is full; twelve months make a year, and the sea is overflowing with water."

Half-way the bearer of this present and message met his little son, who, seeing what was in the basket, begged his father to give him some of the food. His father foolishly complied. Presently he saw the young man, and gave him the rest of the present and the message.

"Give your mistress my salam," he replied, "and tell her that the moon is new, and that I can only find eleven months in the year, and the sea is by no means full."

Not understanding the meaning of these words, the servant repeated them word for word, as he had heard them, to his mistress; and thus his theft was discovered, and he was severely punished. After a little while the young man appeared with the old farmer. Great attention was shown to him, and he was treated in every way as if he were the son of a great man, although his humble host knew nothing of his origin. At length he told them everything—about the laughing of the fish, his father's threatened execution, and his own banishment—and asked their advice as to what he should do.

"The laughing of the fish," said the girl, "which seems to have been the cause of all this trouble, indicates that there is a man in the palace who is plotting against the king's life."

"Joy, joy!" exclaimed the vizier's son. "There is yet time for me to return and save my father from an ignominious and unjust death, and the king from danger."

The following day he hastened back to his own country, taking with him the farmer's daughter. Immediately on arrival he ran to the palace and informed his father of what he had heard. The poor vizier, now almost dead from the expectation of death, was at once carried to the king, to whom he repeated the news that his son had just brought.

"Never!" said the king.

"But it must be so, Your Majesty," replied the vizier; "and in order to prove the truth of what I have heard, I pray you to call together all the maids in your palace, and order them to jump over a pit, which must be dug. We'll soon find out whether there is any man there."

The king had the pit dug, and commanded all the maids belonging to the palace to try to jump it. All of them tried, but only one succeeded. That one was found to be a man!!

Thus was the queen satisfied, and the faithful old vizier saved.

Afterwards, as soon as could be, the vizier's son married the old farmer's daughter; and a most happy marriage it was.

"How the Sun, Moon, and Wind Went Out to Dinner." Illustration by John D. Batten and Gloria Cardew for Joseph Jacobs, *Indian Fairy Tales* (London, England: David Nutt, 270, 271 Strand, 1882).

Week Twenty-Four:

How the Sun, Moon, and Wind Went Out to Dinner

Indian Fairy Tale

One day Sun, Moon, and Wind went out to dine with their uncle and aunts Thunder and Lightning. Their mother (one of the most distant Stars you see far up in the sky) waited alone for her children's return.

Now both Sun and Wind were greedy and selfish. They enjoyed the great feast that had been prepared for them, without a thought of saving any of it to take home to their mother—but the gentle Moon did not forget her. Of every dainty dish that was brought round, she placed a small portion under one of her beautiful long finger-nails, that Star might also have a share in the treat.

On their return, their mother, who had kept watch for them all night long with her little bright eye, said, "Well, children, what have you brought home for me?" Then Sun (who was eldest) said, "I have brought nothing home for you. I went out to enjoy myself with my friends—not to fetch a dinner for my mother!" And Wind said, "Neither have I brought anything home for you, mother. You could hardly expect me to bring a collection of good things for you, when I merely went out for my own pleasure." But Moon said, "Mother, fetch a plate, see what I have brought you." And shaking her hands she showered down such a choice dinner as never was seen before.

Then Star turned to Sun and spoke thus, "Because you went out to amuse yourself with your friends, and feasted and enjoyed yourself, without any thought of your mother at home—you shall be cursed. Henceforth, your rays shall ever be hot and scorching, and shall burn all that they touch. And men shall hate you, and cover their heads when you appear."

(And that is why the Sun is so hot to this day.)

Then she turned to Wind and said, "You also who forgot your mother in the midst of your selfish pleasures—hear your doom. You shall always blow in the hot dry weather, and shall parch and shrivel all living things. And men shall detest and avoid you from this very time."

(And that is why the Wind in the hot weather is still so disagreeable.)

But to Moon she said, "Daughter, because you remembered your mother, and kept for her a share in your own enjoyment, from henceforth you shall be ever cool, and calm, and bright. No noxious glare shall accompany your pure rays, and men shall always call you 'blessed.'"

(And that is why the moon's light is so soft, and cool, and beautiful even to this day.)

Week Twenty-Four:
"All Things Bright and Beautiful"

All things bright and
  beautiful,
All creatures great and small,
All things wise and wonderful,
The LORD GOD made them all.

Each little flower that opens,
Each little bird that sings,
He made their glowing colours,
He made their tiny wings.

The rich man in his castle,
The poor man at his gate,
GOD made them, high or lowly,
And ordered their estate.

The purple-headed mountain,
The river running by,
The sunset, and the morning,
That brighten up the sky—

The cold wind in the winter,
The pleasant summer sun,
The ripe fruits in the garden,
He made them every one.

The tall trees in the greenwood,
The meadows where we play,
The rushes by the water,
We gather every day; —

He gave us eyes to see them,
And lips that we might tell,
How great is GOD Almighty,
Who has made all things well.

CECIL ALEXANDER
(1818–1895)

WORKS CITED

Guroian, Vigen. *Tending the Heart of Virtue: How Classic Stories Awaken a Child's Moral Imagination*. Oxford: Oxford University Press, 1998.

Kalpakgian, Mitchell. *The Mysteries of Life in Children's Literature: Books That Inspire a Love of Life*. Charlotte, NC: Neumann Press, 2014.

Lewis, C. S. "On Three Ways of Writing for Children" from *Of Other Words: Essays and Stories*. New York: Harper Collins, 1966.

FOR FURTHER READING

For further reading, check out public domain collections of children's stories and poetry online at Gutenberg.org.

STORIES:

1,001 Arabian Nights (various editions)

Beautiful Stories from Shakespeare by Edith Nesbit (or longer *Tales from Shakespeare* by Charles and Mary Lamb

Fairy Tales of Hans Christian Andersen by Hans Christian Andersen (various editions)

Folk Tales from the Russian by Verra Xenophontovna Kalamatiano de Blumenthal

Grimm's Fairy Tales by Jacob Grimm and Wilhelm Grimm (various editions)

In the Days of Giants: A Book of Norse Tales by Abbie Farwell Brown

Indian Fairy Tales by Joseph Jacobs

Japanese Fairy Tales by Yei Theodora Ozaki

Just So Stories by Rudyard Kipling

King Arthur and His Knights by Maude Radford Warren

Stories from The Faerie Queen by Jeanie Lang

Stories of Robin Hood by Bertha Bush (or longer stories by Howard Pyle)

The Jungle Book by Rudyard Kipling

POETRY:

A Child's Garden of Verses by Robert Louis Stevenson

Poems Every Child Should Know by Mary Burt